Slackermedia

The Multimedia Distro-from-Text

Seth Kenlon

Klaatu la Terible

slak magik

Slackermedia

978-0-9847842-2-6

Slackermedia
The Multimedia Distro-from-Text

Author	Seth Kenlon	*seth@straightedgelinux.com*
Author	Klaatu la Terible	*klaatu@member.fsf.org*
Author	slak magik	*info@sbopkg.org*

Slackermedia is documentation providing the information a user will need to create a full multimedia studio from a Slackware base install. Inspired by Linux-From-Scratch, it is intended to be a "distro from text", a do-it-yourself Linux distribution beginning with installing Slackware and ending with what we will call "Slackermedia" with all the custom-compiled and configuration of only the best in multimedia content creation tools that Linux offers and the user requires to achieve their artistic goals.

Dedication

Slackermedia is indebted to the Slackware Linux project, the Slackbuilds.org website, and the sbopkg.org application.

GNU Linux users often cite the "community" as one of the greatest appeals of using their OS. This holds true for Slackermedia; this book would not exist without the collaboration, hours of troubleshooting, and tech support from everyone in the freenode channels #oggcastplanet, #opensourcemusicians, #openmolar, and of course #slackbuilds and ##slackware.

Oh yeah and their friendship, that's important too, I guess.

Preface

1. Document Conventions

This manual uses several conventions to highlight certain words and phrases and draw attention to specific pieces of information.

In PDF and paper editions, this manual uses typefaces drawn from the *Liberation Fonts*[1] set. The Liberation Fonts set is also used in HTML editions if the set is installed on your system. If not, alternative but equivalent typefaces are displayed. Note: Red Hat Enterprise Linux 5 and later includes the Liberation Fonts set by default.

1.1. Typographic Conventions

Four typographic conventions are used to call attention to specific words and phrases. These conventions, and the circumstances they apply to, are as follows.

`Mono-spaced Bold`

Used to highlight system input, including shell commands, file names and paths. Also used to highlight keycaps and key combinations. For example:

> To see the contents of the file **`my_next_bestselling_novel`** in your current working directory, enter the **`cat my_next_bestselling_novel`** command at the shell prompt and press **Enter** to execute the command.

The above includes a file name, a shell command and a keycap, all presented in mono-spaced bold and all distinguishable thanks to context.

Key combinations can be distinguished from keycaps by the hyphen connecting each part of a key combination. For example:

> Press **Enter** to execute the command.

> Press **Ctrl+Alt+F2** to switch to the first virtual terminal. Press **Ctrl+Alt+F1** to return to your X-Windows session.

The first paragraph highlights the particular keycap to press. The second highlights two key combinations (each a set of three keycaps with each set pressed simultaneously).

If source code is discussed, class names, methods, functions, variable names and returned values mentioned within a paragraph will be presented as above, in **`mono-spaced bold`**. For example:

---

[1] https://fedorahosted.org/liberation-fonts/

File-related classes include **filesystem** for file systems, **file** for files, and **dir** for directories. Each class has its own associated set of permissions.

Proportional Bold

This denotes words or phrases encountered on a system, including application names; dialog box text; labeled buttons; check-box and radio button labels; menu titles and sub-menu titles. For example:

Choose **System → Preferences → Mouse** from the main menu bar to launch **Mouse Preferences**. In the **Buttons** tab, click the **Left-handed mouse** check box and click **Close** to switch the primary mouse button from the left to the right (making the mouse suitable for use in the left hand).

To insert a special character into a **gedit** file, choose **Applications → Accessories → Character Map** from the main menu bar. Next, choose **Search → Find...** from the **Character Map** menu bar, type the name of the character in the **Search** field and click **Next**. The character you sought will be highlighted in the **Character Table**. Double-click this highlighted character to place it in the **Text to copy** field and then click the **Copy** button. Now switch back to your document and choose **Edit → Paste** from the **gedit** menu bar.

The above text includes application names; system-wide menu names and items; application-specific menu names; and buttons and text found within a GUI interface, all presented in proportional bold and all distinguishable by context.

Mono-spaced Bold Italic or *Proportional Bold Italic*

Whether mono-spaced bold or proportional bold, the addition of italics indicates replaceable or variable text. Italics denotes text you do not input literally or displayed text that changes depending on circumstance. For example:

To connect to a remote machine using ssh, type **ssh** *username@domain.name* at a shell prompt. If the remote machine is **example.com** and your username on that machine is john, type **ssh john@example.com**.

The **mount -o remount** *file-system* command remounts the named file system. For example, to remount the **/home** file system, the command is **mount -o remount /home**.

To see the version of a currently installed package, use the **rpm -q** *package* command. It will return a result as follows: *package-version-release*.

Note the words in bold italics above — username, domain.name, file-system, package, version and release. Each word is a placeholder, either for text you enter when issuing a command or for text displayed by the system.

Aside from standard usage for presenting the title of a work, italics denotes the first use of a new and important term. For example:

Publican is a *DocBook* publishing system.

1.2. Pull-quote Conventions

Terminal output and source code listings are set off visually from the surrounding text.

Output sent to a terminal is set in **mono-spaced roman** and presented thus:

```
books          Desktop    documentation   drafts    mss
 photos    stuff    svn
books_tests  Desktop1  downloads          images   notes
 scripts    svgs
```

Source-code listings are also set in **mono-spaced roman** but add syntax highlighting as follows:

```
package org.jboss.book.jca.ex1;

import javax.naming.InitialContext;

public class ExClient
{
   public static void main(String args[])
       throws Exception
   {
      InitialContext iniCtx = new InitialContext();
      Object          ref   =
 iniCtx.lookup("EchoBean");
      EchoHome        home  = (EchoHome) ref;
      Echo            echo  = home.create();

      System.out.println("Created Echo");

      System.out.println("Echo.echo('Hello') = " +
 echo.echo("Hello"));
   }
}
```

1.3. Notes and Warnings

Finally, we use three visual styles to draw attention to information that might otherwise be overlooked.

Note

Notes are tips, shortcuts or alternative approaches to the task at hand. Ignoring a note should have no negative consequences, but you might miss out on a trick that makes your life easier.

Important

Important boxes detail things that are easily missed: configuration changes that only apply to the current session, or services that need restarting before an update will apply. Ignoring a box labeled 'Important' will not cause data loss but may cause irritation and frustration.

Warning

Warnings should not be ignored. Ignoring warnings will most likely cause data loss.

2. We Need Feedback!

If you find a typographical error in this manual, or if you have thought of a way to make this manual better, we would love to hear from you, so feel free to email *klaatu@member.fsf.org*

If you have a suggestion for improving the documentation, try to be as specific as possible when describing it. If you have found an error, please include the section number and some of the surrounding text so we can find it easily.

You may also choose to obtain the source code of this book. It is available from http://gitorious.org/slackermedia

An Introduction to Slackermedia

Slackermedia is a book and Linux configuration guide. After reading, comprehending, and implementing the lessons in Slackermedia the book, a user will have a customized Slackware Linux distribution for multimedia production.

The idea is based in part upon the Linux-From-Scratch project and is respectfully the antithesis to Ubuntu Studio, Studio64, DyneBolic, and other (quite good) "multimedia distros".

1. Where's The Installer Disc?

Anyone who has looked into Linux will know that there are a lot of Linux distributions available. Many of them are very good, with a lot of effort going into their production and maintenance. There are distributions for everyone; Linux for the office, Linux for home creativity, Linux for server administrators, Linux for televisions, Linux for the science community, for the electronic circuitry design community, Linux for children, Linux for firewalls, Linux for different languages, Linux for religious communities, and Linux for people who like the color pink, or blue, or orange, and on and on.

It's because GNU Linux distributes its code freely that such a rich ecosystem of operating environments are able to peacefully co-exist in a way that just never happens in commercial proprietary software.

But Slackermedia is *not* one of the discs you can download and install, reboot, and magically find that the multimedia environment of your dreams has been installed on your computer.

Slackermedia is not a CD or DVD or pre-fabricated distribution. In fact, part of the idea behind Slackermedia is that a pre-fabricated environment will be less efficient and less effective for you, the user.

2. So what is Slackermedia?

Slackermedia is a set of tutorials on how to build your own Slackware multimedia environment that will be tailored specifically for you and how you work.

Slackermedia exists for two reasons:

1. To build one's environment is to know one's environment.

2. Slackware is a stable, powerful, unix-like, well-supported, sensible, free and open operating system, ideal for the needs of a multimedia artist.

3. What's Wrong With Multimedia Distros?

Multimedia distros like Ubuntu Studio, Studio64, DyneBolic, Startcom, Musix, Indamixxx, and others, are *great* solutions for the artist whose goals and workflow match up with the distribution's maintainers.

They also serve as a good starting point if an artist is unfamiliar with the artistic tools available in Linux. A good multimedia distribution comes pre-configured with all the usual media creation apps, so you can try them out and determine which application best fits your needs.

For some artists, however, a pre-built distribution means that the video editor might have to wade through ten different hobbyist video cutters before finding a good solution, and yet will still have to uninstall ffmpeg in order to configure it with all the codec support required by professional video work. Conversely, a hobbyist user who wants to play around with some software synths may have to download a dozen synths but never understand how to load patches into them or what sequencer to use to make them work.

Slackermedia tries to be a "workflow" distro. It teaches the user how to build their own environment, how to leverage the inherently modular Linux system, and how all the different parts work together. And most importantly, it lets the user get their artwork done.

After building and using Slackermedia, you will better understand how the unix philosophy. You will understand how it applies not to just computing, but to large multimedia projects, and you might even come to a better understanding of your craft.

In short, for some people, no distribution will ever be a perfect fit unless the user has custom-designed it.

4. Why Slackware?

Building a multimedia system on any OS is a precarious task; the goal is always to maximize flexibility, have every tool available to the user with as much integration as possible, have the latest features, a good understanding the tools of the trade, and a solid system that is stable and powerful.

Linux makes an ideal platform for multimedia based on many of those requirements. It is inherently flexible, and if configured correctly it can be everything the user needs in the exact way that the user prefers. For Slackermedia, the base system is the famously stable and powerful Slackware.

There are a few advantages to Slackware over other varieties of Linux:

- *Solid.* Slackware prizes stability over jumping to the latest-and-greatest features. This means, for instance, that Slackware has not included new technologies like HAL and Pulse Audio and udev until they have proven to be reliable, finished products. To users itching for the neatest, latest features, this may appear an inconvenience, but for mission-critical machines it is far better to wait on flashy new features than have beta-quality technology cause unforeseen delays in the workflow.

- *Manual Updates.* Many computer users are very accustomed to their computer blinking an icon at them every week or month, urging them to accept a series of updates to their operating system. Most users accept these alerts blindly and let their OS be updated right out from under them. Sometimes this adds new features and new security patches; other times, it breaks a critical component of an intricate workflow.

For mission-critical systems, auto-updating is not a user-friendly feature, it is bothersome at best, and at worst it's an unknown variable that could all-too easily bring production to a halt.

Similarly, many Linux distributions advertise frequent releases of the OS itself. Ubuntu and Fedora both strive to release a new version every six months, and many users jump to upgrade. This generally demands a time-consuming reconfiguration of the entire system; extremely unrealistic for a serious production studio. Ubuntu and Red Hat do offer longterm stable releases but the general hype tends to lean toward upgrading over conservatism, while Slackware is known for its infrequent upgrades, unless the user wants to update packages manually.

- *Unix-like functionality.* GNU and Linux, the two basic components of what is colloquially called "Linux", were modeled on AT&T's UNIX operating system, and more broadly on the "unix philosophy" as demonstrated in the book Linux and the Unix Philosophy™ by Mike Gancarz. Ideas such as re-using other people's work, keeping things modular, stringing together existing small applications to functionally achieve larger ones are all part of the "unixy" way of doing things. Slackware strives to be as true to UNIX as possible. In fact, its mission statement from the *slackware.com*[1] website is: *The Slackware Philosophy: since its first beta release in April of 1993, the Slackware Linux Project has aimed at producing the most "UNIX-like" Linux distribution out there. Slackware complies with the published Linux standards, such as the Linux File System Standard. We have always considered simplicity and stability paramount, and as a result Slackware has become one of the most popular, stable, and friendly distributions available.*

- *Control.* In Slackware, the user has control over almost every aspect of the system. While other distributions have successfully made some things very easy and almost invisible to the user, such as adding packages via friendly package managers like **RPM** and **yum** or **apt** and **aptitude**, the user also loses a degree of control over the way applications are compiled, what options applications have enabled, where applications and libraries get installed in the system, what gets added and removed upon the instalation and removal of packages, and so on. Slackware leaves all such control firmly with the user, and for this reason the resulting system is precisely the sort of system the user needs.

5. Prerequisites

This book attempts to make no assumption about the reader's experience level, and ideally the Slackermedia tutorials will be able to be used by everyone. Realistically, however, in order to use this book a user will probably need:

- Familiarity with Linux and unix. Obviously, the more familiar you are, the easier the process will be.

---

[1] http://www.slackware.com

- Some familiarity with compiling source code is helpful but not strictly necessary. Slackermedia advises the user to compile from source on a number of important programs, but if the user's needs are simple - or the user wishes to start out simple - then manually compiling from source may never be necessary.

- It is recommended that the user be comfortable with installing and configuring Slackware. While Slackware is not difficult, it does allow for quite a bit of customization and configuration. If the user does not feel comfortable doing this (ie, if the user has only ever run a distribution that largely installs and configures itself, like Fedora, Mandriva, Ubuntu, Suse, and so on), then before Slackermedia is attempted, some degree of comfort with Slackware should be attained.

  If you have not already, then you should read the Slackbook, available online at *slackbook.org*[2], and available as a hard copy from *store.slackware.com*[3] as "Slackware Essentials".

- Familiarity with Linux multimedia applications. It will be difficult to custom design a multimedia distribution if the user does not know what applications they want to install. While Slackermedia gives plenty of good examples and suggestions, it is heavily biased toward what the author knows best and the applications that the author uses most. If a user knows that they prefer **Ardour** to **Qtractor**, then the user should implement an **Ardour**-based Slackermedia design; if the user doesn't know one from the other, then the user may not be getting the best solution for their needs.

All in all, the more experience a user can bring to Slackermedia, the easier the process will be, and the more purposeful it will be able to be. However, if a user wishes to create a Slackermedia system solely based on the tutorials in this Slackermedia book, the result will be a well-tuned and efficient multimedia OS. The learning experience might be beneficial even if the studio isn't tailored to the user, and hopefully Slackermedia is clear enough so that users of all experience levels will benefit.

6. Footnote Regarding the Printed Edition

For its first two editions, Slackermedia was exclusively an online and downloadable electronic book and was bound to a specific version of Slackware itself; the first edition was written for 13.1, and the second for 13.37.

The problem with computer books lately is that the moment they are committed to paper, they are already out of date because some programmer somewhere makes a code commit that changes a menu or an icon or the way something works. Keeping that in mind, Slackermedia, from the third edition onward, seeks to stay clear of any specific version numbers or discussions of specific bugs in one version of software which will likely be solved by the next code commit.

---

[2] http://www.slackbook.org
[3] http://store.slackware.com

This ensures that Slackermedia will remain a good reference for years to come; regardless of version numbers or new software features, Slackermedia will help you understand how multimedia works, how multimedia on GNU Linux works, and how to design a multimedia system that works for you.

Updates, corrections, and important changes are available on the *slackermedia.info*[4] website.

---

[4] http://slackermedia.info

Multimedia Workflow on GNU Linux

Slackermedia is a blank canvas. There is not one "right" way to create your Slackermedia system. While Slackermedia does divide packages into broad sets, there is no pre-set that says "install this if you want to make music" or "install this if you want to make videos" and so on. You need to know what you want to do, and how you intend to do it, before building your system.

In other words, this chapter contains a bunch of advice, which, as the cliche goes, is the one free thing in this world that no one really wants. You don't really *want* to read this chapter; you want to build Slackermedia. However, unless you've got experience as a production co-ordinator, this chapter will probably do you some good. Think of it as the green vegetables of Slackermedia and give it a read not because it's all that good, but because it's good for you.

1. What is a Workflow?

Different disciplines have different methods of creating content, and different people work in unique ways. However, there are common elements from any production to another, and the basic methodology of getting a production from idea to finished product is called the "workflow".

The term "workflow" refers to the entire process of production, not just what happens in the computer system being used on the project. However, since so much of modern production happens on a computer, the computer workflow is a often a determining factor in how the rest of the production will happen. It is important, therefore, to understand certain unique aspects of the Free Software workflow.

2. Monolithic vs Modular

Much of the GNU workflow is defined by its inherent modularity. This is very different than the popular tendency to consolidate broad functionality into one "one-stop shop" application. They are two different philosophies that are not really exclusive of one another; it makes sense to keep different tasks confined to specialized applications because this divides work among many applications and makes troubleshooting much easier, but it also makes sense to have an application designed to a specific goal to also include capabilities to complete all the steps required to achieve that goal.

You may be used to the popular mega-applications that provide methods for everything in a perceived workflow, and you may see the logic in that kind of design, but consider the two approaches carefully:

Monolithic
The Video Editor
> You are an editor who has footage on harddrives delivered to you each week. You have no deck, camera, or other capture device and you will probably never need to capture footage into your non-linear editing solution. Why then does your NLE of choice feature eight different ways to capture footage but no way to do something simple like

color code the video regions in your timeline, and no capability to understand divx or wmv or flv, much less xvid or theora?

The Photographer

You are a photographer who requires a digital darkroom for re-touching. You do not need watercolor emulation in your brushes, you do not need to be able to open images from x-ray machines, you do not even need typesetting. Why does your bloatware digital darkroom software feature all of this and more in the main application when it could instead be included as stand-alone plugins or insertable plug-ins for those who do need these kinds of features?

The Graphic Designer

You are a graphic designer working on websites, promotional materials, invitations, logos, and any other job you can get. Your needs are diverse and unpredictable. You are trying to choose between a few popular software titles but find that they are all major investments both in terms of money and their learning curve. While they all seem to do the same thing, it also seems that one specializes in photography, another specializes in materials emulation, another in design layout, and so on; you need a little of it all, but you want each part to be done well.

Modular

The Slackened Video Editor

You're a video editor who gets footage delivered to them on harddrives and will never need to capture footage. You find **kdenlive**, an application that edits video without enforcing logging, organizing, and capturing footage. It's sleek and fast, and even has a plug-in architecture for effects that you may or may not use (it's up to you!).

It also doesn't ship with 20gb of pre-fabricated motion graphic effects that you'll never use, but you know that there's **blender** or even **Libre Office** for that. You like that you're free to use **ffmpeg** or **dvgrab** for importing footage if you need to, or you can fall back on the user-friendly GUI of **kdenlive** if needed.

The Slackened Photographer

You're a photographer with simple digital darkroom needs. You've taken the plunge and switched to GNU Linux, opting for Slackware with the Slackermedia tutorials helping you set it up. You find that **digiKam** handles your digital darkroom needs and even allows you to upload instantly to a wide variety of sites, so you can deliver proofs to your clients quickly and easily, regardless of what vendor-specific sphere they happen to be associated with. It's lightweight, task-specific, and it doesn't try to manage your files for you with over-complex database backends that separate you from your data.

It also lets you do minor retouching, but knows that for serious retouching and compositing, you'll simply open the picture in an external image manipulation application. Because it it is designed to integrate with the KDE software suite, **digiKam**'s interface is familiar and easy to use.

The Slacker Graphic Designer

> You're a graphic designer with diverse and unpredictable needs, depending on the job you've managed to pick up. You find that on GNU Linux, the applications are smaller and less feature-rich, and you like this. When you need paint-brush emulation, you launch **Krita** and plug in your graphics tablet and create the textures you require. You bring that layer into the **GNU Image Manipulation Program** and do the integration of photographs with the textures from **Krita**. You bring a low-res version of that into **Inkscape** for elaborate vector-based layers and fanciful type-setting. You re-integrate all of that with **GIMP**, as needed. Depending on what the graphic will be used for, you pre-flight in **Scribus** or simply export straight from **GIMP** and upload to the client's server right from your **Dolphin** file manager.

> On a rare occasion, you find yourself in need of importing some rare formats that even **GIMP** will not recognize, but you find a plethora of small applications on sourceforge.net or Slackbuilds.org (like **luminance HD**) that will import these formats and convert them to something the other applications in your workflow will understand.

As you can see, there are many times when the modular approach makes more sense than the monolithic. There is an immediate convenience sometimes with the monolithic; depending on how well-structured your workflow is, you may find yourself confounded when you suddenly have to find a new application to do a task that you'd never had to do before. While in a monolithic application, the solution to that may be found in a sub-menu of the sub-menu of a menu, in the modular approach you may be faced with no hint or indication of where to turn. However, these are mere growing pains that are eliminated once you've found the solution; they tend to happen only once: the first time you are faced with the issue that requires a new solution. And in the mean time, you have no need to deal with bloated software with more menus and features than you can ever hope to either understand or use.

3. What is a Workflow?

It is important that you approach your workflow carefully and deliberately when setting up your multimedia studio. Simply throwing together a collection of applications that are tagged as "multimedia" or "graphics" or "audio" is not the correct solution in GNU Linux any more than it is on blackbox vendor software. The artist knows best what s/he needs from the computer, so the artist should determine what s/he must have on the computer in order to get the work done.

If you have never served as a producer (or in software terms, "project manager") before, then this concept may be new to you, so we will review it here.

1. List all of the major tasks you are expecting to do on the computer system. Use general, broad terms here, such as "edit video", "retouch photos", "motion graphics", "clean up audio", and so on.

2. Do a second pass of this list for the specific steps involved in each major task you wrote down for the first step. For example, a video editor might list:

Edit Video
Log footage
> Review all footage with video player with variable speed control and spreadsheet for notes

Capture
> Capture video from tape or drive

Organize
> Organize by scene number and take number

Edit
> Video editor with sync sound and color correction tools

Print
> Export full quality for director's approval

Edit
> Re-edit, rinse and repeat

Motion Graphics
Spec
> Get initial sketches from director

Create
> Create graphic sources with graphic applications

Animate
> Do first draft of motion graphics

Render, Export
> Export low res version for approval

Render, Deliver
> Do full quality render, deliver for integrate into final edit

3. Now do a third pass of your list and assign known software applications to each task. If you are familiar with only the mass-market blackbox applications, then list these. If you know some Free Software solutions as well, then list those. If you are uncertain what application addresses a list item, then do not make an assumption or guess; list it as something that requires more research.

4. Do some research to learn what application will address each list item. Make sure that everything you know you need to do can effectively be achieved with what is available to you. Be prepared for many different applications to surface in the Free Software world; due to the modular nature of its design, it's only natural that there will be a software application just capture video from a deck, or a separate application from

your graphic design application just to change color space and compression settings, and so on.

5. Look for ways to automate your workflow. If there are repetitive tasks that you may have had to do one-by-one in your old non-Free workflow, you should look at these tasks in a new light. Quite possibly there will be scripts that you can write (or find someone to help you write) that can be run on your Free Software system to automatically perform adjustments or processing without any intervention from you.

6. With the help of Slackermedia, build your Slackware GNU Linux system according to the requirements you have specified in your list.

7. Gather raw material. This is a step that is easy to overlook in Free Software because it is not often addressed, but the fact that many of the vendors providing the non-Free applications package gigabytes of extra content for you to use in your work means that whenever the artist needs something random like a cursive font or a paint brush shaped like an oak leaf or a bear paw print, or a music loop of South American drums, or a high-res sand-texture, and so on, the artist has it available to them within a few clicks.

Note

Free Software lacks the luxury of having gigabytes of licensed content to ship along with their software. Again, this is a double-edged sword that has the benefits of cutting download size by orders of magnitude, and also fights the pre-fabricated feel of art produced on Free Software as opposed to the off-the-shelf solutions, but means that when you do need some extra raw materials, you must go out and find the content yourself.

Sites like *flickr.com* [1], *freesound.org* [2], and *openclipart.org* [3] are veritable bastions of free culture, offering Creative Commons content for easy download.

To further address this need, the Slackermedia project itself gathered supporters from around the globe to do an initial crawl of the Internet to find free raw materials for artistic endeavor (such as fonts, clip art, sound banks, and so on). The content can be found as a torrent file on the *Slackermedia.info* [4] website.

---

[1] http://www.flickr.com
[2] http://www.freesound.org
[3] http://www.openclipart.org
[4] http://www.slackermedia.info

4. Sample Workflows

Only you know your specific needs, but sometimes it helps to get an idea of how other people work. Here are some sample workflows to get you going in the right direction:

Video Editing

Log footage

> Use **Dolphin** and **Mplayer** to review and use Dolphin to organize and name your footage; this gives you the advantage of having filenames that match their content, regardless of what video editing application the clips are being used in.

Editing

> Use **Kdenlive** for its robust editing features, transitions, effects, colour correction, and even basic compositing (chroma keying, etc).

Titling

> For quality titles, use **Blender** for is ability to integrate 3d space into motion graphics and titling and overlays. Its learning curve might make it impractical for quick and basic titling.

> The animation program **Synfig Studio** will also do titles and effects, although a learning curve applies here as well.

> If your titling needs are basic, use **GIMP**, **Inkscape**, or even **Libre Office** to create high-quality .png or .tif files and import them as images into **Kdenlive**.

Audio Correction

> For minor corrections (lips smacking, pop removal, plosive softening, etc), open a sound file in **Audacity** and correct the problems. Your changes will update automatically in **Kdenlive**.

Soundtrack, Soundmix

> After you obtain picture lock, start the sound mix on either **Ardour** or **Qtractor**. To do this, export each individual track from **Kdenlive** and import them into the DAW of your choice. When the mix is finished, export a final mix and re-import that into Kdenlive for final output.

Visual Effects

> Export scenes as image sequences and import them into **Blender** for some of the industry's most powerful compositing, particle emulation, 3d modeling, and other visual effects.

Final Render

> **Kdenlive** offers uncompressed output in the form of huffYUV/PCM, as well as compressed output to all major formats (xvid, mp4, ogg theora, webm, h.264 via x264, and more). For customized compression schemes, use **ffmpeg** directly.

Always export an uncompressed final version of your work first. View it for quality assurance. Upon approval, label it `Goldmaster` and then generate compressed versions as needed.

Audio Production
DAW

Use **Ardour** or **Qtractor** or **Rosegarden** as the main hub of the audio production.

> ### Note
>
> If you're doing basic audio editing, then **Audacity** may be all you really need.

Waveform Editing

Use **Audacity**, which specializes in waveform editing, for cleaning audio, removing clicks and pops and plosives, and so on. If you edit the original file then the changes you make in **Audacity** will update automatically in your DAW.

Effects

Effect packages include the **Steve Harris LADSPA collection**, the **Calf** suite, and **Jamin**. The **Steve Harris** set act as plugins to your DAW, while **Calf** can be used as plugins or as an external application, and **Jamin** is external only.

Synths

Any DSSI software synth can be used as a plugin for your DAW, and synths like **amSynth** and **QSynth** are external synths that can be routed into your DAW. There are many soft synths available.

Drum Machines

The premier dedicated drum machine on Linux is **Hydrogen**, which can be used as an external application routed into your DAW.

Samplers

Linux Sampler is the primary sampling engine for Linux and can be routed into your DAW.

Mastering

Once your sound has been mixed to near-perfection, plug **Jamin** into your master output channel. With **Jamin**'s powerful compressor, you can adjust final output levels. With its customizable EQ, you can ensure optimal sound for different types of speakers.

Once you're finished mastering, export your work as final, uncompressed gold masters.

Graphic Design and Print

Layout

> Use **Scribus** as the central hub for bringing together the different elements in a layout. **Scribus** is a powerful layout program, good for books, pamphlets, posters of any size, banners, single pages, album art, and anything else going out to CMYK printers. It is resolution-independent, can track and embed fonts and color swatches, produce reader and printer spreads, and much more.

Graphics

> Use **GIMP** to create or adjust rasterized (bitmap) images. It's not, in spite of the cliché, a Photoshop clone; it has a language and structure all its own, but once it's learned it is a powerful imaging environment.

Illustration

> Use **Inkscape** for vector-based graphics such as logos, illustration, sketches, or even page layout or over-all design, quick mock-ups, and much more. It can also embed or link to rasterized images, perform masks, and a number of advanced imaging functions that will tempt you to make it the center of your graphic production.

> **Krita** is also vector-based but focuses more on materials emulation, making is a powerful tool for trained illustrators.

> **MyPaint** lies somewhere between Inkscape and Krita, with a dynamic brush set that interacts nicely with tablets.

> Finally, the **Gimp Paint Studio** set of mods for GIMP will provide material emulation for GIMP, but as rasterized images only.

Conversion

> For colorspace or format conversion, or batch processes that you repeat frequently in your workflow, the command line application **Image Magick** (or its variation **Graphics Magick**) is priceless. It can be complex but the website and the internet at large offer enough recipes and examples to make most common tasks trivial to learn.

Font Management

> **Font Matrix** activates, deactivates, sorts, and previews your system's fonts.

Photography

Digital Darkroom

> Professional photographers may use **Digikam** as a photograph manager and digital darkroom with the usual powerful set of features associated with most KDE applications. The **Kipi** plugin set adds to its features. And yes, it does RAW, too.

> For HDR photography, there is **Luminance HDR** (formerly **qtpfsgui**), which creates an HDR file from a set of images of the same subject taken at different exposures. Supports basic editing of images plus tonemapping.

Everything Else

See the Graphic Design list for tools relating to image re-touching, design, and presentation.

Web Design

Coding

Use **GNU Emacs** or **vim** as your text editor; both are popular coding environments and each have a variety of modes that will do everything from syntax highlighting to auto-completion and even rudimentary code validation.

Kate is a more traditional text editor, with a visual list of open documents, syntax highlighting, organization of code blocks, and more.

Previewing

Between **Firefox**, **Rekonq**, and **Chromium**, there is little to be desired when test-driving website designs. **Rekonq** has a user-agent switcher built-in and the other two have user-agent plugins available.

Install the **Firebug** addon for **Firefox** to analyze how browsers are rendering your code and to catch problems in your code's structure.

Graphics

See the Graphic Design list for tools when creating graphics for sites.

FTP

Konsole is a one-stop shop for everything you need to push your changes to the web server. With **ssh** and **rsync**, pushing your latest code can be done in a single command.

ncftp is a traditional FTP client, featuring bookmarks for locations, usernames, and passwords. If you do not have ssh access to the server, this is the next best thing.

If you prefer a GUI solution, try **FileZilla**, a simple and convenient FTP application. Or just use **Dolphin**, which seamlessly integrates with remote servers as easily as it does your own computer!

Version Control

Git, the version control system used for little projects like the Linux kernel, the KDE desktop, this book, and much more, can manage all of the changes you make to your codebase, and restore from old versions as needed. A powerful tool that is simply not even on the radar of any proprietary web coding solution.

Step One: Installation

The first step in creating Slackermedia is to install Slackware and configure it for your machine. It is strongly advised that a user be familiar with GNU, Linux, BSD, or UNIX before attempting to build a Slackermedia system. However, it is hardly unheard of (and in fact, arguably best) for someone to start their Linux journey with Slackware. There are many resources online to help a new Linux or new Slackware user through the installation process, including Alan Hicks' *slackbook.org*[1] which is also available in print from the official *Slackware Store*[2]. Support for installation is available via *linuxquestions.org*[3].

Installation of Slackware begins with obtaining a Slackware installation disc, available for free from *slackware.com*[4] or via *bit torrent*[5]. Since an installation disc is a handy thing to have around, and since you'll likely find Slackware a priceless addition to your studio, you can also purchase a disc from the *Slackware Store*[6].

After the Slackware install disc has been obtained, begin installation as with any other distribution; place the disc into your optical drive, reboot the computer with BIOS or EFI settings such that the optical drive precedes the harddrive in boot order, and wait for a prompt. Slackware's installation is menu-based and provides all the information needed to understand the process. This is not necessarily true with all operating system installersf, or even with all Linux installers, but with Slackware, reading the screen makes the installation fairly self-explanatory.

If it is not clear how to install Slackware from simply reading the screen, then refer to *slackbook.org*[7].

Here are a few noteworthy points to keep in mind as you install:

* Slackermedia officially advises against "dual booting", a somewhat popular method of having more than one operating system or versions of operating systems on a single computer. Dual booting is fine for bug testing or trying out various versions of GNU Linux, or for enabling a user to have both a proprietary OS needed for work and one free OS for real life, but it tends to add confusion to the installation process as well as to the stability of the system since one OS may attempt to change the master boot record unexpectedly, or a user of the other OS may accidentally erase or corrupt another partition, and so on.

   Unless you are an experienced Linux user, avoid dual booting.

---

[1] http://www.slackbook.org
[2] http://store.slackware.com/cgi-bin/store
[3] http://www.linuxquestions.org
[4] http://www.slackware.com/getslack
[5] http://www.slackware.com/getslack/torrents.php
[6] http://slackware.com/store
[7] http://www.slackbook.org

- Slackware ships with a variety of desktop environments that can be used by default. You will be asked to choose which desktop to use as default. KDE's Plasma Desktop™ tends to make all of the most common tasks of system configuration, integration, and everyday use both easy and efficient. Slackermedia is tested and configured on the Plasma Desktop™, so it's advisable for new users to default to KDE.

> **Important**
>
> The other desktops bundled with Slackware require more configuration to get everything working together, which this book will *not* cover. If you dislike KDE, you can either configure it to your liking, or use XFCE applications like Thunar from within KDE.
>
> If your computer is so low-end that you feel it can't handle KDE, then probably doing serious multimedia production on it is going to be difficult regardless of what desktop you use; opting for Fluxbox rather than KDE isn't going to make your computer brand new.

- After the installation has finished, reboot the computer. Login to the new system as root and create at least one user. Slackware ships with the script **adduser** for creating new users, making the process quite simple. In fact, as of Slackware 13, **adduser** even offers to place a new user in the appropriate groups that will enable the user to access important multimedia components such as audio, video, optical media, and so on, so take it up on that offer.

- **adduser** allows you to customize the UID (User ID) of the user you create. If you use other GNU or BSD systems, you will probably want to make your UID and username the same on your Slackermedia system as on your other systems, simply to avoid small but annoying permission problems when using external drives.

- After creating a user, log out from root user, and log back in as a normal user. To start a graphical environment, enter **su -c 'kdm' ; exit** at the Bash prompt, which will start a graphical login screen.

Step Two: Understanding Package Management

Before you begin to build your multimedia system, it's important to understand how software is installed, uninstalled, and upgraded on a Slackware system. Generically, this is referred to as "package management".

GNU Linux systems have become known for having a progressive and unique method of installing software, referred usually as the "repository" or "package management" systems. Red Hat Linux introduced this idea when they created, essentially, a database to keep track of all software installed on the computer. This database could then be automatically checked to see if newer versions of the software existed on a remote server, and in the event that a newer version was released then the user's local computer could be updated. Other distributions have since either re-invented this methodology or adapted it, or they use it directly. There are a few notable exceptions, one of which is Slackware.

Slackware has three primary methods of managing the software installed on a system:

1. **pkgtool** and related tools like **installpkg** and **slackpkg**

2. Slackbuilds

3. Source code

Each of these offers the user a variety of choices with regards to how a user manages the software on a computer; none of them impose update schedules, automatic dependency installation and removal, or demand a complex system of database calls be learned.

1. Slackware Packages

Slackware packages are simply a collection of pre-defined files that have been archived; they generally have the file extension `.tgz`, `.tbz`, or `.txz`, although not all `.tgz`, `.tbz`, or `.txz` are necessarily Slackware packages.

Those that are Slackware packages contain, generally speaking, these files:

- slack-desc

   A description of the application this package will install.

- doinst.sh

   A shell script doing post-install tasks, like adding support in one program for the application just installed.

- /usr, /usr/share, and similar

   The folders into which the executable application itself exists and from which it will be copied out into the rest of the system.

A traditional package, therefore, is a mimicry of your Linux system; it contains a few descriptive files or scripts to do a few specialized tasks, but mainly it is simply an isolated / usr, /etc, and whatever else is required for the application to run, with all the compiled files in place.

The install process is to take all of these files and to impose them upon your existing Linux system. In other words, you could literally go through each file in the package and copy it over to the corresponding folder on your computer; ie, `cp package/usr/bin/foo /usr/bin/foo` and so on. Once the files are copied from the package to your larger system, the application can be run on your computer.

This would be tedious and impossible to track and therefore difficult to reverse, so it would be smarter to have a shell script do it for you. The scripts included on Slackware for these and related tasks are:

- installpkg

- removepkg

- pkgtool

2. The pkgtool, installpkg, and removepkg Utilities

installpkg is a simple front-end to the process of decompressing, copying files from, and keeping a record of a Slackware package.

```
$ su -c 'installpkg
/media/cdrom/extra/wicd/wicd-version.txz'
```

Once a package is installed, all of the files that have been placed on your system are recorded in `/var/log/packages`. Using this information, two other scripts can upgrade packages, or remove packages.

```
$ su -c 'upgradepkg
  /var/log/packages/wicd-version.txz'
$ su -c 'removepkg
  /var/log/packages/wicd-version.txz'
```

To see exactly what is going to be installed before installing it, you can use the **explodepkg** command, which shows a list of all the files in the Slackware package.

Most of these commands can be done with **pkgtool**. **pkgtool** is an empty shell that looks for Slackware packages in any directory defined by the user. **pkgtool** is able to install a package, remove a package that has once been installed, and even upgrade packages. It is a graphical tool that runs in the terminal, so its use is fairly self-explanatory; simply choose whether you want to install packages from a directory, remove packages, or view a list of installed files associated with a package. Since Slackware itself uses Slackware packages to install itself in the first place, you can also run the initial install scripts again, including the **font cache**, **lilo** config, choose a default window manager, and more.

3. Slackware Packages and slackpkg

The first Slackware packages you'll deal with are the ones installed onto your system during the normal installation process. You probably won't interact with these directly, but they are always available for reinstallation, either from your install media or via the internet.

Aside from the default packages installed with a full install, there is an **/extra** directory containing additional packages. To install them from the install DVD, use **installpkg**:

```
# installpkg /dev/cdrom/extra/foo-0.1.tgz
```

If you don't have the install media, then of course all of this is possible from the internet.

To install a package from the internet, you could download the .tgz file from a Slackware mirror and then use **installpkg** or **pkgtool**, but there is a simple shell script that can make the process easier, called **slackpkg**.

To configure **slackpkg** so that it knows where online to look for packages, open **/etc/ slackpkg/mirrors** (a text file) as root and find the mirror that is associated with your Slackware version and that is geographically close to you, and uncomment it. This list of mirrors offers ftp and http access, but you must uncomment only one.

Note

In terms of **slackpkg**, there is no functional difference between ftp and http. But if you use a network that restricts, for instance, ftp traffic, then http would have the obvious advantage for you.

Using **slackpkg** is simple and much like using tools like **yum** or **aptitude**. You should update your list of available packages by issuing the initial command **slackpkg update** and from that point on, the repository can be searched by using the command **slackpkg search foobar** as root, and an application can be installed with **slackpkg install foo**. As usual, reading the manual page for **slackpkg** will reveal a full listing of associated commands.

Once a package has been installed with **slackpkg**, it can be removed or upgraded using **pkgtool** and the other package management commands.

4. Finding Additional Slackware Packages

If you installed the full Slackware install base, then the only additional packages that **slackpkg** provides are applications found in the /extra and /testing directories. Aside from these folders, everything else on the server or DVD has been installed on your system.

Slackware packages can be found elsewhere online, but you should make sure you trust the source of those packages, just as you would when considering installing applications on any other operating system.

There are many places online that offer Slackware packages, and many tools available to help you install them in such a way that you can keep track of what you have installed, and also remove them cleanly.

4.1. rpm2tgz

A useful command that can be used in conjunction with **pkgtool** is **rpm2tgz**, which converts a pre-built package for Red Hat Linux into a slackpkg (ie, a .tgz file) that can then be installed via **pkgtool**. This is similar to finding a pre-built .tgz on any given software's download page, except that rpm files are ubiquitous to Linux package formats and the liklihood of finding a .rpm file often exceeds the likelihood of happening across a Slackware package.

Once you've downloaded the .rpm file, use **rpm2tgz** to convert it:

```
rpm2tgz foobar-x.x.xx.rpm
```

The result is a .tgz file, so after the conversion is finished the original .rpm can be discarded and **pkgtool** can be used to install the **.tgz** file. You will need to ensure that the computer contains the dependency code for the application to function; this means that you might need to install other software before installing the application you really want to install. For instance, the Red Hat documenation tool **publican** offers an .rpm, but in order to install it there are about twenty perl modules that must be installed first, which must be done manually.

Warning

The user should also trust the source of the package such that they can be sure there is no broken, disabled, or malicious code present.

4.2. SlackBuilds and sbopkg

One of the hallmarks of Slackware is its SlackBuild system, a powerful yet easy-to-understand and easy-to-learn method of scripting how an application will be built. The SlackBuild system enables the user to script exactly how applications are compiled so that the same SlackBuild can be used on a variety of computers (useful in a production studio) or from computer to computer after a major system upgrade has been performed. SlackBuilds result in .tgz files as well, so managing the applications after they have been compiled is as easy as using **pkgtool**.

This essentially combines the best of both worlds; it allows the user to compile from source code and to enable all the options required for the application to work best for the user, but also feels like a pre-built package since it requires very little interaction from the user in order to be installed.

Note

There is a unixy beauty to this system in that there is really nothing distribution-specific to it, and nothing redundant about it. It consists simply of a shell script which can be easily hosted on minimal storage, quickly downloaded, and used by anyone. Consider for a moment .deb or .rpm files, which in their most popular and common forms literally contain compiled code of the software it intends to install. This means that the source code itself is hosted on the appliction's homepage, it is possibly then modified by the .deb or .rpm maintainer, so that the application is now stored in at least two separate locations (its source homepage and the repository containing its `.deb` or `.rpm`), it can be a hefty download, compiled without any involvement from the user, and installed without any involvment from the user. Such complexity is un-unix-like, but fortunately Slackware doesn't use this method, using instead build scripts that are clean and efficient.

This system was so powerful that, for Slackware 11.0, a group of Slackware users decided to establish a community around it, which can be found at *SlackBuilds.org*[1]. An advantage to slackbuilds.org is that hundreds of applications have had scripts built for them, which are all fully editable by the individual user so that the compiling options are exactly the way the user wants them. Each user can then either maintain their private repository of customized SlackBuilds or simply continue to use the Slackbuilds.org versions. All of the scripts are reviewed and tested by the Slackbuilds.org administrators but can also be reviewed in advance by the user for security and functionality.

Just prior to the release of Slackware 12.1, a frontend to Slackbuilds.org called **sbopkg** was released. **Sbopkg** is a local application which looks to the Slackbuilds.org server and synchronizes the list of available Slackbuild scripts. The user can then navigate through **sbopkg** similar to how **pkgtool** is used, and install packages from the Internet.

4.2.1. Introduction to sbopkg

Sbopkg is a command-line and dialog-based tool to mirror the SlackBuilds.org repository and to operate on the local copy or to operate on a user's own repository of SlackBuild scripts. **Sbopkg** allows the user to browse the local copy, read associated ChangeLogs, view pertinent **README** files, read and modify the SlackBuild script itself, the **.info** file, and the **slack-desc** files. **Sbopkg** also allows the user to select packages to build and it will download the source code for the user, check the md5sum, and build a Slackware package. It will also optionally install the package onto the system.

Sbopkg does not check or resolve dependencies. It does not automatically install packages. It does not track what has been installed. In other words, this is in no way **apt-get** or **rpm** for Slackware; it is a local front-end for Slackbuilds.org and does not duplicate or overlap the function of **pkgtool** or the responsibilities of the user as the primary manager of the system.

To better understand **sbopkg**, it is good to understand how a SlackBuild traditionally works. Traditionally, the workflow to install from a Slackbuild from Slackbuilds.org might be something like this (performing all but the first step repeatedly in order for any required dependencies):

1. Open a web browser

2. Download the SlackBuild script

3. Search for, or navigate to, the tarball of the SlackBuild files and download it and the source code

4. On your local machine, navigate to the downloaded file and untar it

---

[1] http://slackbuilds.org

```
tar -xzvf foo-sbo.tar.gz
```

5. Move the source code tarball into the SlackBuild directory

```
mv foo-src.tar.gz foo-sbo/
```

6. Change directory into the SlackBuild directory

7. Allow the SlackBuild script to be executable

```
chmod +x foo.SlackBuild
```

8. Become root with su and run the SlackBuild

9. Install the resulting package

```
installpkg /tmp/foo_sbo.tgz
```

Sbopkg enables the user essentially to skip all but two of these commands, and can optionally perform the final step of installation as well.

To obtain sbopkg, visit *sbopkg.org*[2] and download the Slackware package. Then, open a terminal and use either **pkgtool** or **installpkg**:

```
$ su -c 'installpkg sbopkg-VERSION-noarch_1-cng.tgz'
```

Among the files installed along with **sbopkg**, there is **/etc/sbopkg/sbopkg.conf**, which contains all pertinent configuration options for sbopkg. It is safe to use the default settings. To start sbopkg, launch it as root by typing **su -lc sbopkg** (The **-l** is to obtain the root environment some packages require).

Upon first launch, sbopkg creates, as defined in the **sbopkg.conf** file, a local copy of the scripts available from slackbuilds.org in **/var/lib/sbopkg/SBo/x** (where **x** is

---

[2] http://www.sbopkg.org

the latest stable release of Slackware), a log in **/var/log/sbopkg**, a queue directory in **/var/sbopkg/queues**, a cache in **/var/cache/sbopkg**, and a local tmp directory called **/tmp/sbopkg**.

After **sbopkg** has launched, the user is delivered to an ncurses interface; use the **Up** and **Down** arrow keys to navigate through the main menu, **Return** to make a selection, and the **Right** and **Left** arrow keys to select which button on the bottom of the menu (**OK, Cancel, Back,** etc) the **Return** key activates.

The first step with sbopkg is to sync with the remote server; this is the top selection in the **sbopkg** main menu. This copies all available scripts from SlackBuilds.org and saves them into directories corresponding with the categories defined by SlackBuilds.org (academic, accessibility, audio, etc). This allows the user to browse the mirrored repository in **sbopkg** whether or not the user is online, and also modify the scripts before using them to install software.

After the initial rsync, the user can view the SlackBuilds.org **ChangeLog**, which documents the most recent updates applied to the SlackBuild repository, whether these are bug fixes in the scripts or updated packages. A user may also subscribe to the SlackBuild user mailing list at *http://lists.slackbuilds.org/mailman/listinfo/slackbuilds-users*[3].

A list of all SlackBuild packages installed on the user's system may be viewed via the **Packages** menu selection, which looks at **/var/log/sbopkg** and displays the packages installed whose tags match the currently active repo's tags (by default, _SBo). Similarly, selecting the **Update** menu item will compare installed packages to those available in the local mirror and identify any packages that have updates available.

Finding a package to install is done with the **Browse** menu selection, or the **Search** selection. **Browse** takes the user to a list of top-level categories as defined by SlackBuilds.org; use the **Return** key to select a category and browse through the packages. Hitting **Return** again will display the details about a package, such as the **README** file, the SlackBuild script itself, and more. To go back in the list of packages or to the list of categories, use the **Right** arrow to select the **Back** button on the bottom row of **sbopkg**'s interface, and press **Return** or type **Alt+B**. The convention of using the **Up** and **Down** arrow keys (or accelerators) for the top menu of **sbopkg** and the **Right** and **Left** arrows (or **Alt+accelerator**) for the bottom row is used throughout **sbopkg**, except in textbox dialogs where the arrows scroll the text.

The search function in **sbopkg** works as would be expected: hit **Return** on **Search** to be taken to a pop-up search field, type in the term you are searching for (it is case-insensitive) and hit **Return** again. **Sbopkg** returns all packages matching the search term; i.e., if a search is performed for the term "ink" then **sbopkg** will return "link-grammar", "inkscape", "libnfnetlink", "elinks", "wink", etc. Common **bash** wildcard characters are also supported, such that a search for "?ink*" returns the same list minus "inkscape" which has no character prior to "ink".

---

[3] http://lists.slackbuilds.org/mailman/listinfo/slackbuilds-users

4.2.2. Building and Installing Software with Sbopkg

Sbopkg can build and install software. These are two separate processes. If you elect to only build software, the resulting Slackware package (`.tgz` file) is left in `/tmp` by default. This location is controlled by the OUTPUT variable in the config file. It can then be installed via **pkgtool** or **installpkg**, or taken to other machines of the same architecture and installed on those, or simply stored for later use. Alternatively, **sbopkg** can be set to install the software after it has been compiled.

Building and/or installing can be done from different places; the **Build** item is the final menu item on each individual package menu of unbuilt packages, and it is invoked with the **Process Queue** item in the **Queue** sub-menus. **Sbopkg** will prompt the user to perform only a build of the software or a build-and-install. Slackermedia recommends build-and-install for single or small groups of users in which compile time is not an issue; for building larger install bases, it may be more efficient to build once and install the resulting binary rather than having each computer compile it individually.

To build or install a package via **sbopkg**, the first step should always be to view the **README** file. This displays a brief description of the application about to be installed, any options that may be passed to the SlackBuild, and any applications upon which the application depends (required dependencies can always be found on SlackBuilds.org). **Sbopkg** does not automatically resolve dependencies so it is up to the user to ensure that all listed dependencies are installed on the system before proceeding. **README**s can be viewed from various places, including selecting **Queue** → **Process** → **View READMEs** when using the dialog interface or using the **−R** flag from the command line.

Assuming, for the purpose of this example, that there are no dependencies, the next step might be to view the `.info` file, which is a SlackBuilds.org-specific file of metadata which lists the canonical program name, the version for which the SlackBuild script was written, the project's homepage, the exact link where the source code for the program can be downloaded, the md5sum of that downloadable package, the SlackBuild script's maintainer's name and email, and the SlackBuilds.org administrator who approved the script.

Next, the SlackBuild script itself can be reviewed. Although all SlackBuild scripts have been reviewed and tested by SlackBuild maintainers, it is a good idea to review the script, both for security purposes as well as to ensure that the application is going to be installed the way the user thinks it's going to be installed. There are some scripts that feature options that the user can take advantage of (like turning off or on codec or plugin support), while other scripts simply help elucidate optional components that the application will use if available but that are not dependencies themselves. Other applications feature an unusual build process such that a SlackBuild script may be more convenient for most users but a disadvantage to a user who relies on that program and would be better off installing directly from the project's code repository.

If additional options are available in the SlackBuild script, the user's local copy of the script and/or `.info` file can be edited from within **sbopkg** by selecting the **Custom** menu item. This will open the SlackBuild script in the user's text editor of choice (defined by the EDITOR environmental variable). For example, if the SlackBuild script for **LiVES** was written for version 1.1.8 but a new version of LiVES has been released and a user wishes to install the newer version, all that is required of the user is that the version number be changed from 1.1.8 to, for instance, 1.2.0 (making the corresponding changes to the `.info` file's `VERSION` and `DOWNLOAD` fields). The script can be saved and run in **sbopkg** and the correct version of **LiVES** would be downloaded, compiled, and optionally installed.

Any change can be made to a SlackBuild script in this way, whether the user wishes to hard code a unique feature into the script, or define a variable that is described in the **README** file, update the version number, modify build paths, and so on. If the only thing that is desired is to set a build option, however, this can be done by selecting the **Options** item and typing *OPTION=value* ... in the entry field. While editing the SlackBuild is a persistent change, the edited version would have to be kept in sync with version changes which happen often. Using custom options also persists but only needs to be kept in sync with option changes which happen rarely. Changing a SlackBuild script, of course, requires at least some very basic knowledge of **bash** scripting and the installation process. It may be that a software package has changed substantially from one version to the next and so a simple update of the version number may not be all that is required, so if a user is opening a SlackBuild script for modification then the user should truly understand what is being done in the script, or be prepared for the build to potentially fail.

4.2.3. The Sbopkg Queue

One of the most powerful features of **sbopkg** is its queue, which makes it possible for a user to create a list of packages to have installed in a particular order and use the list on other computers. Slackermedia makes extensive use of queue files to co-ordinate which packages should be installed as a basis for a good multimedia system. From the main **sbopkg** menu, select **Queue** and press **Return**. The **Queue** menu contains items to view the current queue, to modify the queue, load an existing queue, save a queue, rename or delete existing queues, add all installed packages to the queue (for creating package templates to enable restoration of the current package list or to transfer to another machine), and to process the current queue.

A queue is created from the **sbopkg** GUI by finding a package via either **Browse** or **Search** and selecting **Add to Queue**. This adds the package to a temporary session-only queue file.

A typical use for this would be, for instance, when installing **Inkscape**. Doing a search for **Inkscape** reveals that there is a SlackBuild available, but that it depends on a number of other packages such as **gc**, **pangomm**, **cairomm**, and others. Adding **Inkscape** to the queue allows the user to then go seek out SlackBuild packages for **Inkscape**'s dependencies and either install them one by one, or add them to the queue as well. If they are added to the queue, then obviously the queue will attempt to install **Inkscape** before it installs the dependencies, so there are special functions in the **Sort Queue** submenu of **sbopkg**'s **Queue** menu to either manually rearrange the order of the queue, or simply reverse the queue such that it is processed in reverse order. A simple reversal of the queue sometimes does work, but it may be insufficient since a dependency of one application may have its own dependencies which may require manual re-ordering to do subsorts in the queue. Alternatively, queuefiles can be created and edited with a text editor.

The **Queue** menu is accessed from the main **sbopkg** menu by selecting **Queue** and contains items to view the current queue, which is dynamically created by the user during an **sbopkg** session and will be erased (unless saved) when **sbopkg** is stopped. The **Sort** item allows the user to reorder the list of applications in the queue while **Remove** allows the user to delete items from the queue. **Save** allows a queue file to be saved to the harddrive for later use; this is useful when doing multiple installs of Slackware on a number of machines; a queue file can be used on each machine so that the same packages are installed with minimal effort. By default, queue files are saved in **/var/lib/sbopkg/queues**.

To load a pre-existent queue file into **sbopkg**, select **Queue** → **Load** and check the desired queuefile(s) in the list. To run a queue file, select **Process Queue** from the **Queue** menu.

For example, if you have downloaded the **av** queue file from Slackermedia, then to load it into **sbopkg**, simply invoke **sbopkg** as **QUEUEDIR=/path/to/dir/ containing/queuefile sbopkg** and it will appear in the checklist and can be checked as usual. The queue file would then be loaded into **sbopkg** and you can view it, modify it, remove or reorder applications, and finally process it.

4.2.4. Advanced Uses of sbopkg

Sbopkg can also be used directly from the command line. Its options can be listed with **sbopkg -h** and details can be found via its manual page (**man sbopkg**), but the most direct and simple command is (to use the earlier example) **su -lc 'sbopkg - i av'** which will search for an application or queue file called "av" and install it (if an application) or the programs in it (if a queuefile). If both a program and queuefile exist with the same name, you'll be prompted to specify which. If a queuefile is intended, specifying the **.sqf** extension will avoid the prompt. If you know the name of an application and feel confident that you you have met all its dependencies (or can meet them all within the same command), this is probably both easier and simpler than loading **sbopkg**'s graphical environment.

Other command line options include causing **sbopkg** to rsync to slackbuilds.org, building without installing, diverse search options, viewing changelogs, and so on.

It is also possible to maintain a local repository of customized SlackBuilds rather than, or in addition to, synchronizing with SlackBuilds.org. The local repository is stored in **/var/lib/sbopkg/local** by default and can be made active by either selecting it from **Utilities** → **Repository** or by invoking **sbopkg** as **sbopkg -V local**. Additionally, the location of the **sbopkg** repository can be defined in the **/etc/sbopkg/sbopkg.conf** file. If necessary, you may also pass the **-d** flag to specify an alternate directory for SlackBuilds repositories or by maintaining two configuration files, since **sbopkg** can be passed an alternate configuration file (**sbopkg -f FILE**) on the command line.

4.3. Source Code

Slackware users often prefer to compile the software they install themselves; that is, they take the raw text files containing the application's code and process it through the GNU **gcc** compiler, and then move the executable result of this process into their system. This has a wide variety of advantages:

- It allows the user to control where the executable binary (the application) is installed.

- It allows the user to enable or disable features of the application before the application is built.

- It allows the user to optimize the application for a specific processor.

- It allows the user to review the code that goes into the building of an application should the user wish to do so.

- It ensures the availability of applications to all users on any GNU, Linux, or unix-like system; if applications are distributed as **.rpm** or **.deb** files then a user must hunt for the proper format for their computer but source code is universal in that if an application was written for a GNU Linux system then it will compile and run on any GNU Linux system regardless of distribution.

The general process of compiling is in theory simple; it is merely a matter of going to a website or code management site and downloading the source code of an application. Typically, free software is available in both a work-in-progress ("current") form as well as a packaged "stable" release version. Slackermedia reccommends with few exceptions downloading the stable version, which indicates that the code has been tested to some degree and that the programmers of the application feel confident enough in the code to package it into a **.zip** or **.tar.gz** or **.tar.bz2** archive, give it an official number and sometimes a release name, and offer it for download to the general non-programmer public. Once the code has been downloaded, it is uncompressed, and a series of two or three commands are issued which starts GNU **gcc** compiling the code and then placing the binaries into the system.

In practise, there is potential for error, just as with any part of computing. Some piece of code that the softare relies upon to run correctly may no be present on the user's system, or the user may have attempted to customize the build process in some impossible way, or the user may have configured the rest of the system in a unique enough way that another program cannot compile against it. This is one major advantage to using stock Slackware as the install base for Slackermedia; in all regards, the foundational code will be the same on the user's system as on the system used for all examples in Slackermedia. In any case, if a user believes there will be an advantage to compiling an application from source code then the user should make the attempt. A failed compile is harmless and can be deleted easily, but never having tried could mean a missing feature on the user's Slackermedia system.

There is not just one way to compile software. There is the usual way, but any programmer may choose a different method to have software compiled. The compilation itself is usually performed by the GNU C Compiler (**gcc**). The way that **gcc** knows what steps to take during the compile is with a **makefile**; that is, a document written in a syntax specific to a compiler, which informs the compiler what code to use while building the application. The **Makefile** may contain pointers to other code that is expected to already exists on the user's system, or to other parts of code within that application's project, and it may contain special instructions for installing the software after it has been built as well as instructions on how to uninstall that application should the user decide it is no longer needed.

It is worth noting that the source code downloaded may or may not include all of the code it actually requires to compile and run. If, for example, Developer Foo has developed code for a graphics application that requires heavily on Developer Bar's **libjpeg**, a set of code that enables the computer to handle jpeg images, then Developer Foo is obviously not going to distribute **libjpeg** along with the application's code, because **libjpeg** is maintained by Developer Bar. It is up the user, therefore, to read the **README** file (or similar) packaged along with Developer Foo's application and find out what other code is required to be present on the computer for Application Foo to work. This is called "dependency resolution".

The canonical user commands to compile software are:

```
./configure
make
su -c 'make install'
```

The version of this you can do on Slackware:

```
./configure
make
su -c 'makepkg ../foo.txz'
su -c 'installpkg ../foo.txz'
```

The application is built as usual in the first two steps, but the third command (**makepkg**) creates a Slackware package file (a simple **.tar.xz** file with the extension .txz) and then installs it upon the final command. The advantage to installing in this way is that there is then a record of what has been installed and where it has been installed, and the **removepkg** can be used to uninstall the application if desired.

5. Bottomline for Slackermedia

If nothing else, **sbopkg** provides an easy way to ensure that a certain layer of common packages are installed, much as using Slackware as the foundation for the system ensures that the install base is constant across all Slackermedia systems. Therefore, with the appropriate use of **pkgtool** and **sbopkg**, anyone's system may be made into a Slackermedia system.

---

⁴ http://www.slackermedia.info

To begin this process, go to *www.slackermedia.info*[4] and locate the **sbopkg** queue files, which are, much like Slackware's install files, grouped into a logical set of "series". For example, to download and install everything in the "huge" series (which contains everything for a full Slackermedia install), one would use the following command:

```
$ wget
http://slackermedia.info/downloads/slackermedia-
huge.txt
```

This leaves the user with the file **slackermedia-huge.sqf**, an **sbopkg** queue file.

To synchronize with SlackBuilds.org and build and install all of the Slackermedia applications that can be or are recommended to be installed via **sbopkg** use the following command:

```
$  su -lc 'sbopkg -r &&
QUEUEDIR=$PWD sbopkg -i slackermedia-huge.sqf'
```

To use the GUI, use the following command:

```
$ su -lc 'QUEUEDIR=$PWD sbopkg'
```

Then scroll down to the **Queue** item (or type **Q** and **Return**), choose **Load**, check the **slackermedia-huge.sqf** file and hit **Return**, and choose **Process. Sbopkg** will build and install the applications.

Step Three: Getting the Deps and Libs

Only three steps into the process, and you're ready to start building your multimedia studio!

There are a number of small programs, libraries, and small applications that a typical multimedia system, regardless of what you intend to do on it, should have installed, simply because they are so ubiquitous that nearly ever major media app you will install will probably require them anyway.

These deps and libs are usually small pieces of software that you will not use directly, but that are important for the larger applications to be able to function properly. In some cases, these dependencies are also fully-featured applications in themselves, and are also used by other applications. In any case, they are good to have as a common base from which you can build upon; think of it as the missing "base install" components that you didn't get with stock Slackware.

Determining what your system will need in order to process all the different kinds of media that a multimedia artist typically encounters can be confusing and overwhelming. This is alleviated in this chapter.

1. Which Dependencies Should You Install?

Slackware is a nice all-purpose distribution, so many of the dependencies, libraries, and backend apps required for a Slackermedia system are already installed by default, and many others can be obtained easily and quickly via **sbopkg**. The question is whether or not you should build a given dependency or application from source code yourself.

Building from source code gives you the ability to build the application so that it has the features that you need, whereas relying on an unmodified Slackbuild or a prepackaged binary will not give you the same control over what you are installing.

For the most part, it is safe to install most all libs and many dependencies from **sbopkg** or other trusted sources. Read the **README** files and Slackbuild information that comes along with software packages to determine whether you might need to compile the application with custom options. If you are not sure, then it is safe to install the software as it is configured by default, and if something does not work that you believe should work, then identify what component that function is dependent upon, and investigate online documentation and forums for whether or not more can be gotten from that component by custom compiling it.

You may have to install more than those listed here, depending on what you intend to install for your multimedia work. But if you performed the default, full Slackware install and do a complete Slackermedia dependency install, then most everything you'll need will be ready for you when you need it.

Important

Mind the order in which you install libraries and dependencies; if you attempt to install, for instance, **Inkscape** before you install **gc** or **libsigc++** then the install will obviously fail since **Inkscape** depends on **gc** and **libsig++**, so the sequence of install *is* important.

2. Structure of Slackermedia Queue Files

The lists of Slackermedia libraries and dependencies can, like the rest of Slackermedia, be divided into roughly-defined modules according to what kind of multimedia the system will be used to create. For the best possible system, it is recommended to install all of the advised dependencies and libraries.

To use the Slackermedia lists of dependencies and libraries, you may download sbopkg queue files from *slackermedia.info/downloads*[1]. When you launch **sbopkg** to use this queue file, become root and then define QUEUEDIR as the directory containing the **slackermedia*sqf** file and launch **sbopkg**:

```
$ su -lc
'QUEUEDIR=/directory/containing/queuefile sbopkg'
```

Once **sbopkg** is launched, select the **Queue** submenu. From there, load the appropriate queue file, and then select the **Process Queue** option.

While the exact contents will change from release to release (as Slackware brings in certain dependencies as part of its default install, or the applications themselves start to require different libraries, and so on), the following lists give you a general idea of what kinds of dependencies and libraries are common for each artistic discipline:

3. huge set

huge [2] installs all slackermedia deps and libs; everything from groups **avg**, **av**, **vg**, and **a**. Highly recommended.

---

[1] http://slackermedia.info/downloads
[2] http://www.slackermedia.info/downloads/slackermedia-huge.sqf

4. a/v/g set

avg [3] provides common deps and libs for Audio, Video, and Graphic Designers, and everyone else. In other words, if you are not installing the **huge** set, then you should be installing this even if you don't intend to specialize in audio or video or graphic design; these are just good tools for anyone dealing with media.

Manifest (subject to change):

scons
OpenAL
freealut
locale-gettext
ftgl
exiftool
gtk-engines
gtk-qt-engine
wxGTK
imlib2
giblib
scrot
fftw
icu4c
cppunit
lua
podofo
libdvdnav
dvdauthor
lsdvd
unrar
p7zip
pyicu
fontmatrix

5. a/v set

av [4], when combined with the **avg** set, provides important deps and libs for Audio and Video content creators, and excludes things that would be more specific to a Graphic Designer, painter, photographer, and similar.

*Requires **sdl libvorbis libtheora**, all included in a stock Slackware install.*

Manifest (subject to change):

---

[3] http://www.slackermedia.info/downloads/slackermedia-avg.sqf
[4] http://www.slackermedia.info/downloads/slackermedia-av.sqf

yasm
ladspa_sdk
set_rlimits
libmp4v2
faad2
faac
libdv
x264
libquicktime
libsndfile
twolame
xvidcore
libdca
lame
libmpeg2
liblo
speex
smpeg
aften
a52dec
mjpegtools
lv2core
vorbisgain
aacgain
mp3gain
swh-plugins
ogmtools
oggvideotools
libvpx
rtmpdump
opencore-amr
orc
schroedinger
mplayer-codecs
jack-audio-connection-kit
qjackctl
fluidsynth
libdvdcss
vobcopy
frei0r
libdvbpsi
libzen
libmediainfo
mediainfo
mediainfo-gui

6. v/g set

vg [5], when combined with the **avg** set, provides important deps and libs for Video and Graphic creators while excluding packages important to audio specialists.

*Requires **exiv2**, **libkdcraw**, **libkipi**, included in a stock Slackware install.*

Manifest (subject to change):

libwpg
libdc1394
libopenraw
openjpeg
SDL_gfx
gc
gsl
graphviz
liblqr
gimp-lqr-plugin
gimp-fourier-plugin
gimp-registry-plugins
gimp-wideangle-plugin
resynthesizer
gimpfx-foundry
separate+
iccprofiles
kipi-plugins
lensfun
dcraw
gtkimageview
ufraw
gdk-pixbuf
potrace
lcms2
libraw
luminance-hdr
raw-thumbnailer
unpaper
libsigc++
mm-common
glibmm
cairomm
pangomm
atkmm
gtkmm

---

[5] http://www.slackermedia.info/downloads/slackermedia-vg.sqf

Cython
pysetuptools
lxml
numpy
inkscape

7. a set

a^6 set, along with **avg**, provides deps and libs for Audio creators.

Manifest (subject to change):

id3lib
id3v2
freepats
TiMidity++
mm-common
libsigc++
glibmm
graphviz
cairomm
pangomm
atkmm
gtkmm
amsynth

8. Coffee Break

This gives you a solid foundation for a wide variety of more discipline-specific applications. Feel free to customize this base install as you see fit; you may not need so many video codecs, or you may opt for a different id3 tag editor, and so on. However, installing the above layer of dependencies and libraries prepares your system quite well for a more discipline-specific set of applications.

A very robust Slackermedia install will involve over 50 packages from **sbopkg** and more to be built from source. The sbopkg queue file for all the packages listed on this site can be downloaded at *slackermedia.info/downloads/slackermedia-huge.sqf*[7] and then loaded into sbopkg as a queue to process. Feel free to add to it or subtract from it as needed.

So, you may as well download a queue file now and start the installs. It may take a while, so you may find this to be a good time for a coffee break.

The above lists install important libraries (like **libsigc++**) and dependencies (such as **openAL**) , as well as ubiquitous applications such as **Inkscape** or **qjackctl** or application

---

[6] http://www.slackermedia.info/downloads/slackermedia-a.sqf
[7] http://www.slackermedia.info/downloads/slackermedia-huge.sqf

---

plug-ins (such as **GIMP** plugins and mplayer codecs), but your Slackermedia build is far from over.

Next, we will look at a number of important multimedia components that you can install to get your artwork done, different options you have while installing them, as well as how many of them work together.

Step Four: Application Sets

With the basis for Slackermedia now complete, the system is ready for the main multimedia applications that you want to use for your multimedia content creation.

By now you are familiar with the different methods of installing software on Slackware, so all that remains is to choose the applications you want to use, and use either **slackpkg**, **Slackbuilds.org**, **sbopkg**, **rpm2tgz**, or (if all else fails) the old, traditional method of compiling directly from source code, to install them.

There are a great many multimedia applications available for Linux, and if Slackermedia attempted to list them all it would turn into a catalogue of hundreds of applications without much room for anything else. Lists and blog posts of all the "best" multimedia applications abound on the internet, so if you are completely new to GNU Linux, then shop around. Try some ready-made multimedia distros to sample the multimedia applications they offer.

It's also worth noting that application versions and stability change over time; use your best judgement when installing applications and when choosing versions.

Listen to oggcasts (a good master-list of Linux-related shows can be found at *thelinuxlink.net*[1]) to hear about the applications that are available and, more importantly, the ones that are stable and mature enough to actually be in use by real users.

It's important to understand the difference between an application-in-development and an application ready for production use. It's natural that sometimes an application is not really aware of this itself, since the programming team is usually busy creating the application and not as busy actually utilizing it for full-time creative works.

In an ideal world, rigorous quality assurance testing would be done on all applications by professionally trained beta-testers. On the other hand, this *is* done on most proprietary "professional" applications and yet often they are still nowhere near ready for real-world use even as they sit on a shelf with a price tag of hundreds of dollars attached to them.

Therefore, the process might be for you to first assemble a list of candidates for the tasks you'll need to do on your media workstation, and then to install those applications and test them. Eventually you will assemble a collection of applications upon which you can rely.

1. The Slackermedia Sets

The maintainers, friends, and users of Slackermedia use quite a few multimedia applications in real-world production environments. The applications that have proven themselves in everyday stress-tests are considered to be members of the Slackermedia software sets, which are loosely organized by discipline.

---

[1] http://www.thelinuxlink.net

The following is a list of the applications you should look at while building your system. It is obviously not an exhaustive list of all possible multimedia applications for Linux; but it's a good starting point:

1.1. Audio Workstation

DAWs and Editors
qtractor
> MIDI and Audio sequencer

ardour
> Audio and MIDI sequencer

rosegarden
> MIDI sequencer

hydrogen
> Drum Machine

lmms
> Audio and MIDI sequencer

schismtracker or milkytracker
> Tracker

Score Editors
tuxguitar
> Multitrack tablature editor and player

nted or mscore
> WYSIWYG score-editors

Waveform Editors
audacity
> Multitrack waveform editor

mhwaveedit
> Waveform editor

Samplers and Synths
linux sampler
> Sampler for Linux

whysynth
> Soft synth

qsampler
> Frontend for Linux Sampler

qsynth
>Frontend for Fluidsynth

gigedit
>Sample editor

Mixing and Effects
jamin
>Audio mastering

calf audio plugin pack
>Audio effects and processors

streamripper
>Ripper of streams

Related Tools
kid3
>GUI id3 tagger

id3v2
>id3 tagger in the shell

Support Libraries and Miscellany
soundtouch
>Audio processing library

shorten
>archive and compression of sound files

pd
>Pure Data, realtime audio processing and synthesis

lilypond
>musical typesetting

frescobaldi
>score editor

solfege
>A learning tool for musical notation

abcde
>a better cd encoder

Already Installed...
>JACK and related tools, vorbis and related tools, id3 support, freepats, normalize, libsamplerate, and others

sox
> Should be re-compiled to include all codec support

Because GNU Linux does not have a staff of musicians packaging sets of samples, synth banks, drum loops, and so on, it is up to the artist to create and/or compile the components of their art work. This means that either you should spend time gathering together whatever raw materials you will require for your art, whether by creating your content or gathering it from outside sources like *freesound.org*[2], *soundcloud.com*[3], *ccmixter.org*[4], or *Computer Music Magazine*[5].

There is also the so-called "Great Linux Multimedia Sprints" which have rendered free collections of Creative Commons and Public Domain content (such as soundfonts, samples, loops, et cetera). You may download these from multiple mirrors. See *slackermedia.info/downloads.html*[6] for more information.

1.2. Graphic Designer

Slackermedia Base System

GIMP
> Bitmap image manipulation

GIMP Paint Studio
> Materials emulation

DigiKam, luminance hdr
> Digital darkroom

Inkscape
> Vector art

Image Magick, tiff2pdf
> Image processors

gimpfx-foundry and gimp-registry-plugins
> GIMP plugin pack

fontmatrix
> Font manager

povray, yafaRay
> Rendering engines

---

[2] http://www.freesound.org/
[3] http://soundcloud.com/
[4] http://ccmixter.org
[5] http://www.computermusic.co.uk
[6] http://www.slackermedia.info/downloads.html

Additional Graphics Applications
scribus
> Page layout and design

graphics magick
> alternative to Image Magick

scrot
> screen capture utility

fontforge
> Font designer

ttf-ubuntu-font-family, ecofont-ttf, google-droid-font
> Just a few fonts available from SlackBuilds; see the Multimedia Sprint for a few thousand more :^)

As with the music module, you will need to gather together your raw materials since, luckily, Linux does not come pre-packaged with a standardized set of pre-fabricated artistic components or raw materials. Typically helpful for the graphic artist is a good set of fonts, which you should collect and back up for re-installs; many good free fonts (many are available from *openfontlibrary.org*[7] and *theleagueofmoveabletype.com*[8]), gimp paint brushes, patterns, and more can be via *the Great Linux Multimedia Sprint*[9]. Stock photography also often helps; a good resource is *flickr*[10] which allows (via the Advanced Search) within various Creative Commons licensing schemes. If it is vector art you seek, try *openClipArt.org*[11], a vast library of public domain vector art with contributors from around the world (including many of the respected Fedora Art Team) resulting in art suitable for a wide variety of projects and styles.

1.3. Film and Video Production

Slackermedia Base System
ogg theora, webm, dirac, xvidcore
> Flexible, robust, free video codecs

Mplayer
> Video player, processor, and editor

rtmpdump
> Support for RTMP streams, because you never know when 1995 might come back around

---

[7] http://openfontlibrary.org/fonts
[8] http://www.theleagueofmoveabletype.com/
[9] http://slackermedia.info/downloads.html
[10] http://www.flickr.com
[11] http://www.openclipart.org

libdvdnav, dvdauthor, lsdvd, libdvdcss
  DVD support libraries

Video Editors
kdenlive
  Professional-level video editor

LiVES
  Video editor and VJ toolkit

Animation, Compositing, and Effects
Blender
  3d modeler, compositer, animation editor

k3d
  3d modeler and animator

synfig studio
  Vector animation and compositing

gaupol
  subtitle editor

Video Tools
ffmpeg, libav
  video processor, player, and editor

avidemux
  Video de-muxer and editor

HandBrake, ogmrip
  DVD ripper

transcode
  Video transoder

guvcview
  Video capture frontend

smpte calculator
  SMPTE calculator

Imagination
  Slideshow builder

video-meta
  Video analysis tool

frames.sh
>   Frame conversion calculator

Distribution
rtorrent
>   Commandline torrent client

miro
>   Internet TV aggregator and viewer

bombono-dvd
>   User-friendly DVD authoring

1.4. For Writers

Slackermedia Base System
emacs, vim, kate
>   Text editors with plugin structures

kword, libre office
>   Word processors

Docbook
>   Publishing markup

Writers Tools
screenwriter.el, screenplay-tools, celtx, trelby
>   Screenwriting applications

nXML-mode
>   XML plugin for Emacs

org-mode
>   task management and outlining plugin for Emacs

publican
>   Perl frontend for Docbook

text2pdf
>   plain text to pdf conversion

Writing, either creative or technical, requires the fewest tools and yet seems to have some of the most variations of them. In essence, a writer needs a basic text editor; something that can be written by even a modest programming student in a day or two. Yet there is a proliferation of text editors and office suites. The appropriate choice for your writing environment will be whatever is familiar and comfortable to you, and whatever is most appropriate for your genre.

Charles Olson (formerly of the podcast Mintcast) provides an overview of writer's tools on Linux via the *Linux Reality podcast*[12], which may help with understanding some potential workflows for writing on GNU Linux.

---

[12] http://www.linuxreality.com/archives.php#94

Step Five: Real-Time Kernel

For audio and video content producers, it will probably be necessary to work with a low-latency or even realtime kernel (often indiscriminately referred to as an "RT Kernel"). During the dark ages, it was necessary to download realtime-kernel patches from obscure repositories, manually patch the kernel, and then re-compile. However, Linux kernel 2.6.38.4 received a 200-line block of code that drastically changed its ability to work with near-realtime performance.

Therefore, there are two reasons why you might want or need to compile a kernel:

1. Because you are using a version of Slackware that did not ship with a kernel 2.6.38.4 or above

2. Because you have new hardware that has linux support in a newer kernel than the kernel you are currently running

In those two cases, compiling a new kernel is simpler than its reputation. In fact, there is a discouraging mythology against compiling kernels, but Slackware has always made the process quite easy. Slackware (or any operational Linux system) already contains a config file for the kernel in use, making a re-compile a trivial task.

It's not recommended for production use, but if you need a newer kernel in order to support new hardware, then also check the Slackware changelogs (some Slackware users set their architecture's changelog as their web browser home page in order to stay informed) at *slackware.com/changelog*[1] to find the latest kernel packaged as a downloadable, installable binary (via **installpkg**); no compiling necessary.

1. Compiling the Linux Kernel

Here is a step-by-step tutorial on configuring and compiling the Linux kernel for low-latency performance.

1. First, download the source code for Linux kernel. Download as root and place the sources into **/usr/src/linux**

```
# wget http://kernel.org/pub/linux/kernel/vX.X/
linux-X.X.XX.X.tar.bz2 -P /usr/src/linux/
```

2. Uncompress the sources and **cd** into the folder.

---

[1] http://slackware.com/changelog/

```
#   cd /usr/src && bzip2 -d
linux*XX.X*bz2
```

```
#   cd ./linux-X.X.XX.X
```

3. Download the config file into the kernel sources folder.

Look for a kernel config file in **/media/{cdrom}/testing/ source/linux-X.X.XX.X-configs** or on any Slackware mirror; for example, **ftp://ftp.slackware.com/pub/slackware/ slackware-XX/testing/source/linux-X.X.XX.X-configs/**

Presuming an SMP-capable CPU, you will notice that there are two configuration files; the "generic" kernel configuration and the "huge" kernel configuration. By default you are using the huge config, but this doesn't mean you have to keep using it. If you feel that your hardware is well-supported by the Linux kernel, then you may wish to try operating on a more lightweight kernel. You can always re-compile to a huge kernel if it turns out to be necessary.

```
#   cp /media/cdrom/testing/source/ linux-
X.X.XX.X-configs/config-generic-smp-X.X.XX.X-smp /
usr/src/linux/linux-X.X.XX.X/.config
```

Note

If Slackware does not offer a config file for the kernel you wish to build, then run:

```
# make oldconfig
```

This command brings in your current kernel configuration, leaving you to configure only the new options available with the newer kernel code.

Configuring your kernel is mostly a question of choosing which drivers you want to load into upon boot. Chances are, most of the new options are safe to accept at their default values, unless you are specifically attempting to get a piece of new hardware to work, in which case you should look for the device drivers and choose to build them into your kernel.

4. Launch the **menuconfig**, an ncurses-based, menu-driven list of possible options for your new kernel. The menu can be overwhelming, but as it starts off with the default Slackware configuration, there will not be much you really need to change. The most common point of failure is filesystem support; without the ability to read your harddrive the kernel will not be able to load your operating system. So make sure that you go into the **File System** menu and activate the filesystem support you need (not as modules, but as code to compile into the kernel).

As an example, if I chose to use ext4 filesystem when I installed Slackware, then I must enable ext4 support as part of my kernel. I would then save and exit the menu to commit the change to the config file.

Note

Strictly speaking, there are better ways to configure the kernel. You could drop support for hardware you don't actually have in your machine, you could compile dynamically-loadable modules to keep the actual kernel small, you could use an initrd, and so on. On the other hand, you could also give up art and become a computer scientist ;^)

That said, it is a good idea to have a look through **menuconfig**, just to see what options are available in that monolith of code that runs your computer. You may also find, unfortunately, that you will need to revisit this menuconfig in the event that your new kernel does not boot, or you may get brave and try to trim down your kernel some lazy afternoon, so getting accustomed to the layout and interface of the configuration menu might be helpful.

If you are not sure what kind of filesystem you chose, simply **cat** your **fstab**:

```
#  cat /etc/fstab
```

5. With your new configuration file saved, compile the kernel and its modules.

```
#  make bzImage
#  make modules
#  mv /boot/vmlinuz /boot/vmlinuz.stock
#  cat arch/x86_64/boot/bzImage > /boot/
vmlinuz # or arch/i386/boot/bzImage

#  mv /boot/System.map /boot/System.map.stock

#  cp System.map /boot/System.map
#  make modules_install
```

6. The new kernel is now in place and its modules are installed. Still as root user, edit **lilo.conf** and run **lilo** to reflect the new topography of your system:

```
#  vim /etc/lilo.conf
```

Duplicate the current entry, but change the label to reflect that it will boot the realtime kernel, and change the vmlinuz reference in the stock kernel so that it points to vmlinux.stock rather than vmlinuz. In the end, you will have entries quite similar to this:

```
image = /boot/vmlinuz
root = /dev/sda1
label = slackermedia
read-only
image = /boot/vmlinuz.stock
root = /dev/sda1
label = slackware
read-only
```

And then run **lilo** to complete the change.

```
#  lilo
```

Reboot the machine and boot using the realtime kernel. It should boot as quickly or quicker (depending on how much customization you did in **menuconfig**) as the stock Slackware kernel.

If the new kernel does not boot as expected, then it will most certainly provide errors during the boot process. Take note of the errors, reboot to with the stock kernel, and research what the errors mean.

 Warning

Always remember to run **lilo** after doing a new kernel installation!

Typical errors are that the user has left some important code to be built as modules rather than building them into the kernel. Most often this is the filesystem, so verify that you have the proper filesystem(s) included.

Another possibility is that the user has removed some vital component of the kernel altogether in an effort to reduce its size. Research the issue, cd into /usr/src/linux and run (as root) **make clean ; make menuconfig** and include what you had previously taken out of the kernel.

Otherwise, the kernel is no different from a stock Slackware kernel configuration and should work as expected. If you had installed Slackware with the huge kernel and are trying to use the generic, then it's possible that you do need the huge kernel after all, meaning you'll need to download the huge configuration file and make that into the config file.

1.1. Setting Real-Time Priorities

Now that the realtime kernel has been installed and boots as expected, an interface for the user to assign realtime priorities must be installed and implemented. The application is **set_rlimits**, and it is installed by default along with the audio or huge Slackermedia dependency installs.

After installation, there will be a new file in **/etc** called **set_rlimits.conf.new**. It is well commented and the man page is well written. Re-name the **set_rlimits.conf.new** to **set_rlimits.conf** and edit it so that the important realtime-dependent applications get escalated realtime priviledges. For example:

```
@audio /usr/local/bin/jackd nice=-1 rtprio=80
memlock=100000
```

Repeat this for each application you wish to elevate to higher realtime priorities. If you are not sure what applications need to have realtime priorities, you can always come back to this file to add priviledges as you encounter the need to do so. Certainly add **jackd**, and your DAW will certainly require it. Other applications may or may not require it.

The **set_rlimits.conf** only grants permission to certain processes to be realtime, it does not actually force them to use that priviledge. Any application you want to have running as a realtime process, you must launch through **set_rlimits**, which can be done either by launching the application from the terminal or by modifying your KDE menu.

Launching each application from the terminal can be cumbersome, so you'll more likely want to modify your menu:

1. Right-click on the **K-menu** and select **Menu Editor** from the contextual menu that appears.

2. Find the application you wish to launch with realtime priorities in the left pane (for example, **QJackCtl**).

3. In the right pane, edit the Command field to include the realtime priority command (for example, **set_rlimits qtractor %F**. Save your changes. From now on, when you go to the **K-Menu** to launch **Qtractor** it will launch with realtime priorities enabled.

If you launch applications with a keyboard shortcut, then you will need to edit the command your custom key binding sends to your desktop environment. In KDE this would be via the **System Settings** in the **Shortcuts and Gestures** (formerly the **Keyboard & Mouse**) menu.

Compiling Software

Some applications are so integral to an artist's workflow that it is probably best to compile from source code. This will ensure that the application is built with the options that the artist expects. Without custom compiling some of these applications, certain file types (particularly files with codecs associated with them) will not open and will not be available as an export option, or there may be no plugin architecture built into the application, and so on.

Compiling software, second only to compiling a custom Linux kernel, is often discouraged by proponents of a so-called "user friendly" system. They assert that a truly user friendly system is already set up and configured for the user, ignoring that the user may want something completely different than what the system designer has given them. GNU Linux makes no such assumption, leaving you free to compile your own software so that it does what you want it to do, and then to configure the applications so that you may interact with them the way you want to.

1. Audacity

Audacity is a time-honored and widely used free software audio editor, used by a staggering number of audio hobbyists and professionals alike. As such, it probably deserves to be compiled from source. Luckily, Chess Griffin's slackbuild for it applies all the right options although it does leave the soundtouch and twolame features optional. To ensure that soundtouch and/or twolame compatibility is compiled in, make sure that you have soundtouch and twolame support installed and the ./configure process should auto-detect the support and compile accordingly. You can also simply modify the slackbuild script so that support is *definitely* built in rather than left to auto-detection.

The version of Audacity is extremely important. Releases are frequent with Audacity, but not all releases are equal, and so you may want to find a good release and stay with it for as long as it continues to meet your needs. There are official "stable" releases as well.

If you find the need to change the version that you are compiling with Slackbuilds, modifying the VERSION line in the slackbuild script to the desired version, and downloading that source into the slackbuild directory will allow you to properly build and then install it. If you are doing this from within sbopkg, then change the version number and the download link so that it downloads the proper version.

You may also download the official Slackermedia *Audacity power-user config file*[1] and place in your ~/.audacity-data directory for a better UI layout.

---

[1] http://slackermedia.info/downloads/audacity.cfg.zip

2. Blender

Blender is a powerful application that you can use for graphics, video editing (or both) as well as motion graphics, game programming, desktop publishing, and quite a lot more. It is also very actively developed, with new features arriving fairly often. While there are pre-compiled binaries available on the blender.org site (and through **sbopkg**) for 32-bit and 64-bit systems, the binaries force you to use their version of **ffmpeg** which may not be the best version of ffmpeg for your needs.

The compilation process of Blender is not as complex as it might seem at first glance. On a default Slackware system, most of Blender's dependencies are already installed and there is no need for "development" versions of anything as there are on distributions like Fedora or Ubuntu.

If you installed all of the dependencies (primarily for Blender: scons, openAL, ftgl, smpeg, and gettext) listed as the starting point for this multimedia version of Slackware, then the process is simple:

1. Download the source code from their site. The development team offers you a stable release tarball as well as the development code from svn; Slackermedia recommends the stable release.

2. Untar the downloaded archive and cd into it:

```
$ tar -xzf blender-2.x.tar.gz
$ cd blender-2.x
```

3. And invoke the build script.

```
$ scons
```

The binary itself will be located in a directory called **build/linux2/bin/** and will be called, of course, **blender**. You may move this executable file to whatever location is most convenient for you; such as **/usr/local/bin**

Unexpected errors are common enough to warrant a note about them. Blender is frequently developed, and building it from source will sometimes render a puzzling error. Chances are, of course, that someone before you has experienced the same error, so simply do an internet search on the error in order to find a solution or work-around.

For best results, search the internet for the exact error that you receive, such as:

```
yasm: FATAL: unable to open include file `nasm.inc'
```

Searching for very specific errors often return existing issues and their solutions. Whether it's a bug or simply something that you overlooked when preparing for the compile, the answers are often a simple matter of installing another dependency or commenting out a bad line of code. Errors do happen, but they needn't dissuade you from compiling important applications from source.

3. Digikam

Digikam is a direct competitor to powerful digital darkroom applications as well as to photo managers. It is fully featured, powerful, and has a rich plugin structure which enables even more features. Even if a graphic artist or photographer is happy using **GIMP**, **digikam** is an important tool for its workflow and image manipulation ability.

There is a build script available on *Slackbuilds.org*[2] which should suit most people's needs.

Compilation is fairly simple, although it uses **cmake** rather than the usual **./ configure && make && make install** sequence. Instead, you first have the options to export key variables such as the location of the Qt libraries you wish to use, and then issue **cmake** with whatever options you feel are necessary, and then (as root) make install. Here is an example:

```
$ export PATH=$QTDIR=/usr/lib64/qt
$ cmake . -DCMAKE_INSTALL_PREFIX=/usr -
DCMAKE_BUILD_TYPE=release
$ make
# make install
```

---

[2] http://slackbuilds.org

4. ffmpeg and libav

Important

ffmpeg has been forked into *libav.org*[3], and there is not yet a clear indication of which project has the better features. In fact, the two projects seem to nearly mirror one another in progress and features. They are completely interchangeable, so flip a coin and install one or the other.

Currently, the maintainer of Slackermedia uses **ffmpeg** on his workstation, and **libav** on his laptop. Or is it the other way around? Point taken?

ffmpeg is the backbone of many video-related applications from players to editors (and is in fact even both of these things in itself). For the most flexible video and audio system possible, **ffmpeg** should be installed directly from source code. You can find the code at *ffmpeg.org*[4]. It's a big application with many options and you will want to have control over whether these options are enabled or disabled. To learn about the options, read the ffmpeg compiling documentation found in the source code tarball, and then try ./configure --options

A sample configuration of ffmpeg-0.x for a diverse system:

```
./configure --enable-nonfree --enable-avfilter
--enable-avfilter-lavf --enable-x11grab --enable-
gray --enable-small
--enable-encoder=amrnb --enable-encoder=amrwb --
enable-libdc1394
--enable-libdirac --enable-libfaac --enable-libfaad
--enable-libfaad
--enable-libmp3lame --enable-libschroedinger --
enable-libspeex
--enable-libtheora --enable-libvorbis --enable-
libx264 --enable-gpl
--enable-libxvid --enable-postproc --enable-shared
--disable-static
--enable-pthreads --disable-debug --mandir=/usr/man
```

---

[3] http://libav.org
[4] http://www.ffmpeg.org/

There is a build script available on *Slackbuilds.org*[5] but it requires basically the same level of enabling codecs; rather than doing them as traditional ./configure options, either define them definitively in the Slackbuild script itself, or as preceding variable arguments before executing the Slackbuild.

```
# VPX=yes XVID=yes DIRAC=yes AND SO ON
./ffmpeg.SlackBuild
```

5. Fonts

Fonts are vital to creativity and good design. Slackware comes packaged with the Red Hat set of Liberation Fonts, which are drop-in replacements for fonts like Helvetica and Times. There are a number of sources of more fanciful free fonts available online.

First, look on *Slackbuilds.org*[6] either in your web browser or via sbopkg. Do a search for "font" and you will find a number of installable packages of fonts.

Secondly, *the League of Moveable Type*[7] features aggressively open source and free fonts.

You will also find quite a few font packages available from the Fedora Linux repositories. Fedora has long been considered to have on of the finest graphic design teams of all Linux distributions, and also dedicated to freely licensed content, so pillaging their repositories for **.rpm** files is both helpful and simple. Take any **.rpm** from an official Fedora repository and turn it into a Slackware package using **rpm2tgz**, and then use **installpkg** to install.

And finally there is *the Great Linux Multimedia Sprint v1.0*[8], which has over 2455 free fonts to use and re-distribute.

 Important

Note that most applications scan the font directory every time they launch, so keeping hundreds of fonts in your font directory may make applications slow to load. It may, therefore, behoove you to familiarize yourself with the fonts you own, and only keep your favourite fonts in the font directory, until developers come up with a more dynamic way to load fonts.

[5] http://slackbuilds.org
[6] http://www.slackbuilds.org
[7] http://www.theleagueofmoveabletype.com/
[8] http://www.slackermedia.info/downloads

5.1. Installing Fonts

Generally speaking, there are two different philosophies on installing fonts:

1. Install fonts on a systemwide basis so that all users of a computer has access to them

2. Install fonts on a per-user basis

Traditionally, installing fonts systemwide made most sense; it was economical on disk space and made sure all users had access to the same fonts for design work. This is still true if you actually manage a multi-user system but in today's world when each person has a desktop and a laptop to themselves, the multi-user aspect seems less important, and disk space is cheap.

In fact there is a distinct advantage to installing fonts on a per-user basis; it makes keeping track of those fonts and porting them or syncing them over to another computer a lot easier.

5.1.1. Manually Installing Fonts as User

To install fonts into a user's home folder, place a font file into a directory (it may or may not yet exist) **~/.fonts** and then run this command:

```
$ fc-cache -f
```

5.1.2. Manually Installing Fonts for All Users

To install fonts on a system-wide basis, the font files (usually *.ttf) should be copied to /usr/share/fonts/foobar where foobar is the type of font. Usually they are TTF fonts, so they are copied into /usr/share/fonts/TTF. Keeping this in mind, here is an example of installing a font, all done as root user:

```
$ su -c 'cp foo.ttf /usr/share/fonts/TTF/'
$ cd /usr/share/fonts/TTF
$ su
# enter root password
# mkfontscale .
# mkfontdir .
# /usr/bin/fc-cache -f
```

5.1.3. Installing Fonts via KDE

If you are running KDE, you may use KDE's Font Viewer (which will launch automatically if you click a **TTF** file in **Dolphin**). This shows you a feature of all the glyphs in the font set and even allows you to enter your own preview text). If you choose to install the font, click the **Install** button in the lower right corner of the window. Enter the root password to install the font system-wide, or choose to install it for only the current user.

6. GIMP Brushes

Ever since version 2.4, **GIMP** can use Photoshop ABR brushes, so almost any website offering free brushes for image manipulation programs will have something to offer an artist in need of new brushes. These sites seem to come and go at random, but *the Great Linux Multimedia Sprint v1.0*[9] has plenty for you to freely install, use, and re-distribute.

Installing GIMP brushes is simple:

- To install them on a system-wide basis, move the brush files (*.gbr *.arb *.vbr etc) to the /usr/share/gimp/2.0/brushes/ directory

- To install them on a per-user basis, copy the files to that user's ~/.gimp-2.x/brushes directory

Launch GIMP (or quit and then launch, if it was already running) and the brushes will in the brush palette. Notice that GIMP scans the brushes directory every time it launches, so keeping hundreds or brushes in the the brushes directory will make GIMP slower to launch. It may behoove you to familiarize yourself with the brushes you own, and only keep your favourite brushes in the brush directory, until GIMP developers come up with a more dynamic way to load brushes.

6.1. Gimp Paint Studio

GIMP Paint Studio ("GPS" for short) is a sort of project-within-a-project; it is an add-on pack for GIMP itself and brings with it a whole new personality by adding sets of brushes, color swatches, and presets so that you can achieve everything from realistic materials and brush emulation, airbrushing, inking, and any variety of special effects.

In other words, if you have been looking for a solid digital painting application, your search has probably just ended.

GPS is available from *code.google.com/p/gps-gimp-paint-studio*[10] as a zip file. It releases as a traditional software appliation would, and it's currently on 1.4 (or 1.5 if you want to test newer features). The install is simple; unzip the file and then copy the brushes into your GIMP brushes directory.

---

[9] http://www.slackermedia.info/downloads
[10] http://code.google.com/p/gps-gimp-paint-studio

Warning

If you have custom ***rc** files, **GPS** will overwrite them during installation. Backup your GIMP ***rc** files before proceeding, or do not copy the ***rc** files.

```
$

    curl
    http://gps-gimp-paint-studio.googlecode.com/
files/GPS%201_5_final%20release.zip
    -O GPS1_5_finalrelease.zip; mkdir GPS_source

$

    unzip GPS*zip -d GPS_source ; cd ./GPS_source

$

    for gps in $(find ./* -type d) ; do cp $gps/*
    ~/.gimp*/$gps ; done

$

cp ./GPS_source/*rc ~/.gimp*/
```

Once the files are copied, launch or re-launch **GIMP** and explore the new options. The new brushes are stored in the **Restore Options From...** button at the bottom of the **Paint Brush** tab. Everything else is easily accessible in their respective tabs.

7. HandBrakeCLI

HandBrakeCLI is a commandline DVD ripper that will read DVDs and convert the native muxed mpeg2 files to some other format, like Ogg Theora, xvid, x264, and others. It is one of the many invaluable tools for the video editor, who can typically expect to receive video from every imaginable source. The compilation is simple, but requires both **yasm** (an extra on the Slackware install disc) and **jam** (available via sbopkg).

Similar to **Blender**, the build process results in a binary called **HandBrakeCLI** that should be moved to a more suitable location, like **~/bin** or **/usr/local/bin**

Note

> Klaatu and XGizzmo's slackbuild of **HandbrakeCLI** is now available on slackbuilds.org

8. Kdenlive

Kdenlive is a professional-grade, industry-strength video editing application that can ingest, edit, affect, correct, and render motion pictures.

Kdenlive has many dependencies not included in the default Slackermedia sets due to them being highly unique to Kdenlive:

- codecs: x264, xvidcore, schroedinger, lame, libdv, libquicktime, faac, faad2, gsm, amrnb

  *If you installed the **slackermedia-huge** set then you have all of these already*

- libiec61883

- libavc1394

- dvgrab

- recordmydesktop

- qjson

- mlt

Once these are installed, the Slackbuild for Kdenlive is simple.

Please read the Kdenlive Quick Start Guide in this volume for more information on configuring and using **Kdenlive**.

9. Qtractor

Qtractor is a Qt4-based multi-track audio editor with LADSPA, LV2, DSSI, and even VST support. It still claims to be alpha software, so you will want to give it a few test runs before integrating it into your production workflow, but Slackermedia's maintainer has used it for music and voice work for months without incident.

Compilation is a little complex for its multitude of options.

It requires JACK and LADSPA (available via Slackbuilds.org). Optional installs are libvorbis, libmad, libsamplerate, liblo; all available via slackpkg or Slackbuilds.org.

You may also choose to download and install:

- Download the source for *librubberband*[11]

- This in turn depends on *vamp-sdk*[12]

  1. *Compile and install liblo (via Slackbuilds.org or **sbopkg**) and Vamp-SDK*

     ```
     tar -xzf rubberband-x.x.tar.gz && cp -r
     ./rubberband-x.x/vamp ./rubberband-x.x/ladspa
     ./rubberband-x.x/src/
     ```

  2. *add this line to rubberband-x.x/src/system/sysutils.h (thanks to jlindsay for figuring this out)*

     ```
     #include <cstdio>
     ```

  3.
     ```
     ./configure && make && su -c
     'make install'
     ```

  4. *If you receive errors that vamp-sdk cannot be found but you have installed vamp-sdk, then you may need to set $PKG_CONFIG_PATH*

     ```
     PKG_CONFIG_PATH=$PKG_CONFIG_PATH:/usr/local/
     lib/pkgconfig
     ```

- *dssi*[13]

Install is trivial.

---

[11] http://breakfastquay.com/rubberband/
[12] http://sourceforge.net/projects/vamp/
[13] http://dssi.sourceforge.net/

- *VST SDK 2.4*[14]

  In order to enable VST functionality you must:

  1. Establish a developer account at *steinberg.net*[15], confirm registration, and log in.

  2. Download VST 2.4 (technically you can use 2.3 as well)

  3. Unzip the source directory

```
su -c 'cp vstsdk2.4/pluginterfaces/vst2.x/
aeffect*
/usr/local/include/'
```

With so many options available to you, be sure to check the enabled options after ./configure has finished. Only if you have installed components to non-default locations should you need to define paths. Obviously, reading the documentation included with **Qtractor** would clarify extra configuration options.

Please read the full Qtractor user Guide for more information on configuring and using **Qtractor**.

10. Synfig Studio

Synfig Studio is a vector animation tool for Linux. Generally, it is similar to something like Flash or creating animated GIFs in Photoshop. Technically, it consists of two elements: **synfig**, the backend, and **synfig studio**, the GUI front end.

In order to compile it, you first must install **ETL**, then **synfig**, and finally **synfig studio**. All of these packages are available via its *project page*[16]. Note that also included on the project page are rpm packages for both 32bit and 64bit systems, so using Slackware's **rpm2tgz** utility seems to work quite well.

Compiling from source code requires nothing special, although on 64bit systems there may be confusion between /usr/local/lib and /usr/local/lib64 directories, which could cause compiling errors. Should this occur, define the appropriate paths with the --libdir=/usr/local/lib64 or --libdir=/usr/local/lib, and possibly set PKG_CONFIG_PATH as needed.

---

[14] http://www.steinberg.net/en/company/3rd_party_developer.html
[15] http://www.steinberg.net
[16] http://www.synfig.com/download

11. Transcode

Transcode is similar to **ffmpeg** but has some unique features, and is also a recommended dependency on some other major applications. Like **ffmpeg**, it has many options that you will want to ensure are enabled and others that can safely be left disabled. There is a slackbuild for it but if you wish to build from source here is a sample configuration:

```
./configure --enable-libavcodec --enable-
libavformat
   --enable-libavformat --enable-libmpeg2 --enable-
experimental
   --enable-v4l --enable-oss --enable-alsa --enable-
freetype2
   --enable-lame --enable-xvid --enable-x264 --enable-
ogg
   --enable-vorbis --enable-theora --enable-libdvdread
   --enable-libdv
   --enable-libquicktime --enable-a52 --enable-faac --
enable-mjpegtools
   --enable-ibp --enable-sdl --enable-imagemagick --
enable-libjpeg
   --enable-libpostproc --with-libavformat-libs=/usr/
lib
   --with-libavformat-includes=/usr/local/include
   --mandir=/usr/man --with-libpostproc-libs=/usr/lib
```

12. SoX

As **transcode** is to video, so **SoX** is to audio; therefore, to have maximum flexibility in your multimedia studio you will want to create a custom compile of SoX. Since SoX probably installed itself when you installed Slackware, first do:

```
$ su -c 'removepkg sox'
```

Then download the sox *source code*[17] and compile. This is a good set of **./configure** options:

```
./configure --with-distro='Slackermedia13'
--with-ladspa-path='/usr/lib64/' --with-oggvorbis=dyn
```

---

[17] http://sourceforge.net/projects/sox/files/sox/14.3.0/

```
--with-flac=dyn --with-amrwb=dyn --with-amrnb=dyn --
with-wavpack=dyn
--with-alsa=dyn --with-ffmpeg=dyn --with-oss=dyn --
with-sndfile=dyn
--with-mp3=dyn --with-gsm=dyn --with-lpc10=dyn --
with-ao=dyn
--libdir='/usr/lib64'
--mandir='/usr/man/'
```

 Note

Note that if you are doing customization that differs from what Slackermedia does, then one of the **--with-foobar=dyn** options may cause your **./configure** to exit with an error. This is probably because, for instance, you have defined **--with-flac=dyn** but you have no flac support on your system; either install flac (or whatever there is a problem with) or remove that option from your **./configure** command.

13. ffmpeg2theora

ffmpeg2theora is a frontend of sorts for **ffmpeg** that specializes in converting any format that **ffmpeg** can read into the free Ogg Vorbis and Ogg Theora codecs.

There may be no real advantage to using **ffmpeg2theora** rather than just using **ffmpeg**, but it does have an abbreviated set of options since its goal is far more focused than the near-infinite possibilities of **ffmpeg**.

The command structure is similar, so if you've used **ffmpeg** or **mencoder** to transcode media then it will all feel very familiar:

```
$ ffmpeg2theora input_file.avi -x 1080 -y
720 -V 10000kbps -A 320kbps -c 2 -H 48000 -o
output.ogv
```

In other words:

```
$ ffmpeg2theora [input filename] -x
[target horizontal pixel count] -y [target vertical
```

```
pixel count] -V [target bitrate in kbps] -A [audio
bit rate] -c [audio channels] -H [audio sample
rate in Hz] -o [output filename]
```

ffmpeg2theora is available from Slackbuilds.org and requires no special compile options.

14. video-meta

Mike Schilli's perl script to show metadata on a video file is a helpful "video forensics" tool that invokes the **Video::FrameGrab** module which in turn invokes **mplayer**. This tool can quickly help a video artist determine codecs, frame sizes, bitrates, frame rates and other properties of video clips at a glance. The installation is easy but unique in that it involves perl, which has its own way of installing modules. It also depends upon **yaml**, available from SlackBuilds.org

1. Install the *video::framegrab*[18] perl module with the command:

```
$ su -c "perl -MCPAN -e
'install Video::FrameGrab'"
```

2. Install the *data::dump*[19] perl module with the command:

```
$ su -c "perl -MCPAN -e
'install Data::Dump'"
```

3. The script **video-meta** itself requires no installation, although the initial line of the script needs modifying so that the script can find perl on the system.

```
$ wget
ftp://linuxmagazin.de/pub/magazin/2010/01/
Perl/video-meta -O video-meta.pl
$ sed "1s#/local##"
video-meta.pl > video-meta
$ chmod +x video-meta
```

---

[18] http://cpan.uwinnipeg.ca/search?query=Video%3A%3AFramegrab&mode=module
[19] http://cpan.uwinnipeg.ca/module/Data::Dump

```
$ su -c 'cp video-meta /usr/local/bin/'
```

The script can then be used by simply invoking it before the name of a video file, such as: **video-meta foo.avi**, which will list all metadata attributes associated with foo.avi

Soft Synths and Effects Explained

Soft Synths are the software versions of the big and bulky synthesizers that electronic musicians used to lug around to gigs and studios. The concept of using a synthesizer is simple if expressed in hardware terminology; if you have a recording device and a synthesizer, then you connect the synthesizer sound Out to the recorder's sound In, press record on the recording device and play on the synthesizer. If you want your music to be more complex, then you'll purchase an 4-track recorder, a mixer, and mulitiple synthesizers. To make it more automated, you'd use MIDI so that you can trigger sounds and pre-recorded phrases on cue.

In the software world, the equivalent setup would be a good multi-track audio editor like *Qtractor*[1] or **Rosegarden** (from **sbopkg**) and some soft synths. To record, then, you will start the **Qtractor** application, add a new track, open the mixer window, and define the track as containing a plugin that is a synthesizer of your choice. The soft synth then appears onscreen as a plugin into **qtractor**, which you can then sequence and play and record.

In the hardware world, we might have experienced issues with cable sizes (eighth-inch connectors, quarter-inch connectors, mono vs stereo, and so on) or MIDI compatibility; in the software world we experience issues with soft synth plugin formats. Specifically, soft synths and effect units are created in a variety of different formats. For **Qtractor**, we have access to:

- DSSI

- LADSPA

- LV2 (LADSPA's second-coming)

- VST (Linux-Native)

VST is the most ubiquitous of soft synth formats and via a combination of Steinberg's VST SDK and **Qtractor**, you can have Linux-Native VST synths or effects on your Slackermedia machine. Note that the VST plugins must be *Linux-Native*, which are far fewer in number than Windows and Mac VST plugins, making the best support for soft synth and effects available via DSSI and LADSPA.

Installing soft synths and effects is simple; find the synth or effect you want, download the source code, build and install. The default install location rarely needs to be altered. Then, in **Qtractor**, go to the **View** menu, select **Options**, and click on **Plugins** and define where all of your installed plugins are located in your system.

---

[1] http://qtractor.sourceforge.net/

> **Important**
>
> The paths to audio plugins are usually /usr/local/lib or /usr/lib on 32bit systems, and either /usr/local/lib64 or /usr/lib64 on 64bit systems.

Once these paths are defined, you will be presented with, when you create a track and insert a plugin, a list of auto-detected LADSPA, DSSI, and VST plugins that you may use on that track. The plugin may be a soft synth that you want to use to generate sound, or it may be an effect that you wish to process the track through. It may be a combination of both.

Keep in mind as you search the internet for new synths and plugins that you are looking for DSSI or LADSPA plugins unless you intend to do quite a bit of hacking to get VST plugins to work. Also keep in mind that if you decide to use a stand-alone soft synth or effect, that they must be JACK-aware.

1. Finding Soft Synth Plugins for Linux

One source for good soft synths and effects is *Planet CCRMA*[2] (pronounced "Planet Karma"), a well-maintained and respected site that hosts audio software for Red Hat and Fedora. This provides an exhaustive list of all the audio software available for Linux, a brief description of each application and its function, and even RPMs that could be utilized by Slackware's *rpm2tgz* for a quick and easy install.

Outside of this, the usual Linux search locations apply.

2. Some Popular Soft Synths for Linux

2.1. whySynth

In terms of instant gratification, *whySynth*[3] is one of the best. If you require a synth fully loaded with diverse pre-made patches, install this first. With over 200 synth sounds ready-to-use and a friendly interface, **whySynth** is the synth to install if all you want to do is get started making synth music on Linux.

---

[2] http://ccrma-www.stanford.edu/planetccrma/software/soundapps.html
[3] http://www.smbolton.com/whysynth.html

The interface for **whySynth** at first is simply a list of available patches; if you want to create new patches or edit current ones, you can select **Edit > Edit Patch** and you will be shown a full synthesizer interface.

To install **whySynth**, download the source code from *dssi.sourceforge.net*[4] and set the PKG_CONFIG_PATH:

```
$
PKG_CONFIG_PATH=/usr/local/lib/pkgconfig
$ export PKG_CONFIG_PATH
```

And then compile as usual with `./configure && make && su -c 'make install'`

Access **whySynth** via **Qtractor** or other DAW as a plugin for a MIDI track.

2.2. Xsynth-DSSI

Xsynth[5] is part of the basis for whySynth but may require more setup than whySynth and, for those not familiar with synthesis may be overwhelmed by its interface. Installing it is the same as with whySynth.

2.3. hexter

Hexter[6] is a Yamaha DX7 emulator that also can import native Yamaha DX7 patch files (many are available with a simple internet search). The user interface is simple with more complex controls accessed via the **Edit** button on the synth itself. It comes pre-packaged with 70 patches and has moderate control over each. Installation is the same as **whySynth** and **Xsynth**. Be sure to read the README for links to sites with DX7 patches and information.

2.4. nekobee-DSSI

Nekobee[7] is a simple synth for DSSI with modest controls. Installation is same as whySynth.

2.5. Fluidsynth

Fluidsynth is a command-line synthesizer that utilizes E-MU's Soundfont format. Soundfonts are a flexible format and provide high quality sounds to a variety of platforms. Because they can be used on a variety of platforms, there are many soundfonts available,

---

[4] http://dssi.sourceforge.net/
[5] http://dssi.sourceforge.net/download.html
[6] http://dssi.sourceforge.net/download.html
[7] http://dssi.sourceforge.net/download.html

many entirely free. In a sense, soundfonts are akin to sample banks, with Fluidsynth acting as your host and soundfont as the source of any variety of soundwave.

Fluidsynth is available via Slackbuilds.org, as well as a DSSI plugin from *dssi.sourceforge.net*[8]

2.6. Fluidsynth-DSSI

There are two notable frontends for Fluidsynth: the plugin *Fluidsynth-DSSI*[9] and the stand-alone **Qsynth**.

Fluidsynth-DSSI is installed and used like all other DSSI plugins, while **Qsynth** requires further MIDI and Audio routing.

2.7. Soundfonts

In order to utilize **Fluidsynth**, **Qsynth**, or **Fluidsynth-DSSI**, you must have soundfonts on your system. Soundfonts are plentiful online, but unfortunately, like GIMP brushes and free fonts, there seems to be no central repository for them. This means that each artist must go online and hunt for soundfonts. So that you have to do this only once, it is advisable to archive all soundfonts you download.

Soundfonts require no installation, as such. Simply unzip or unrar or untar the soundfonts that you download and place them in a directory somewhere on your system. They are loaded manually into **Fluidsynth-DSSI** by clicking the **Load Soundfont** button on **Fluidsynth-DSSI**'s interface, and they are loaded manually into **Qsynth** via the **Setup** button.

One good source of free soundfonts is *Hammersound.net*[10]. This site merely lists soundfonts available and links to files hosted elsewhere, so some links will have expired, but hammersound.net remains an invaluable resource.

Note

The Great Linux Multimedia Sprint v1.0[11] features over 350 soundfonts in one easy-to-use zip file. All of the fine Hammersound collection is included in this bundle, as well.

---

[8] http://dssi.sourceforge.net/download.html
[9] http://dssi.sourceforge.net/download.html
[10] http://www.hammersound.net/
[11] http://www.slackermedia.info/downloads.html

3. Finding Effect Processors for Linux

Effect processors are those devices (or in this case, software plugins) that take sound and process them to combine them with some effect, like reverb, a bitcrusher, echo, guitar amp emulator, and so on. They are often available separate from one another but typically it is more convenient to simply download a package of plugins.

3.1. Steve Harris LADSPA Plugins

The Steve Harris LADSPA plugins are perhaps the most ubiquitous package of plugins, featuring almost every effect imaginable. They are high quality plugins well worth downloading and installing. Install via **sbopkg** and find them in your DAW's LADSPA plugin window.

3.2. Calf Plugins

The *Calf plugin*[12] set features common effects like delay, phaser, reverb, an organ synthesizer, and others. By default, it installs the plugins as both DSSI and LADSPA plugins, so no matter what DAW you are using you should see them as available plugins. As long as you have installed the Audio module of **Slackermedia**, then installation of Calf is a simple `./configure && make && su -c 'make install'`

3.3. Jamin

Jamin is a powerful audio mastering suite with full-featured compressors and EQ to make the most out of the master output of your digital audio workstation. It is a stand-alone application, so must be utilized as an Aux Send from your DAW; for details, read the Qtractor User Manual.

4. Stand-Alone Synths

Stand-alone synths exist outside of the **Qtractor** interface, and must be tied into the **Qtractor** workflow via JACK. The key to doing this successfully is to make sure that the stand-alone synth is JACK-aware, and knowing your MIDI drivers.

To understand the specifics of using stand-alone synths in **Qtractor**, see the updated **Qtractor** User Manual. Here is a quick overview:

1. Start **Qtractor** (which in turn starts **jackd**)

2. Then start the stand-alone synth

3. Set the MIDI driver of the stand-alone synth to **alsa_seq**, the Slackware default MIDI driver.

---

[12] http://calf.sourceforge.net/

4. Make sure, via **QJackCtl**, that **Alsa Sequencing** is enabled (in the **Misc** tab)

5. Load a soundfont and set the bank to something other than zero and populate its MIDI channels with the soundfonts you wish to use

6. Create a new MIDI track in **Qtractor**, setting the MIDI channel to whatever soundfont you want that track to speak to

7. Once the track appears in your workspace, right-click the track name and select Outputs

8. Connect the Master MIDI output of **Qtractor** to the stand-alone synth

9. Now all MIDI data you enter into that track will trigger the stand-alone synth

4.1. Qsynth

Qsynth, from the developer of **QJackCtl** and **Qtractor** itself, is a solid, intuitive, and attractive GUI frontend for **Fluidsynth**. It uses, therefore, soundfonts for its sound sources and therefore is almost endlessly diverse. From one **Qsynth** instance, you can create multiple **Qsynth** engines, and each engine may have a variety of soundfonts loaded into it.

Get Qsynth at *qsynth.sourceforge.net*[13]. Installation is achieved with the standard `./configure && make && su -c 'make install'` sequence. It depends upon **fluidsynth**, available via **sbopkg**.

4.2. Linux Sampler

The *Linux Sampler*[14] is a stand-alone sampler as well as a DSSI, LV2, and Linux-native VST unit. It uses the *GigaStudio* sample format, used in many of the de facto soft sampler applications. The compile options are many, but the download page of linuxsampler.org provides a good guide on how to proceed.

The source code for Linux Sampler consists of a minimum of two components (**libgig** and **linuxsampler**) with an option of using up to seven components. To compile it as a stand-alone application as well as a DSSI and LV2 (the two free formats Qtractor supports) this is the order that the compilation must occur:

*   Install `libgig` with the usual `./configure && make && su -c 'make install'`

*   For linuxsampler:

    1. `$       ./configure       --libdir=/usr/local/lib PKG_CONFIG_PATH=/usr/local/lib/pkgconfig`

---

[13] http://qsynth.sourceforge.net/
[14] http://www.linuxsampler.org/downloads.html

2. $ **make**

3. $ **su -c 'make install'**

- For gigedit:

    1. $ **./configure   PKG_CONFIG_PATH=/usr/local/lib/ pkgconfig**

    2. $ **make && su -c 'make install'**

- For Qsampler:

    1. First install **liblscp** with **./configure && make && su -c 'make install'**

    2. Then install Qsampler itself with **./configure && make && su -c 'make install'**

Note

The main source of trouble during compiling these components will most likely be the order in which everything is installed. The above order is correct, and should render no errors. Defining the PKG_CONFIG_PATH variable helps define the presence and version of **libgig**.

As the download page of **Linux Sampler** says, **Qsampler** is independent of linuxsampler itself. Therefore, if you build the backend (libgig+linuxsampler +gigedit) then you can choose to download and install **Qsampler** and its dependency or a different frontend, like **Jsampler** and its dependency, or both, or neither.

The example above renders both a simple DSSI plugin immediately accessible via your DAW (such as Qtractor), and a stand-alone application that can be utilized either independely or with a DAW via JACK -- the same as with Qsynth and other stand-alone sound generators.

4.3. Sooper Looper

Sooper Looper is a digital tape loop device, or a looping sampler. It requires JACK and, notably, a 1.2.x series libsigc++. Please note that libsigc++ 2.x which is available via Slackbuilds is not sufficient; a libsigc++ release in the 1.2.x series must be downloaded from *http://ftp.gnome.org/pub/GNOME/sources/libsigc++/1.2/* and installed. It will co-exist peacefully with libsigc++ 2.x but it must be present for Sooper Looper to build.

Aside from that, Sooper Looper builds relatively easily with `./configure && make && su -c 'make install'` although depending on what it is set to, you may need to set PKG_CONFIG_PATH to `/usr/local/lib`

Sooper Looper itself can be run on the command line or with a GUI. The command for the command line application is sooperlooper while the command for the gui application is **slgui**.

4.4. Hydrogen

Hydrogen is a software drum machine with the traditional pattern and song paradigms of traditional hardware sequencers. Creating custom drum kits is very easy, and the interface is both intuitive and powerful. Hydrogen is readily available for other operating systems, as well, so it has a good community surrounding it and a good repository of custom drum kits available via *a dedicated sourceforge project page*[15].

Download the source code from *hydrogen-music.org*[16] and untar it. Compilation uses **scons**, which will be installed if you have done the basic installs recommended by Slackermedia. It also depends on **zlib** or **libtar** and **liblrdf**, all available via Slackbuilds.org

After all dependencies have been installed, run `scons --help` and verify that the configuration options are satisfactory. Then simply run `scons`, followed by `su -c 'scons install'` and **hydrogen** will be installed and ready to use.

Using **Hydrogen** with a DAW, like **Qtractor**, is fairly trivial with **QJackCtl**; simply ensure that **Hydrogen**'s MIDI driver is set to ALSA and then direct the DAW's master MIDI out to **Hydrogen** via the **Connection** screen in **QJackCtl**.

---

[15] http://sourceforge.net/projects/hydrogen/files/Sound%20Libraries/
[16] http://www.hydrogen-music.org/?p=download

The Patchbay That Jack Built

Since **Qtractor** relies upon **QJackCtl** as its signal routing backend, it can take full advantage of **QJackCtl's Patchbay** feature. The **Patchbay** is basically an interface that allows you to define pre-set routing configuration so that needn't re-do all your routing every time you start either **QJackCtl** or **Qtractor**.

Note

This chapter paraphrases a blogpost on developer Rui Nuno Capela's *blog*[1], which in turn quotes a mailing list post by user Simon W. Fielding.

To create a preset configuration for your gear and software:

1. Plug in all devices and activate the applications you intend to connect to.

Note

You may wish to connect everything manually first, although it's not necessary. It may help guide you, however, as you will be re-creating the configuration manually.

2. Click the **Patchbay** button in the lower left of the **QJackCtl** window. If needed, you can also open the **Connections** window as reference.

3. In the **Patchbay**, click the **New** button located in the top left corner of the window.

4. You will be asked if you wish to create a snapshot of your current configuration. Somewhat counter-intuitively, the answer is **No**.

---

[1] http://www.rncbc.org/drupal/node/76

Warning

If you answer Yes to this question, this process *will not work*. The correct answer is **No**.

5. Obviously there are nearly infinite varieties of possible configurations, so the following example is only one of many. The principle will be the same regardless of your setup.

    Click the **Add** button on the left side of the patchbay to create a new Output Socket. An Output Socket in this context is a source of sound or some kind of signal; it's an output of itself, and it will be sent as an Input to the computer!

6. In the **New Output Socket** window, provide a logical, human-readable name for your new socket. If you are defing where you'd like your USB keyboard to be routed, for example, you might name this socket **USBKeyboard_AKAI**.

7. Define the type of socket; the three types are Audio, MIDI, or ALSA. These correspond with your **Connections** window, so refer to it if you're unsure. If you had your USB keyboard working as a MIDI device, then simply look in connections and see how you had it routed, and emulate that for your socket. In my example, I would set this socket to **ALSA**, since I am using ALSA as my MIDI driver.

8. Set the **Client** to reflect the device you are routing. In my example, I would choose the LPK25_AKAI.

9. Choose from any available plugs that you wish to use. In my example there is but one; choose yours, and click the **Add** button to add it to the socket.

10. Click the **OK** button to confirm. You now have an output socket available in your custom patchbay. Next, set an Input socket for **JACK**.

11. The process for the Input socket is basically the same; click the **Add** button on the right of the patchbay. In the **New Input Socket** window, give a logical name for your socket; in my example, I might use **Qtractor_AKAI** or similar.

12. Set the type to the same as your related **Output** socket; in this example, I would choose ALSA.

13. Choose the destination client from the **Client** dropdown menu. In this case, I would choose **Qtractor**, but if I have a dedicated keyboard for a specific synth, then I might

just as likely choose **amSynth** or any other potential destination for a keyboard. Again, your previous experience with your known setup should be your guide here.

14. Choose the plug to use for the socket; in this case I have only one available, so I would select it and click the **Add** button, and then the **OK** button to confirm the socket creation.

15. Back in the **Patchbay** window, there are now two sockets. Within each socket there is one device. Click these devices and click the **Connect** button.

16. Repeat this process for each source of sound or signal and each destination, until you have replicated your typical setup in this patchbay form.

17. When you have finished setting up the patchbay definition, click the **Save** button to save it as a preset. Save a copy of the configuration to both a standard location in your home directory, as well as into your project folder for safe keeping.

18. To load this configuration manually, simply click the **Load** from the **Patchbay** window of **QJackCtl**.

    If you want this to be your default configuration, then click the **Setup** button on the right of the **QJackCtl** window.

    Click the **Options** tab and place a checkmark in the **Activate Patchbay Persistence** option. Choose the preset you wish to have automatically loaded.

19. Click the **OK** button to save your changes.

20. Restart **QJackCtl** to test the auto-load.

You now have persistent connections for **QJackCtl** and **Qtractor**.

Slackermedia for Writers

GNU Emacs is a robust writing environment for both creative and technical writers alike. This, in part, is due to its high level of customization and extensive plug-in structure. There are many "modes" that you can use from within **Emacs**, allowing it to become the ideal editor for whatever kind of writing or writing-development that you do.

For creative writers, the default **Emacs** environment is sufficient. To add to it, you might want to look at *org-mode*[1], which can help you organize notes and thoughts about your writing project.

For screenplays, of course there is **screenwriter.el**

For technical writers and creative writers seeking to self-publish rich pdf documents, there is Docbook XML and the emacs *nXML mode*[2], which will help validate the XML markup that Docbook uses. There is also a handy Docbook Menu for emacs, available at *sourceforge.net/projects/docbook/fiels/emas-docbook-menu*[3].

And there is always the online version of the authoratative *Docbook Reference Manual*[4], as well as the source code of the *Slackermedia book*[5] itself, with a customized Docbook workflow described in detail in the HOWTO file.

Installing extras in **Emacs** is usually described in the code of the `.el` file itself. Reading the comments of an `.el` file is often all that you will need in order to know how to install it and start using it in **Emacs**. However, the process can be summarized in these general, typical steps:

1. Download the mode from its website

2. Place it in your ~/elisp directory (you will want to create this directory if it does not already exist)

3. Make sure that the ~/elisp directory is in the load-path of emacs

4. Add the mode as a loadable plugin in your ~/.emacs file

1. Installing a single .el mode

More explicitly, if you are downloading a mode that is distributed as a single `.el` file, the process would be this:

---

[1] http://orgmode.org
[2] http://www.thaiopensource.com/nxml-mode/
[3] http://sourceforge.net/projects/docbook/files/emacs-docbook-menu/
[4] http://www.docbook.org/tdg5/en/html/docbook.html
[5] http://gitorious.org/slackermedia

```
$ wget http://www.example.com/foo.el -P ~/elisp/
```

This downloads the `.el` file to your ~/elisp file, which is essentially a plug-ins folder for emacs.

```
$ echo "(add-to-list 'load-path \"~/elisp\")"
>> .emacs
```

This ensures that ~/elisp is in your load-path. This only need to be done once, as once ~/elisp is in your load-path it will always be in your load-path.

```
$ echo "(require 'foo)"
>> .emacs
```

This tells emacs to load (or "require") the mode that you want to use. Note that you require the mode by name, not by file name (ie, you do not include the `.el` extension).

2. Installing a bundled .el mode

Sometimes a mode comes bundled with other related files. For instance, nXML-mode is distributed as nxml-mode-20041004.tar.gz. To install this sort of mode, download and untar the directory of code to ~/elisp:

```
$ wget
http://www.thaiopensource.com/download/nxml-
mode-20041004.tar.gz
$ tar -xf nxml-mode-20041004.tar.gz -C
~/elisp/
```

Tell **emacs** to load the mode each time it is launched:

```
echo "(load \"~/elisp/nxml-mode-20041004/rng-auto.el
\") >> ~/.emacs
```

Notice that we use "load" rather than "require" and provide the full path to the `.el` file, mainly because the `.el` file does not exist directly in the ~/elisp directory (there are more technical differences between the load and require functions; see emacs documentation for more information, if interested).

3. The dot-emacs file and You

It is not uncommon for Unix traditionalists to carry around source code and handy scripts for years, from computer to computer. It is not a bad idea to get into this habit yourself, should you find emacs modes that become indispensible to you, or docbook schemas that you require, or bash or python or perl scripts that make your life easier. Download the code, keep them organized in your ~/elisp directory, backup your .emacs file, and keep track of your ~/src directory. Most of these simple (yet life-changing) scripts and programs will quite likely work for you for the rest of your computing life.

4. screenwriter.el

The most universal and simple solution is **Screenwriter.el** a fork of **Screenplay.el** by Vance L. Simpson. This is an excellent screenplay (major) mode for **GNU Emacs** that is easy to use, efficient, and will work on any and every platform that the ubiquitous and revered **GNU Emacs** works on.

If you are running a default install of Slackware, as Slackermedia recommends, then you will have **Emacs** installed already. If you have not installed **Emacs**, you will find it in the **e** package set.

Installing `.el` files for **Emacs** is as simple as placing the `.el` in a user-owned **~/elisp** directory, and then adding that **~/elisp** directory into **Emacs'** load directory if it is not already there:

```
$ mkdir ~/elisp
$ wget
http://cvs.savannah.gnu.org/viewvc/*checkout*/
screenwriter/screenwriter/screenwriter-1.5.tar.bz2
$ tar -xf screenwriter-1.5.tar.bz2
$ mv ./screenwriter-mode/screenwriter.el ~/elisp
$ echo "(add-to-list 'load-path \"~/elisp\")"
  >> .emacs
$ echo "(require 'screenplay)" >> .emacs
```

Start **emacs** and press **meta x**, and type **screenwriter-mode**. You are now in **screenplay-mode** and can start writing in proper screenplay format. Read the comments in **~/elisp/screenplay.el** for instructions on how to use the application, or read on for use and optimization, Slackermedia style.

4.1. Using and Optimizing Screenwriter-mode

There are three elements in screenplays:

• Slug Lines (scene headings, such as INT. CAFE - NIGHT)

- Screen Direction (blocks of action text, wherein the screenwriter describes what a character is doing physically during a scene)

- Dialogue (heavily indented blocks of text in which characters speak)

Accessing each element is done with keyboard commands that can be easily remembered with the mnemonic SAD:

- **Control-c**   **s**   Slugline

- **Control-c**   **a**   Action (Screen direction)

- **Control-c**   **d**   Dialogue

Additionally, you can use **Control-c t** to insert **Transitions** (indented and capitalized blocks for CUT TO:, FADE IN, FADE OUT, and so on).

Whitespace is handled for you, so there is no need to place a blank line between the actor's lines, or between a slugline and the beginning of the action, and so on.

Note

Alternate keybindings for each element type centers around the **tab** key:

- **tab**   **return**   Slugline

- **tab tab**   **return**   Action

- **tab tab tab**   **return**   Dialogue

- **tab tab tab tab**   **return**   Transition

4.2. Streamlining Screenwriter-mode

Make **screenwriter-mode** a quicker launch from within **emacs** by adding a global keyboard shortcut for it, and defining the expected file suffix:

```
; a quick and easy way to enter screenplay-mode


(global-set-key (kbd "<f5>")
'screenplay-mode)
```

```
; open any file with a .scp or .screenplay suffix
in
  screenplay-mode


  (setq auto-mode-alist (cons '("\\.scp" .
screenplay-mode)
    auto-mode-alist))


  (setq auto-mode-alist (cons '("\\.screenplay" .
screenplay-mode)
    auto-mode-alist))
```

Save your **.emacs** file and launch Emacs. Pressing **F5** should place you in **screenplay-mode**. Pressing **control-c s** will start a new slugline for you, **control-c a** an action block, and **control-c d** a dialogue block.

Save a sample screenplay (sample.scp, for example), and then close **Emacs**. Open **Emacs** again and open a file via the **File** menu or by using the **control-x control-f** key sequence. Open your **sample.scp** and note that **Emacs** opens it in **screenplay-mode**.

In Dolphin, you can right-click on **sample.scp** and choose to **Open With Emacs**, and it will be opened in **screenplay-mode** in **Emacs**. However, default KDE uses the much faster single-click method, so it would be nice if a single click on any **.scp** or **.screenplay** file would open prompt KDE to launch **Emacs**, and **Emacs** in turn to open in screenplay mode.

Emacs is already set for **.scp** and **.screenplay**, so only KDE now needs to be configured:

1. Open **System Settings**; open it and select the **File Associations** panel.

2. Click the **Add...** button on the left of the panel to add a new file type.

3. Place it in the **Text** category. It will be placed at the bottom of the text list; select it and configure it on the right side of the panel.

4. You may give it a custom icon, such as something from the Oxygen Icon set that suggests movies or the default **Emacs** Document icon, and define the file extension as both ***.scp** and ***.screenplay**.

5. Give the **Application Preference Order** a sensible set of applications. The documents are in plain text, so they may be opened in any text editor; **Emacs** as the first is obvious, **Kate** and **KWrite** are likely candidates for fallback applications.

6. Click the **Apply** button in the lower right corner to save your configuration.

Now if you click on sample.scp from **Dolphin**, KDE will open it in **Emacs**, and **Emacs** will enter **screenwriter-mode**.

You now have a screenplay authoring program for Slackermedia, and quite likely for any other platform you possibly run.

5. screenplay-tools

screenplay-tools is a powerful set of helper scripts developed by Slackermedia to aid:

1. The screenwriter in formatting and printing a screenplay written in **screenwriter-mode** in **emacs**

2. The Assistant Director or Producer in getting important scheduling-related reports from the screenplay

screenplay-tools[6] is free under the GPLv3 license and requires no external dependencies. To install into ~/bin, the recommended location, simply cd into the screenplay-tools directory and run the install script:

```
$ tar -xf screenplay-tools.tgz
$ cd ~/screenplay-tools
$ ./install.sh
# enter your password
```

This obviously assumes you already have a ~/bin. If you do not, then you should do this first:

```
$ mkdir ~/bin
$ PATH=$PATH:/home/$USER/bin
$ export PATH
```

This does NOT require root privs because by default it installs everything into your home bin directory. If you prefer the commands to be available for all users of the system, just **cp** them, as root, to **/usr/local/bin/**

You can also install man pages by running, as root, **installman.sh**, which installs man pages to /usr/share/man/man1/

You can also find an in-line quick-reference guide by running screenplay-help

---

[6] http://www.gitorious.org/screenplay-tools

5.1. screenplay-tools

A convention that **Slackermedia** uses is to name *scenes* written in screenwriter.el with the extension `.scp` and either complete screenplays or blocks of text to be processed as screenplays with the extension `.screenplay`. This is obviously not a requirement, but **screenplay-tools** is written under these assumptions (although it is free software, so you are free to change it to suit your own workflow).

An example screenplay directory might, therefore, look like this:

```
$ cd ~/slackermediaTheMovie
$ ls
00.scp
01.scp
02.scp
03.scp
# and so on..
```

In this way, scenes are easily re-arranged, shelved, archived, printed, etc. In other words, take advantage of the UNIX philosophy and keep it modular.

screenplay-tools itself is only the application suite. The actual commands are:

- screenplay-build - to preview your screenplay as a single document

- screenplay-title - to easily generate a formatted title page

- screenplay-print - to create a printable document

- screenplay-location - to generate a report on locations and sets

- screenplay-character - to generate a report on characters and casting

- screenplay-help - instant stdout help

5.2. screenplay-build

For a quick preview of your screenplay as one big document, use

```
$ screenplay-build ~/myScreenplayDir
```

which concatenates anything appended with `.scp` into one complete **preview.screenplay**, indents it for readability, and places that preview file in whatever directory you currently are in.

If you've configured your system with the Slackermedia .emacs file, then preview.screenplay will open in screenplay-mode in Emacs, and is obviously also readable (being plain text) in any other text editor you choose.

Note that this is intended as a quick, single-file preview of your screenplay only and does not contain page-numbers or scene numbers.

5.3. screenplay-title

To generate a properly formatted title page for your screenplay, use:

```
$ screenplay-title
```

which interactively creates and saves the file **title.page** with a capitalized and centered title, a correctly placed by-line, and your contact info.

5.4. screenplay-print

Once you're ready to print the screenplay, and after you have generated a `title.page`, use

```
$ screenplay-print [directory with all your .scp
files in it]
```

which will attempt to auto-detect the title and author from your `title.page` (although it allows for override), indent your script by 8 spaces to provide for a left margin, number scenes by occurence of SLUGLINES, add the `title.page` to the front of the document, and insert form feed characters to enforce page breaks.

Finally, it will ask you to confirm printing via **lpr**

If you are ready to print, then answer **y** and it will send the printable script and the title page to your default line printer.

Otherwise, you'll be left with a `print.screenplay`, which you can review and print at your leisure.

If you do not have an **lpr** printer configured, then you can use the **--no-print** flag. This will not attempt to print but will save a print-friendly version of your script to a file.

If you want the **lpr** printing to work, you should open up the **CUPS** admin panel in a web browser. You reach this by opening a web browser to 127.0.0.1:631, and you will probably need the root password.

In the **ADMINISTRATION** panel of this page, you can **MANAGE PRINTERS** or add a new one if you haven't used a printer on the system yet. Do that, and set a printer as an **lpd://** printer, and set that as your default.

As an example, one might go to CUPS and add a new printer, selecting the production office's Ricoh 1060 printer by way of its IP address:

```
lpd://192.168.1.8
```

Choose the matching driver, which is conveniently already installed (but if yours isn't, go to *openprinting.org*[7] and find the **ppd** file). Mark this printer as your default.

If you want to save your screenplay to a PDF and email it to your production staff and actors, there are a few different options.

The easiest and most direct method is to download *text2pdf*[8], a small application by Phil Smith, which takes plain text and creates a PDF. There is both the source code and a GNU **MakeFile** available from the website.

To compile it, simply download both, place them into a consolidated folder, and run **make**. You can then move **text2pdf** to either **~/bin** or a systemwide **bin** directory.

Once installed, you can do this:

```
$ text2pdf print.screenplay >
  slackermediaTheMovie.pdf
```

This produces **slackermediaTheMovie.pdf**, viewable in any PDF viewer.

---

[7] http://www.openprinting.org
[8] http://www.eprg.org/pdfcorner/text2pdf/

If, on the other hand, you prefer or want to use **CUPS** as a pdf "printer", then you can download the *cups-pdf*[9] ppd from its website, install it, create a printer backend for it, and print.

This is more complex than using **text2pdf** and there is no noticeable advantage, but a good overview of it can be found on *alien.slackbook.org/dokuwiki/doku.php? id=slackware:cups*[10]

5.5. screenplay-location

Once the screenplay is finalized, one of the first things you'll want are LOCATION reports and CHARACTER reports.

You should have a **preview.screenplay** or a **print.screenplay** for these to work the way they are intended to work. But there's nothing stopping you from running it on individual scene files, either.

To get a list of all locations in your screenplay, run this:

```
$ screenplay-location [input file] [output file]
```

This will interactively generate one of 4 types of location reports, or one that includes them all:

1. List of all (unique) locations

2. List of all INT. locations

3. List of all EXT. locations

4. List all locations in script order

5. Generate all of the above in one report

By default, you end up with a printable report with appropriate headings to indicate what report it is.

---

[9] http://www.physik.uni-wuerzburg.de/~vrbehr/cups-pdf/
[10] http://alien.slackbook.org/dokuwiki/doku.php?id=slackware:cups

Warning

screenplay-location is programmed to eliminate common transitions and other capitalized words from its list, but there is obviously a chance that something will get listed as a location when it is not. You may need to review your location list for these quirks before sending it out to your entire production crew.

If you prefer to keep the reports digital, you can specify an output file with the `.org` extension, such as `locations.org` to produce a document without enforced page breaks or headers, formatted for use in **org-mode**'s outline view.

Note

Org-mode is a major mode for Emacs which excels at project management and is, along with screenplay.el and screenplay-tools, all a movie production needs for its organizational and scheduling needs. Learn more about it, and download it, from *orgmode.org*[11]

5.6. screenplay-character

Before you start casting, you will want a report of all the characters you've written into your movie so that you know what casting slots you must fill.

screenplay-character searches for all the CAPITALIZED character names with dialogue. It will also therefore catch transitions, but it uses **grep** and **sed** to eliminate as many false positives before you see the final report. Also eliminated from the list are transitions, like CUT TO, FADE IN, FADE OUT, etc. but you should review the output before distributing the report to your casting director.

By default, this list is formatted for printing with appropriate headers and page breaks as needed. As with **screenplay-location**, if you prefer to keep the reports digital, you can specify an output file with the **.org** extension, such as **characters.org** and a document without enforced page breaks or headers, formatted for use in **org-mode's** outline view will be produced.

---

[11] http://www.orgmode.org

6. celtx

Another free alternative is a multi-platform app based on the Mozilla codebase, called **Celtx**. This has many of the features one would expect from a commercial application, including integration with a scheduling module, database for characters and props and breakdown sheets, an outline or notecard view, and so on. There are extra modules available for fees, such as online collaboration and "writer's tools".

Warning

There are some disadvantages to Celtx, not the least of which includes a lackluster response from the development team when community members ask for the source code in accordance with the license.

Trelby is probably a better option, unless it is compatible collaboration with others that you require; **Celtx** does have a userbase and is already completely cross-platform.

Celtx installation is simple as long as you are using it on the 32bit x86 architecture. There are downloadable packages available from in a variety of languages and one especially for the eeePC form factor. Using Celtx is therefore as simple as downloading the tarball, untarring it into your ~/bin directory, and adding it to your application launcher.

```
$ wget http://download.celtx.com/2.7/
Celtx-2.7.tar.bz2
$ tar -xf Celtx-2.7.tar.bz2 -C ~/bin/
```

To add **Celtx** to your **K Menu**, right click on the **K Menu** and select **Menu Editor**. Create a new menu entry with `control N`, and set the **Command** field to `~/bin/Celtx/celtx`. Save the change, and from now on you will have a **Celtx** entry in your application menu.

7. Trelby

A new project, called *Trelby*[12] shows promise in becoming a properly free GUI-oriented screenwriting program. Initial tests prove an impressive import feature and all the usual GUI bells and whistles. It is licensed under the GPL.

---

[12] http://trelby.org

The developers of **Trelby** are active and responsive, and Trelby's source code is easily obtainable. The interface is attractive and even though it is a relatively new program, its stability and feature set leaves little to be desired.

For GUI-oriented screenwriting, **Trelby** is Slackermedia's recommendation.

The End

You have reached the end, meaning that you are now ready to start creating your art. Having made this journey, you are probably now far better equiped to be a truly independent artist than ever; you not only understand your system, you understand how it was built, why certain technologies require others, why some technology must be hacked around, and how to fix things when they go wrong (or at least where to ask for help).

You may also find that some of what you have learnt about the Unix philosophy and even the broader models of Software Development may help you in creating your artwork and refining your workflow.

Whatever path you have chosen to take from a basic Slackware install toward a multimedia "Slackermedia" system, you are now prepared to use Free Software for your own brand of creativity. There is freedom in the software you have chosen to use, and so you should exercise the same freedom in your creativity.

To this end, you may find it helpful to support the *Creative Commons* [1] and "Free Culture" movements, by using and contributing to sites such as *freesound.org* [2], *openclipart.org* [3], and even the extended search for cc content on sites like flickr.com

I think you'll not regret choosing Slackware GNU Linux as your operating system, and Slackermedia as your tutorial. Remember to share successes with everyone, and don't be afraid to ask for help when the going gets rough.

And it will get rough. But then that's why you're an artist, no?

Well, OK, maybe that's not why, but you know already that art is tough, you know it's challenging, you know you're going to have to work for results, and you know that it's in your blood to make art nevertheless.

On Free Software and in the Creative Commons, you're not working just for yourself any more, but a whole community of people who can follow in your footsteps, use the workflows you've developed, maybe even some of the scripts you write or the techniques you pioneer. And that's the real reason to run Free Software; to be a part of something bigger than the crowd that submits to a marketing campaign to validate themselves as artists, or the crowd that uses the latest pro software because, well, everyone else does. Free Software is about building something real people can use for real art, real work, and real life. And hey, it's free, so if your art is purchased by three people in the entire world, you've already broken even ;^)

Enjoy!

---

[1] http://www.creativecommons.org
[2] http://www.freesound.org
[3] http://www.openclipart.org

Appendix A. Customizing the Slackermedia Desktop

One of the main reasons a typical GNU Linux user switches to GNU Linux in the first place is customization. On GNU Linux, the user is in control and can, quite literally, customize anything.

Short of programming a new desktop, there are many options both in the KDE **plasma desktop** and in Slackware in general. Officially, extreme customization like using the **Fluxbox** desktop instead of **Plasma Desktop** is not advisable for new Slackermedia users, as customization really does complicate troubleshooting when something doesn't seem to be working quite right. KDE abstracts many basic tasks like routing sound and accessing external media so that the user doesn't need to know how it is happening and can instead concentrate on creating art.

Warning

For experienced or haphazard users only! If you're new to Linux, wait on playing around too much with how it all works.

Some minor customization is good, though, since it will increase efficiency. This appendix contains both minor and major customization options; read it over as a reference, or to get ideas on how you might change the GNU Linux desktop to suit your work style. But if you're new to Slackermedia or GNU Linux, use it sparingly at first.

A.1. KDE Plasma Desktop Optimization

KDE's **Plasma Desktop** is a powerful desktop environment suitable for all styles of computing and is feature rich with a full suite of powerful applications. To take advantage of the **Plasma Desktop**, it is possible for the user to customize it. The programming toolkit used to create KDE sotware is state-of-the-art and yet user-friendly and intuitive; along with visual cues and the Settings menu, customization is straight-forward.

In fact one of the major advantages to using KDE software as a desktop environment is its persistent use of common conventions across applications. The programmers creating applications for the KDE Software Compilation use many of the same design concepts and interface conventions so that after a user has used basic applications like the **Konqueror** web browser or the **Dolphin** file manager, the user is equally prepared for multimedia applications like **KDEnlive, Qtractor, Qsynth, QJackCtl, Amarok, Dragon**, and so on.

There are four primary paths to customizing the KDE desktop layout:

1. Customizing the panels

2. Customizing individual windows and applications

3. Adding plasmoids and new interface elements

4. Configuring custom key bindings

A.1.1. Customizing KDE Panels

Customizing panels may involve moving the default panel (once known as the "kicker") from the bottom of the screen to the top, changing its size, adding new plasmoids to it, or adding a second or third or fourth panel to other edges of the screen. Unlike proprietary operating systems, the control is completely in the hands of the user.

The options of panels are achieved by either right-clicking on the panel itself, or clicking the panel's plasma button (usually located on the far right of the panel, and bearing the icon of droplets of plasma).

A.1.2. Customizing Windows and Applications

Customizing individual windows and applications is typically done via either with panel resizing and toggling or the View and Settings menus.

Windows in KDE are made of different panels. For an example of this, open an instance of the **Dolphin** File Manager and go to its **View** menu, and then to the **Panels** submenu. There are four panels available to **Dolphin**: **Places**, **Information**, **Folders**, and **Terminal**. If all are activated, **Dolphin** becomes a tiled display of small panels each with unique information and all completely resizeable by clicking and dragging the panel edge, movable by clicking and dragging the panels within **Dolphin**, extractable by clicking the small diamond pop-out button, and removable by clicking the small close button. This is typical of many KDE applications.

In the **View** menu, there is also the **Adjust View Properties** selection, which allows for general settings of **Dolphin**. Some applications will have this kind of customization available, others will not, depending on the nature of the application.

The desktop itself can be customized by right-clicking on the desktop and selecting **Desktop Settings**. Here, the desktop background and theme can be changed. It is also possible to place the desktop itself in "folder view" mode, meaning that the desktop becomes a folder itself, onto which you can place icons and files. This is the default mode of a desktop in the current proprietary operating systems, and therefore may be more comfortable for new Linux users. Many **plasma desktop** users find this only leads to a cluttered workspace, however, and prefer to leave the desktop as an empty workspace rather than a catch-all folder for whatever file the user happens to decide is important at the time.

The **Settings** menu is generally the home of Toolbar customization and Configuration settings. There will usually be an option to configure related keyboard shortcuts, which icons appear in that application's toolbars, and different attributions of how the application works and what plugins or extensions it uses, and so on. KDE rarely restricts the user, leaving the user free to decide exactly how the environment works. On the other hand,

KDE's default configuration is a powerful and flexible environment; do not feel obligated to change things.

A.1.3. Plasmoids and Interface Changes

Plasmoids are small applications that can be added to the KDE desktop, ideally to enhance efficiency and productivity. To see the plasmoids that ship with KDE, right-click on the desktop and select **Add Widgets**. This will bring up a list of plasmoid widgets, as well as buttons to find new ones from popular KDE-related websites. When the mouse is hovered over a widget that has been added to the desktop, a control panel appears, containing a resize option, a settings button, and a button to close the widget.

Warning

While some plasmoids are infinitely useful, others are more for fun and games. Using too many will consume resources, so it is not necessarily advisable to litter the desktop with useless plasmoids. It is not advised to install new plasmoids on a production machine as they could introduce instability into the work environment; use the plasmoids that ship with the KDE Software Compilation, which have been tested and are considered stable.

A.1.4. Custom KDE Key Bindings

Key bindings ("keyboard shortcuts") are powerful tools for increasing usability and efficiency. Many users have favourite key bindings they like to assign to various applications, whether in an attempt to emulate a proprietary app key binding set that they are accustomed to or an attempt to translate the key bindings of their favourite text editor (such as **gVim** or **emacs**) onto other applications they use on a daily basis.

Plasma Desktop naturally comes with a set of established key bindings, but it is all completely customizable via two setting windows: **Input Actions** and **Shortcuts & Gestures**. These are both found by going to **System Settings** from the **KDE Menu**.

Input Actions allow the user to define any key binding for almost any conceivable command, whether it can be issued at the command line or via a KIOslave or a movement of the mouse or a press of a key. There are some preset actions, which the user may keep or delete. So that user-defined key bindings do not interfere with application key bindings, it is wise to use the Super Key (the "windows" or "command" key on some brand-specific keyboards) as the basis of the new key bindings.

A sample set of new shortcuts might include:

super-d = dolphin
super-n = new folder

super-o = open in new dolphin window
super-3 = ksnapshot
super-f = firefox
super-t = terminal (konsole)
super-shift-a = kfmclient openURL applications:

In the **Shortcuts & Gestures** panel, preset actions such as closing windows, bringing up Krunner (the "run command" interface), switching virtual desktops, and so on, can be re-defined. The existing actions are separated into two separate windows, one called *Standard Keyboard Shortcuts* which includes fairly generic actions like closing windows or configuring toolbars, adding bookmarks, refresh, save, and so on, and a second window called *Global Keyboard Shortcuts* which are more desktop-centric with actions like switching from one virtual desktop to another or triggering the run command interface, switching users, adjusting system volume, and so on.

Customizing the keys associated with the action is as simple as selecting the category appropriate for the shortcut, finding the shortcut in the list, and clicking the button next to the *Custom* label. Again, a sample listing of some re-assigned key bindings:

• super-spacebar = launch krunner

• control-alt-arrowkeys = switch desktop up, down, left, right

• super-w = close window

• super-m = minimize window

• control-alt-super-arrowkeys = move current window to another desktop

Even with so much customization, this is only the beginning. There are other methods of changing the environment, such as mixing-and-matching other elements from other desktop environments or defining sessions and activities. KDE does not limit the user in any way, so it only makes sense to customize it for maximum productivity.

A.2. Fluxbox Desktop Optimization

Ultimately, of course, most of a multimedia creator's work is done in multimedia applications. Some artists might prefer having no desktop environment at all, either to minimize distractions or to conserve system resources. A good possible solution for this is the **Fluxbox** window manager.

Fluxbox is shipped by default with Slackware and is known for giving the user "just enough" of a desktop environment to enable normal graphical user interface activities, and little else. The true power of **Fluxbox** lies in its minimalism and its ability to be a patchwork environment of all the user's favourite GUI tools.

Warning

Fluxbox is not recommended for new users attempting to do complex audio and video work! Take advantage of KDE's built-in abstraction layers and make multimedia easier. If you are primarily a graphic artist and do only basic audio or video work, then Fluxbox is safer to try.

Fluxbox can be enabled as the primary GUI environment in two different ways: either during installation, by selecting **Fluxbox** as the default X environment, or after installation by issuing this command:

```
$ cat /etc/X11/xinit/xinitrc.fluxbox >
    ~/.xinitrc
```

Now, when issuing the command **startx**, **Fluxbox** will start. To change it back, use the command:

```
$ cat /etc/X11/xinit/xinitrc.kde >
~/.xinitrc
```

Fluxbox in its initial state is very minimal, but it can be customized with easy-to-use KDE applications and tools. The important parts of **Fluxbox** are:

- startup - A startup script defining all the utilities Fluxbox should have persistently running from launch. This is located in the file **~/.fluxbox/startup**

- keys - Bindings for keyboard shortcuts within **Fluxbox**. Located in the file **~/.fluxbox/keys**

- Applications - The applications available for everyday work. Not a single file, but what you choose to install and what you choose to list in the menu file.

- Look and Feel - The methods for customizing the look and feel and sense of design unification within Fluxbox.

The startup file for **Fluxbox** is **~/.fluxbox/startup** and is nothing more than a well-commented text document, containing commands that will be issued when **Fluxbox** is starting. To customize it, open **~/.fluxbox/startup** in a text editor and add applications with the ampersand sign after the command so that the applications are started and then sent to the background. The final command in this file must always be **exec fluxbox**

Example of additional applications in the startup file:

```
## Applications you want to run with fluxbox
klipper&
kmix&
xscreensaver&
wmauda&
eval $(cat ~/.fehbg) &

# And last but not least we start fluxbox
exec fluxbox
```

Klipper is the KDE clipboard tool which functions better than most clipboards and is as useful in **Fluxbox** as it is anywhere else. **Kmix** is the volume control also borrowed from KDE, although *dockapps*[1] offers good volume controls as well. **Klipper** and **Kmix** both integrate well with the rest of **Fluxbox** and sit neatly in the **Fluxbox** toolbar because the ability to do so is defined in the **~/.fluxbox/init** file.

Xscreensaver is a lightweight screensaver which will is capable of locking the screen when the user leaves the computer. For it to work quickly and smoothly, it should be loaded in the background. It can be launched with the command

```
xscreensaver-command
 -activate
```

Feh does many things, but in this startup file it sets the Fluxbox desktop background to whatever image it was last set to. The background can initially be set with a command like **feh --bg-center ~/Pictures/wallpaper.png** which is then logged in **~/.fehbg** The startup file evaluates .fehbg and sets the background to the image logged there as long as it is still available in the same path as before.

In this file you also will need to put any service upon which your applications depend that may normally be running as part of the KDE **plasma desktop** but which may not be running by default in **Fluxbox**. If you do not, you will receive errors from the applications when they cannot find essential services like a MIDI driver, or a sound driver, and so on. Often, the easiest way to find out what needs to be started for your multimedia applications is to start **Fluxbox** and launch your usual apps; look at any errors they give you, and reverse

---

[1] http://www.dockapps.org

engineer what you would therefore want to have started automatically each time you log in. Alternately, you can make the conscious decision to launch those services manually on an as-needed basis.

A.3. Custom Fluxbox Key Bindings

Key bindings in **Fluxbox** can provide fast, almost mouseless interaction with the desktop. Since so many applications already have key bindings for the control and alt keys, it is wise to use the Super Key (the "windows" or "command" key on some brand-specific keyboards) as the basis of the new key bindings.

Assigning new keyboard shortcuts in **Fluxbox** is as simple as mimicking the existing syntax in the **~/.fluxbox/keys** file. The **Fluxbox** term for the Super Key is *Mod4* and the syntax is:

```
# open apps
Mod4 t :Exec konsole
Mod4 k :Exec konqueror
#        ### flux run command interface
Mod4 z :Exec fbrun
#        ### kde run command interface
Mod4 l :Exec krunner
Mod4 f :Exec firefox
Mod4 x :Exec qtractor
Mod4 d :Exec dolphin
Mod4 u :Exec audacity
Mod4 j :Exec set_rlimits qjackctl
Mod4 e :Exec emacs -fg Black -bg Wheat
Mod4 q :Exec xscreensaver-command -activate
```

A.4. Applications in Fluxbox

Fluxbox does not inherently promote the use of any particular application set and as with any Linux desktop environment, components can be used in any combination. Launching the applications is typically done either via custom key bindings or via the **Fluxbox** menu.

The **Fluxbox** menu is constructed from a text file in **~/.fluxbox/menu** and is simple to create. The syntax is a series of descending submenus wrapped in [begin] and [end] tags. It is simple to emulate in any text editor. Create a personalized menu file and place it in **~/.fluxbox** and then edit **~/.fluxbox/init** so that session.menuFile points to the new menu. In other words, a menu created and saved as **~/.fluxbox/mediamenu** would require this setting in **~/.fluxbox/init**:

```
session.menuFile:          ~/.fluxbox/mediamenu
```

A sensible multimedia submenu might look like this:

```
[submenu] (Music) {}
    [exec] (Audacity) {/usr/local/bin/audacity}
    [exec] (Qtractor) {'set_rlimits /usr/local/bin/
qtractor'}
    [exec] (Rosegarden) {/usr/local/bin/rosegarden}
    [exec] (QJackCtl) {'set_rlimits /usr/local/bin/
qjackctl'}
    [end]
[submenu] (GraphicDesign) {}
    [exec] (GIMP) {/usr/local/bin/gimp}
    [exec] (Inkscape) {/usr/local/bin/inkscape}
    [exec] (Krita) {/usr/local/bin/krita}
    [exec] (Scribus) {/usr/local/bin/scribus}
    [end]
```

And so on.

A.5. Unification of User Interface in Fluxbox

Changing the theme of **Fluxbox** is fairly easy. By default it comes with numerous themes to choose from, and adding to these themes is trivial. You can find themes on sites like *box-look.org*[2] or boot up a liveCD that uses **Fluxbox** with a desirable theem and "steal" its config files. Wolvix's themes *blind_grey* and *blind_blue*, for instance, are attractive, modern, and professional; to use them outside of Wolvix, find the **/usr/share/fluxbox/themes** directory in which the blind_grey and blind_blue themes are saved, and copy the theme files over to the local **/usr/share/fluxbox/themes** directory. Restart **Fluxbox** and the themes appear in the **Fluxbox** menu.

The background image can be set with *feh* [3]. A typical invocation of **feh** would be:

```
feh --bg-center /home/username/Pictures/
slackermedia.png
```

---

[2] http://www.box-look.org
[3] http://slackbuilds.org/repository/13.37/graphics/feh/

Because the applications used on a diverse Linux system come from many different programmers and programming toolkits, the application's basic look may sometimes vary wildly from the rest of the user's environment. While this is unavoidable and actually desirable in some cases (Blender's interface, for instance, one would not try to mask), sometimes a more unified look and feel helps make the system more integrated. To tie together two of the most common user interface toolkits, GTK and Qt, there is the application *gtk-chtheme*[4], which allows the user to change the GTK theme to something more attractive that the basic box forms of raw GTK widgets.

KDE's set of Qt widgets and styles can be configured by launching KDE's **System settings** which can be done from within **Fluxbox** by launching *krunner* and typing in **System Settings**.

Most desktop activities will be integrated by default, meaning that the same drag-and-drop functionality across separate applications that a user is accustomed to in proprietary applications will also be present in a "hacked together" **Fluxbox** desktop. There may be some actions that will require added configuration; opening a music file in **Firefox** may require the user to define what media player to use, for instance. Overall, however, **Fluxbox** configured to the user's preference will be as robust a desktop environment as any but with a fraction of the memory footprint.

A.6. Other Desktop Environments

There are certainly other desktop environments that can be used within Linux. Some ship with Slackware and are easily implemented in the same manner as **Fluxbox**. Slackware also offers **XFCE4**, a popular desktop built, literally, with the same graphics toolkit that was developed for **GIMP**.

Before investing time and effort in configuring a desktop environment, make sure that all important components work by starting up the applications that will be most frequently used. Ensure that the environment does not introduce complications or inconveniences. While it is important to find a comfortable and inspiring working environment, stability and efficiency must be kept in mind as well.

Once an environment is decided upon, configure it so that it is comfortable and efficient, and then backup the configuration files. All important configuration files will be backed up by default when backing up your **/home** directory, which naturally should be done on at least a weekly basis between projects and at least nightly during active production. Typically all environmental configuration files are found in the **/home/** username directory in hidden folders with names preceded by a dot.

---

[4] http://slackbuilds.org/repository/13.0/desktop/gtk-chtheme/

Appendix B. Choosing the Right Hardware

B.1. Due Diligence in Hardware Selection

The Linux kernel has become famous for its hardware support. When purchasing new hardware for a multimedia system, however, it is important to research what is about to be purchased with real-world case-studies. There are a handful of sites on the internet dedicated to analyzing how different hardware works with Linux, which works best as a boolean determination of compatibility; it can accurately be measured whether something does or does not work with Linux. Degrees, however, are harder to ascertain, since one person's requirements for performance might be drastically different than another person's.

The best way to make sure hardware works to the degree needed from a multimedia artist is to test the hardware. Burning a liveCD of a multimedia distribution and taking that disc to a computer store and rebooting the target machine into Linux is a very good way to judge hardware Linux compatibility and performance. While liveCDs will run slower than running an OS from the harddrive, it should still give the user a good idea of severe problems, and the user should make some allowances for the fact that the test is being performed on a liveCD.

If specific multimedia peripherals are required to work as well, they can be judged separate from the workstation itself. Regardless of what computer is purchased, the Linux kernel either does or does not have support for a peripheral. An online search or tests at home on any computer available should reveal whether or not an interface or peripheral is recognized and usable on Linux.

The computer market can be confusing and it is often difficult to know what actually has a pragmatic significance in multimedia. In other words, all things being equal, where in a computer system should a buyer spend money? Some general things to keep in mind:

B.1.1. CPU

There was a time when every last megahertz really did matter to the end user, but now most CPUs have reached a mostly-equal plateau in speed. Brands and model names will advertise different features but generally speaking any general-purpose computer CPU will do as well with multimedia as another. "General purpose" excludes chips designed specifically for netbooks and other ultra-portable devices.

CPUs process data, so the jobs that benefit most from multiple CPUs or very fast CPUs are processing-heavy activities such as video compression, special effect rendering, audio effect generation, audio effect rendering (sometimes called "freezing" in a DAW), large image conversion, audio file conversion or compression, and so on. Very broadly speaking, it could be said that the CPU matters most on jobs that involve pressing a button and then getting up and going for a cup of coffee in anticipation of having to wait for the job to be complete. Some of these jobs will literally last for days, others may only be a few seconds past the point at which a typical user becomes bored with waiting. Overall, spending less on a processor or opting for a computer with a slightly slower processor than its more expensive competitors is probably fine unless intense audio or video processing is going to be done and realtime results are required. Otherwise, mid-range CPU's will do the same work.

The other side of the argument, of course, is that since the CPU is not a trivial upgrade, spending the money upfront for a CPU that will still feel powerful in a few years would be a good investment. However, if price is a factor, a mid-powered CPU will leave more money to spend on RAM and video card.

B.1.2. RAM

How much RAM you have will dictate, largely, what size projects your system can comfortably handle. **Audacity**. for instance, will be responsive with a 30-second spot but will feel sluggish with longer projects, or projects with a great many tracks. **GIMP** will do well on web graphics but struggle with for-print graphics. This is simply because information is moving in and out of RAM; upgrade the amount of RAM, and the applications will function more consistently.

The speed of RAM is less talked about in consumer electronics, but the overall responsiveness of the system is greatly dependent upon it. The faster the RAM, the faster the information can be moved from RAM to CPU for processing, so given the choice, purchase the faster RAM. On the other hand, if money is an issue, try to find a happy medium between storage space and speed.

B.1.3. Graphics Card

A powerful graphics card is obviously important if you will be doing video and graphics work. For serious visual multimedia, it is very likely that you will need to install a proprietary graphics card driver since the companies do not release their driver code as free software. This is unfortunate and taints an otherwise free system, but the performance increase can be measured in orders of magnitude.

If you are not doing intensive video or graphics work, then probably your only concern with a graphics card is whether it will work, and perhaps provide some moderate level of modern "eye candy". For these, low-end to mid-range cards, the drivers can come from Nvidia, ATI, or Intel, or from the Xorg developers. Performance can usually be gauged in tests at any computer store.

Whether you're looking for a high-performance card or a mid-range card, you can always determine the official support by going to the chipset manufacturer's website and finding a download (or lack thereof) for the card. If the download is there, you are at least guaranteed performance for that chipset, on the kernel or kernels for which the code was released.

Otherwise, look on the Xorg website to see if they have a driver for the card you are looking to buy (or buy along with a laptop or pre-built system), and take note of what kind of performance results are being seen with those drivers on that card.

B.1.4. GPU Tests

A few unscientific tests to determine the real-world performance of a graphics card, should you have the opportunity to test it in a computer store before buying:

1. Launch KDE's **System Settings** and turn on Desktop Effects in the **Desktop** pane.

2. Navigate to the **All Effects** tab and scroll down to the **Window Management** section. Activate the **Cover Switch** effect.

3. Close **System Settings**

4. Open a few windows (**Dolphin**, **Konsole**, **konqueror**, and so on) and play a video in **Dragon**; while the video is playing, use `alt-tab` to switch between the windows.

5. If the video and its reflection continues to play smoothly through the animated switching, the card will more than likely be a suitable card for moderate to heavy video work and other multimedia creation.

6. Continue to add more videos, and continue to `alt-tab` to test the limits of the card. Take note of flickering, stuttering, and other distortion.

And finally there is the obligatory glxgears test. This is fairly meaningless out of context, but running this on all systems being tested provides numerical benchmarks so that they can each be compared. To run the test, open a terminal and type in `glxgears` which launches a window with three turning 3d cogwheels. After some delay, the framerates achieved as these gears turn will be logged in the terminal. Make note of the framerate on each computer being considered for purchase and compare the results to the other computers as they are tested. All else being equal, more is better. Serious video work requires framerates in the thousands. Moderate video work can be done, feasibly, in the high hundreds.

B.1.5. Sound card

Play sound to ensure that the speakers are being recognized and are supported by the Linux kernel. Assuming that the computer does provide sound, try playing multiple sources of sound and test how the audio card handles multiple tasks. Obviously, the more robust the card, the better, but in most computers the real test is simply whether or not the sound card is recognized. For multiple inputs and outputs, an additional, more professional sound card or interface will need to be added.

B.1.6. Wireless card

Although this is less of a problem now than it has been historically, there are wireless network cards that simply do not have Linux drivers. Recently more drivers have been developed and hacks around the lack of drivers have been implemented, but a cursory test of the wireless card is worth while. If it is not recognized, issue the command `lspci` on the command line and look through the listing to find the card's chipset. Perform an online search to find out how well supported the chipset is and review the necessary steps that will need to be taken for the card to function.

B.1.7. Webcam

Webcams are generally well-supported in Linux, even if they are not recognized out of the box. If the webcam is vital, launch VLC to test whether the webcam is recognized.

1. Launch VLC; install if it is not already on the liveCD

2. Navigate to the **File** menu and choose **Open Capture Device**

3. How the webcam will be seen is difficult to predict; it might be listed as **/dev/video0** or it may be some other name, and it may use the **video4linux** (v4l2) driver or the **UVC** driver. Play around with the settings, look at the **/dev** listing in a terminal as needed, and see if you can get an image from the webcam when you press the **Play** button in the **capture device** window.

B.1.8. Miscellaneous Considerations

Anticipate what might be required of the multimedia system and take this into consideration whilst considering the purchase. The outward appearance of a computer matters not at all compared to its capabilities. Proprietary connection types and a lack of common features like an optical drive or SD card reader will only complicate the always complex task of importing media.

If it is not a new computer being purchased, but a used computer, the same tests should be performed, in addition to common physical tests, such as ensuring all of the ports are functioning, the optical drive functions as expected, the harddrive is healthy, and so on.

In all cases, the command *lspci >> lspci_computerModel.txt* should be performed, and the resulting file (lspci_computerModel.txt) should be saved to a thumbdrive for later review. The lspci command lists all internal components such as the graphics card, amount of RAM, wireless card, and so on. Some commands to bear in mind in general:

* **lspci** lists all major internal components including revision numbers and much more

* **cat /proc/cpuinfo** lists all details on the CPU(s)

* **free -g** reveals how much RAM is in the system in gigabytes

* **df -h** reveals free disk space in human readable format; useful for checking the size of the harddrive

B.2. Desktop or Laptop?

It's financially advantageous for computer manufacturers to claim that their laptops are as powerful as traditional desktop computers; it encourages people to buy laptops, which feature lower-specs for higher prices. These claims seem true at first glance. After all, if someone is editing a video clip on a laptop then the marketing must have been right.

The truth, of course, is that laptops have lower-specs than a desktop that is even a fraction of its price, so for the same amount of money as one might spend on a good laptop, an amazing desktop could be purchased. And for every professional artist you see working on their masterpiece on a laptop in either a glossy magazine ad or in a trendy cafe, there are ten real artists working on actual productions at their desktops.

If it is horsepower you seek, then you should invest in a desktop machine. If you are more flexible with how much raw power you have at your immediate disposal and value mobility, then obviously a laptop is probably a better choice.

B.3. Building Your Own System, and Ideal Specs

Building your own system from parts is the best possible option you have in terms of finances and control. Useless parts are not forced upon you, you can achieve a perfect balance of all the different features and capabilities you need, and there always room for expansion.

A computer consists of a few main parts that can be bought individually from any good computer store. You must ensure that all of the parts fit together properly, which can be tricky for beginners, but if you read the descriptions of the items carefully and match all of the part numbers and types together, then you will be able to assemble it with success.

If you are unsure about what you've chosen, find an IRC server where you can chat with Linux geeks, and ask them about the parts you've chosen. Slackermedia itself maintains an open IRC channel on the *irc.freenode.net*[1] network.

Balancing cost with performance is obviously an eternal struggle. Keep in mind what you really want from your computer, and spend your money accordingly. For graphics and video, concentrate on the graphics card; for audio, lean toward the CPU and audio card features, and for writing, well, buy a second-hand netbook and save your money for coffee.

In any case, consider purchasing an SSD drive (solid state harddrive) for your system. The performance increase is mind-boggling and a small 16gb or 32gb SSD drive can easily hold the system partitions for Slackware 13.37; simply place the /home and /tmp and /var partitions on traditional harddrives.

In every case, try to re-use parts from other computers; if you can recycle an optical drive, save yourself the expense. Find an old keyboard you can use, pull a network card from a discarded neighbour's computer. Offer to rescue a poor Window's users data in exchange for the parts of their dead computer. Building your own box makes re-directing cashflow quite easy!

---

[1] http://www.freenode.net

Appendix C. The State of Multimedia on GNU Linux

Multimedia on GNU Linux is still a developing field. On one hand, there are distinct advantages to creating multimedia on GNU Linux, while on the other there are compromises one must make.

Compromises must be weighed against benefits and since these are probably the most influential factors in deciding whether to switch your production to an exclusive GNU Linux solution, they will be examined first.

The correct method of converting to GNU Linux will be to convert one application at a time, and to audition each application as you would audition any other new software or piece of hardware. In people's haste and excitement to change to GNU Linux, or in an evangelist's haste to encourage people to change, there is often the assumption that the "equivalent" Free Software solution to a creative process is equal to its non-free counterpart. This is as realistic an expectation as blindly assuming Sony Vegas is a drop-in replacement for Final Cut Pro. Without proper evaluation, you would never make such an assumption, so you should not make the assumption for Free Software.

Introduce one application or set of applications, test them, evaluate them, and if you see that they are equal to or better than your current solution, make the replacement final. It is important to keep in mind the requirements of an application and the conveniences of an application. While, for instance, your current application may have a nicer Type Tool than the free software replacement, but you never use that application to do Type Setting, then it can be assumed that future improvements to free software will eventually fix the Type Tool but there will be no need to delay making the replacement final if in all other aspects the application is equal. If, however, the free software lacks a vital feature such as realtime previews of effects and you cannot work without the feature, then you will probably be wiser to delay making this replacement.

Learning Curve
> If you have already an established workflow with a set of standard tools that all members of your production team know, then changing the toolset to a GNU Linux workflow will bring production to a halt for an inordinate amount of time as everyone learns the new tools and learns how to integrate all of these tools into a new workflow.

Convenience
> Similar to a learning curve, the convenience of existing software solutions should not be discounted. If your existing workflow works well for you now, it is probably largely because of your investment of fine-tuning it such that the applications more or less the way you want them to work (to the extent that blackbox proprietary software can be fine-tuned) and that they more or less work together the way you need. Implementing a new set of software will require a new investment and will mean temporarily forsaking certain convienences that you and your team may take for granted now.

Conventions

There are conventions that different vendors build upon over time. These are unique ideas or ways of doing things that, if used exclusively, become the accepted way things are done. If a user is then presented a new way of doing the same task, it seems wrong to them.

Conventions like this should not be adopted as the "right" way of doing something, but that if the tendency among most users. If you replace an application with even a drastic update of the same application, much less a Free alternative, which changes a convention, it becomes an inconvenience to the user and slows production. Keep this in mind and make sure that you and your team is prepared to learn new conventions and approach problems with sometimes a drastically different approach.

Compatibility

If your workflow relies on sharing detailed final edits, elaborate graphics with layers, masks, effect layers, or paths saved in non-standard form, and so on, then changing to an application that may not be able to fully support all of those proprietary features may not be wise.

Continuity

Since so many production teams do use very specific proprietary solutions for their work, there has arisen a kind of mass-produced "look" to many creative works. A classic example is the Adobe solar flare, which was distinctively over-used in artwork spanning from still photography retouched in Photoshop and motion photography retouched in After Effects. After a few years it had proliferated to such a degree that even the most casual of audiences could spot this cheap effect.

The opposite side of this pre-fabricated coin is that there is an aesthetic comfort-level that can be satisfied by using old, familiar effects such that your work (or your clients's work) looks like all the other work being produced. It ensures a level of comfortable conformity that you or your clients may not be comfortable either giving up. While many Free Software solutions will have very good emulations of all the most common effects, it may be just different enough to substract from the comfort of precise conformity.

There may also be a technical need to have the exact same effect; if you are trying to match something that was produced entirely in Photoshop with all the classic Photoshop bevels, shadows, light effects, and so on, then the best way to duplicate it may just be to re-produce it in Photoshop. if these tasks are a significant portion of your production needs, then changing to CinePaint or Gnu Image Manipulation Program (GIMP) may be unwise and counter-productive.

Ubiquity

Pragmatically speaking, proprietary applications are the de facto standard in many areas of the creative industry. This means that however miserable you may be, you are not alone. Free Software will alleviate some of the arbitrary blockades that applications impose, but they will introduce new issues certainly, and you will still struggle with creative decisions that no software can make for you. In other words, you may still find yourself miserable, but without the company.

Conversely, there's a lot to be said for the trailblazers and pioneers. You'll be creating multimedia on an exciting and flexible platform that simply refuses to recognize boundaries. When you do need help, tutorials, instructional videos, and ebooks (such as this one) about working with Free Software applications proliferate both online and in stores, so the support structure does exist; it's just a different one than the ones you already have bookmarked.

These are all valid concerns and depending on the urgency and importance of changing your existing production to Free Software, they each may influence your decision to different degrees. Now that you have seen the reasons not to change your studio to a Free Software studio, the rest of this chapter will largely be about why you should take the steps now to convert every element of your production workflow, from the web browsers to the office applications to video editors to audio mixers to graphic workstations to the Operating System itself, to a Free Software solution based on Slackware GNU Linux and why the initial inconveniences of converting to Free Software are outweighed by its many benefits.

C.1. What Free Software Is Not

A typical expectation of many computerists investigating Free Software is that popular Free Software terms are "free versions" of a software term they used previously. It is, after all, common online to see popular Free Software presented as proprietary replacements; ie, "**GIMP**, the free version of Photoshop", or "Inkscape", the free version of Illustrator", and so on.

Such comparisons do neither Free Software or the proprietary software "equivalents" justice, since it ignores the fact that, for instance, **Inkscape** is a masterpiece of programming, a practical, efficient, magically intuitive, and infinitely powerful application, and that Illustrator is an albatross of bloated, confusing, over-thought and under-designed excuse for a professional artist's platform that has skillfully and effectively fooled an entire industry into believing it is the only solution to the very simple task of creating vector graphics.

The fact is that Free Software does not need to replace any software. It does not need to replicate how other software terms handle tasks, or design their interfaces. Free Software has the rare luxury of being able to re-invent paradigms, explore new methods of working, or to choose not to do something that other software packages do.

Free Software is a diverse and self-sustaining system. It is free to join, and even free to contribute, but it is not a movement centered around copying what already exists and ensuring that no-one need ever pay for software or software-related services again. It's a movement dedicated to progress and innovation, to code that is free to use and modify, and re-distribute.

If you want a system that is monetarily free and is an exact duplicate of proprietary systems, then use proprietary software with "illegal" licenses. This will ensure that you are not paying for the software or support, and remain entrenched in the proprietary model.

If you want control over your data, your environment, and you wish to use a self-sustaining, non-consumer model, then investigate Free Software.

C.2. Benefits of Free Software Multimedia

Free Software has many benefits which eventually any production studio has a right to profit from in their own workflow. It is not uncommon for Free Software enthusiasts and evangelists to speak very highly of anything that bears the mark of Free Software, which is not the point or intent of this chapter. However, Free Software, and the philosophy that is its driving force, does have a number of advantages over the idea behind Proprietary "black box" software solutions. This is no secret, which is why in the high-dollar special effects world GNU Linux is an important and major platform. This section examines the benefits that industry leaders have already recognized, and hopefully the rest of the industry will see soon.

Modularity

A deceptively simple concept, the fact that unix-based Free Software systems are written religiously with modularity in mind is a powerful foundation for an entire philosophy that expands into even defining production workflow. By keeping the software components small and self-reliant, unix programmers are able to isolate small problems, solve them efficiently with small programs such that it is done quickly, taking up few system resources, and with less potential for failure. For larger problems, many of these smaller programs can be strung together to create a new solution consisting of pre-existing and known-working programs.

Improved Troubleshooting

When processes do fail, it is often unclear to the multimedia artist wether the root of the problem is the media itself, the program being used to process or effect it, a plugin, or some combination thereof. Blackbox systems are just that: black boxes into which the user cannot see, and for fear of being copied or revealing "trade secrets" these kinds of applications provide very little output when errors do occur, fearing that a descriptive error message will indicate inner processes that they wish to keep secret.

Worse still, companies often feel that imperfections in software reveal problems in with their product, and since clients have paid thousands of dollars for that product, it does not financially benefit the company to admit to any imperfection. A company cannot very well support an imperfection that does not exist.

Free Software has no such concern, and when a process fails, Free Software is able to tell the user exactly why it has failed. Depending on the technical proficiency of the user, the errors may or may not be helpful, but they might be very helpful to their techinical support. It is the difference between receiving "Error 3639" but having no reference to what Error 3639 is, and receiving the error "xvid-devel not installed" where the solution is most likely obvious to even the least technical of users.

Furthermore, Free Software applications seek to find errors and invite their users to report bugs when they have been found on public bug reporting sites. Free Software does not hide problems or solutions; they openly seek both.

Scripting

The modularity of Free Software applications often provides a great flexibility in how the programs are executed. Many Free Software programs can literally be run entirely from a text command prompt, without ever requiring that a user interface be loaded. This means that complex, multi-step, and long processes may be scripted and executed automatically. This goes well beyond simple Action Scripts and Batch Files, and enables the user to walk away from the office secure in the knowledge that the processes will be run, and that the status of the processes can be checked remotely at any time. In fact, it can even be scripted so that a process emails the user when it has been completed successfully.

Customization

Vendors providing expensive, locked-down software spend a lot of time and money on establishing a unique brand and convention for their product. As such, their software must always identify itself clearly so that every time it is run, it is also an advertisement for itself. If you sit down in front of Photoshop, Adobe wants you to know that it is Photoshop. If you look over someone's shoulder and they are using Final Cut Pro, Apple wants you to know that it is Final Cut Pro. It is a "franchise" mentality; the company must ensure that their product and logo is recognized, that the interface remains the same across all implementations so that to sit in front of one workstation is basically the same as sitting in front of another.

While this seems sensible on one level, it is completely restrictive in other ways. If the user wishes to change the way they use an application, most blackbox programs are very limited in their ability to be customized. They would rather the user conform to the company's way of doing things, not break the branding of their product and make the application become foreign to other potential customers.

Free Software has no such agenda. If a user wishes to change how they interface with an application, the user has complete freedom to do so. They may change the look and feel of an application, the keyboard shortcuts, potentially even more beyond that (depending on the technical resources available). Other users may not be familiar with the way such a "hacked" version of the application works, but a standard configuration of that same application is usually an easy thing to create by making a new user account with the default configuration of the application. In this way, you gain the flexibility of customizable applications but do not lose the advantage of standardized interfaces.

Participatory Culture

Free Software exists because people, programmers and end users alike, use and maintain it and contribute to it. While proprietary software companies do generally encourage a community around their products, the community involvement is entirely superficial, since the community has no real say in the product's direction or purpose. Free Software is quite literally built by its community; you needn't be a programmer to help build Free Software, you simply need to participate.

Progressive

Almost any technical group can be argued to be "progressive" or "innovative" in one way or another, but Free Software excels in a number of realms that are of particular interest to multimediaticians.

Delivery

> When it comes to getting content to as many people as possible, Free Software sets the pace to the extent that traditional vendors simply cannot compete. Peer-to-peer file sharing, bit torrent, free video codecs taht will compile and install on every operating system imaginable, open audio codecs, generic vector formats with animation, open web standards for all kinds of content delivery to all kinds of devices, and so much more. The ability of Free Software to proliferate content is unmatched, oft imitated, and sometimes downright reviled.

Networking

> The internet itself is based upon open standards developed for large UNIX data centers, and largely "runs", essentially, Linux. The syntax and structure of URLs that people use every day to get to their favourite websites are simply ways of expressing locations in a unix networked filesystem. Technologies such as HTTP, FTP, ssh, ssl, and a dozen others that few people really think about are in fact very mundane and common to unix and Linux users, and yet they have each revolutionized the level of communication across the globe. Other operating systems use these technologies but they were and are developed on Free Software.

Alternatives

> Free Software is known for its myriad choices. If one solution does not fit your workflow, then surely there is at least one good alternative way of getting something done. These are important not only for the user's sense of freedom, but it is important for progressive technological development. Just because one technology company might design a new system that does things one way, it hardly means that this is the only or best way. Free Software is often the driving force behind finding alternative ways, and often better ways, of achieving the same end goal as a current solution. Sometimes the alternative remains only available in the Free Software realm but frequently it becomes the motivation for improvements in a major company's product.

Investment Security

> Software that is owned by a software vendor means that the user is entirely at the mercy of that vendor. Should the vendor decide to make drastic changes to the software, then the user is forced to change along with it. Should the vendor go out of business, then the software may disappear forever, making the user's data files suddenly obsolete.

> Likewise, if a production studio has designed custom scripts or plugins for a software that they use but do not own, then they are putting resources into a black box that they have no real access to or ownership over. The immediate return on investment is clear; the custom scripts or plugins make a job easier in that moment, but over the course of time these may become obsolete when the platform they are intended to run on disappears.

> Contrast these two scenarios: The non-Free compositing software Shake ran on Linux in special effects houses for years and allowed companies to purchase any hardware they wanted to purchase and run a Free operating system to power the application. Then Apple purchased Shake and gave users two choices: they could purchase Apple's

expensive hardware in order to run Shake with a per-license fee of $500, or they could continue to run Shake on GNU Linux with a per-license fee of $5000 (sic).

The Free Software package Blender, featuring a powerful compositing interface, belongs to anyone who downloads it, and they can use it on any hardware they choose and for as long as the need. No one can purchase it and put restrictions upon it, and anyone can improve and modify it to fit their needs. They can upgrade with every release or never upgrade at all. The user is in complete control.

Forkable

When using Free Software, the user literally owns the application, part and parcel. They are free to download all of the source code that makes the software run, and they could, if they felt it was important enough, hire a programmer to modify and improve that software to fit their exact needs. The benefit is clear; rather than sinking thousands of dollars into hardware required to run a vendor's software plus a version-specific license to use that software, a company could instead sink the same amount into modifying an existing software solution to fit their production needs, and they retain all ownership of the software and require no licensing fees and no special hardware. They are bound to no vendor and they are at no vendor's mercy.

If this sounds too good to be true, or too theoretical, then consider that in fact this is precisely what companies (especially in special effects, computer animation, experimental music production, and so on) are doing today.

No Agenda

Free Software has no real agenda aside from (sometimes) ensuring that Free Software remains Free. This means that there are no arbitrary decisions to exclude a file format or specific competing codec or a diable a feature in order to enable that same feature in a "pro" edition of the same software. Free Software concentrates on getting the most out of current technology, and allowing the user to decide what to use, how to use it, and what to do with it.

Potential

While it's not something you can take to the bank, there is an enormous amount of potential in Free Software. Much of it is being developed and adopted at a breakneck speed, with exciting improvements rippling through its software selection every month. The potential for Free Software to displace the blackbox vendor-lock-in closed-source model has been frightening the established industry (and thereby pushing the industry forward) for years. The even more exciting part about this is that the more people who use Free Software, the quicker the pace will become.

Conversely, proprietary software companies at some point reach a peak in their product life cycle after which they have no place to go, but the product has brand-recognition, industry respect, and is making the company loads of cash. So the company, instead of innovating in a logical direction, or to stop developing it in a useless direction, will do whatever it takes to perpetuate the brand. Not the software, but the brand. This often means radical, pointless changes to the application or its file formats (to force upgrades), left-field additions in functionality, re-structuring of how

the terms are sold in relation to one another, and all the usual tricks you yourself have
surely seen in your computing lifetime.

Idealism

There is an element in many (although not all) free software communities that
champions idealistic concepts having to do with freedom of technology, of making
sure that technology is accessible to everyone regardless of geographic location or
wealth or upbringing, that technology should benefit first and foremost the people
using it and not the companies producing it, that technology should improve quality
of life not frustrate or pollute it.

There can be political idealism behind it as well, such as a preference for lack of central
and dictatorial control (such as a CEO) that inspires many technological decisions
without regard to what effect it might have on the people using it or the world in which
is being produced. And there is also a powerful sense of community, since much of
the Free Software itself is being developed because individual programmers have a
passion for writing code just as much as a painter loves to paint, or a singer loves to
make music. This is where the arts and technology truly intersect, and a collaboration
between the two communities is long overdue.

C.3. Multimedia as a Moving Target

Multimedia itself is an ever-changing industry, with new formats, new trends, new delivery
methods, new platforms, new hardware and gear. Any toolset an artist uses for multimedia
content creation is forced to update catch up to the industry's requirements. Free Software
sometimes does this astonishingly quickly, and other times lags behind, just as any other
platform does. Free Software is no more a "magic bullet" than any other software package,
but for those who value technological advancement, equality, freedom, solidarity, and
community, Free Software offers powerful rewards, and a powerful platform upon which
to build a multimedia studio.

Appendix D. Revision History

Revision 0-3 Mon 29 2012

Seth   **Kenlon**

seth@straightedgelinux.com,
Klaatu   la   Terible
klaatu@member.fsf.org

made the whole book more generic and agnostic of the Slackware-version being used.
Added applicable Qtractor user guide material
Added Kdenlive Quick Start
General corrections and clarifications, added Kdelive as a featured app, added amsynth, graphics, etc.

Revision 0-2 Tue 23 2011

Seth   **Kenlon**

seth@straightedgelinux.com,
Klaatu   la   Terible
klaatu@member.fsf.org

finished updates for Slackware 13.37, including a port of screenplay.el, some new slackbuilds, a publican install hack, and a lot more

Revision 0-1 Wed Feb 23 2011

Seth   **Kenlon**

seth@straightedgelinux.com,
Klaatu   la   Terible
klaatu@member.fsf.org

ported book to publican schemas, much prettier

Revision 0-1 Wed Feb 23 2011

Seth   **Kenlon**

seth@straightedgelinux.com,
Klaatu   la   Terible
klaatu@member.fsf.org

ported book to publican schemas, much prettier

Revision 0-0 Wed Jan 15 2011

Seth   **Kenlon**

seth@straightedgelinux.com,
Klaatu   la   Terible
klaatu@member.fsf.org

official release

Index

Symbols
.el files
    installing , 83

A
adduser
    useradd , 18
animation , 65
applications , 41
audacity
    config file for , 55

B
blender
    compiling from source , 56
brushes , 61

C
CCRMA , 72
changelog , 49
Chess Griffin , 23, 55
codecs
    forensics , 68
    installing , 35
creative commons, 11, 97

D
DAW
    Digital Audio Workstation , 63
dependencies
    dependencies for Slackermedia , 33
desktop , 18
desktops
    alternative , 102
downloads, 11
    Slackermedia dependency queue files , 34
dssi , 71
dual booting, 17
DVD
    ripping , 62
DyneBolic, 1

E
effects processors , 75
elisp , 83
ext4 , 51

F
fc-cache , 60
feedback
    contact information for this manual, x
file associations , 87
fluidsynth , 73
fonts , 59
    installing manually , 60
    installing via KDE , 60

G
Gancarz, Mike, 3
gimp paint studio , 61

H
hexter , 73

I
install
    installing slackware, 17
iso
    how (not) to download Slackermedia, 1

K
kernel
    compiling , 49
    panic , 51
    real time , 49
    realtime priority , 54
kernel panic , 53
keyboard shortcuts
    custom , 101

L
ladspa , 71
lilo , 52
Linux From Scratch, 1
lpr
    printing with , 91
lv2 , 71

Qtractor

User Manual

Seth Kenlon

Klaatu la Terible

Qtractor
User Manual
Edition 0.5.x

Author	Seth Kenlon	*seth@straightedgelinux.com*
Author	Klaatu la Terible	*klaatu@hackerpublicradio.org*

A Guide for audio producers both new and experienced.

Part 1. Quick Start

Diving into Qtractor; a quick start guide for the basic workflow.

Getting Sound Into Qtractor

Getting started with basic music production in Qtractor is simple as long as all of the requirements are installed. Review the Installation chapters to ensure you've installed all the necessary components before beginning. As long as you've done that, you'll find Qtractor a robust digital production environment with plenty of knobs and dials to tweak.

1. Start the **QJackCtl** application (recommended), or start **jackd** from a shell. Once launched, press the **Start** button to start JACK.

2. Launch **Qtractor** from your applications menu, dock, or launcher.

3. It's good practise to start every session by saving. It might seem strange to save an as yet empty session, but it's better to save an empty session that to start creating your masterpiece and have data files and MIDI files scattered all throughout your hard drive. Saving first is a good way to instantiate an environment in which you can keep all of your files and sounds organized and consolodated.

    To save, click the **File** menu and select **Save As**.

    In the **Name** field, name your session. For the **Directory** field, click the **Directory** icon to create a new, empty directory for your session files and click **OK**.

    Save your session by clicking the **OK** button; a **Save Session** dialogue will open so that you can now navigate to the directory you've created and name your session file, which will appear as a **.qtr** file. Click the **Save** button to confirm.

4. Now you're ready to start producing! Obviously there are different means to creating music in **Qtractor**, but nearly each one would create with creating a new track.

    To create an empty track in your **Qtractor** workspace, click on the **Track** menu and select **Add Track**.

    In the **Track** dialogue, name your track in the **Name** field. For **Type**, choose between Audio or MIDI, depending on what kind of data you wish to use in the track. If you have a specific set of inputs and outputs that you wish to use for the track, you can set that here, or you can leave it on the default and manipulate it later as needed. Likewise, if you know the MIDI bank or patch selections, you can set it here, or leave it as default values and configure it later.

    Click **OK** to create the track.

5. Now that you have an empty track, you should put some sound into it. You can do this in three ways:

    *   Record audio directly into the track - to record directly into **Qtractor**, you must define your input device in your central patchbay (ie, **QJackCtl**). To do this, choose **View** menu > Windows > Connections.

In the left column, choose the source of sound (a device that, from **Qtractor**'s perspective, is outputting sound, hence the "output" label). Your microphone exists as part of your computer system, so choose the **System** category, and click a capture device there.

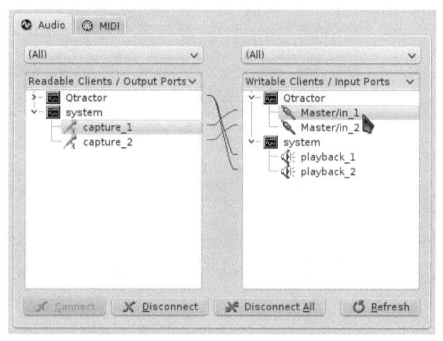

Now choose the sound source's destination in the right column. You are routing the sound from the microphone into **Qtractor**, so choose the **Qtractor** category and select the corresponding input port, such as Master/in_1.

Click the **Connect** button if they are not already connected. Repeat this process for the right channel, and then close the window.

In the track label on the left of the **Qtractor** window, click the **R** button to arm the track for recording.

Click the **Record** button in the top menu bar to activate Recording mode.

Click the **Play** button in the top menu bar to begin.

• Insert an existing audio file into the track - if you're using pre-recorded material from a live performance, a sound booth session, or a sample or loop collection, then there is no need to set up a recording source such as a microphone or line-in. You'll simply add files to your **Qtractor** session and drag them into your workspace.

To add sounds files to your session, go to the **Clip** menu and select **Import**.

Choose the file you wish to import, and it will be added into your empty track. Notice that it is also added in the **Files** panel on the right of the **Qtractor** window; so to add files without adding them to a track, you can right-click in the **Files** panel and choose **Add Files**.

- Play MIDI into the track - similar to recording audio directly into **Qtractor**, you can connect a MIDI controller to your computer and record MIDI data into a track. The MIDI data will be used to trigger a sound source; the simplest and most direct method is to use the MIDI to trigger a software synthesizer, but of course the MIDI signal could also be routed back out of the computer into a hardware synth as well.

Assuming you are using a USB-based MIDI controller such as the Oxygen or Axiom series, or AKAI LPK series, and so on, then you must first define the source of your MIDI signal. Click the **View** menu > Windows > Connections to see your central patchbay (ie, QJackCtl).

In the left column, choose the source of your MIDI signal (a device that, from **Qtractor**'s perspective, is outputting the signal, hence the "output" label). Your USB controller should be listed as a source, so open its listing and click the MIDI channel listed there.

Now choose the MIDI signal's destination in the right column. You are routing the sound from your hardware controller to **Qtractor**, so choose the **Qtractor** category and select the corresponding input port, such as 0:Master

Click the **Connect** button if they are not already connected. Close the window.

If you start playing now, you'll be sending MIDI data without hearing any feedback whatsoever, because you have not yet configured the MIDI signal to trigger sound. So that you can hear what you're playing, you must insert a plugin synthesizer into the track.

With your destination track selected, click on the **Track** menu and select **Track Properties**. In the **Track** dialogue, click the **Plugins** tab.

In the **Plugins** tab, click the **Add** button on the right to see a list of available sotware plugins.

In the **Plugins** dialogue, select the type of plugin you wish to use with the top right button. Software synths on Linux are usually of the DSSI variety; from the list of DSSI synths, select the one you want to play and click the **Activate** checkbox in the lower left corner.

Click the **OK** button in the bottom right corner of the window to proceed.

Note

If you don't have any plugins installed, you can install them from your distribution or directly from their project websites. One of the best soft synths for immediate gratification is **whySynth**, which bundles some nice, ready-to-use patches.

You will need to restart Qtractor in order for your new soft synths to be available.

Back in the **Track** dialogue, select the **Track** tab again. In the MIDI/Instrument panel, choose an instrument from the top dropdown menu; using **WhySynth** as an example, you would select **WhySynth_20100922 DSSI plugin**.

Choose a **Bank** and **Program**. If you're not familiar with **WhySynth**, you can select any of its three Banks and any of the Programs contained in them. You should be able to instantly audition the sounds on your USB controller.

When you've selected the sound you'd like to use, click the **OK** button.

In the track label on the left of the **Qtractor** window, click the **R** button to arm the track for recording.

Click the **Record** button in the top menu bar to activate Recording mode.

Click the **Play** button in the top menu bar to begin.

• Insert existing MIDI data into the track - if you want to use pre-made MIDI files then simply add the files to your **Qtractor** session.

To add MIDI files to your session, go to the **Track** menu and select **Import Tracks > MIDI**

Choose the file you wish to import, and it will be added into a new track. Notice that it is also added in the **Files** panel on the right of the **Qtractor** window; so to add files without immediately adding them to your workspace, right-click in the **MIDI** tab of the **Files** panel and choose **Add Files**.

The MIDI file you import may or may not have generic MIDI instrument assignments. Either way, you can always adjust the MIDI instrument assigned to that track via the **Track Properties** dialogue, as you would for a track into which you're recording MIDI.

Effects and Filters

You know how to create tracks and insert sound either in the form of audio files or MIDI data. In addition to putting sound into tracks, **Qtractor** can pipe tracks through filters and effects.

The most popular format for sound filters and effect units in Linux is LADSPA, providing the free equivalent to VST, RTAS, or AU. The two ubiquitous Linux plugin packs are the **Steve Harris LADSPA Plugins** and the **CALF Plugins**, which should be availble from your repository or from their respective websites.

If you have not installed them yet, install them now and then re-launch **Qtractor** so that it will detect them as available filters.

Effects occur upon the sound itself, so they can be applied to Audio tracks as well as MIDI tracks. To place an effect on a track:

1. Select the track you want to pipe through an effect and select it by clicking the track label on the left of the **Qtractor** workspace.

2. Click on the **Track** menu and select **Track Properties**.

3. In the **Track** dialogue, click on the **Plugins** tab.

4. Click the **Add** button on the right of the window.

5. In the **Plugins** dialogue, choose the type of plugin you want to use with the filter button in the top right corner; more than likely, you will be using a LADSPA plugin.

6. A very common effect, of course, is reverb. Filter the choices from all the LADSPA plugins by typing "verb" into the search bar along the top. You may see one or two results, such as **GVerb** and **Plate Reverb**, so choose one of these. Place a tick in the checkbox in the lower left corner of the screen, labeled **Activate** and click **OK**.

7. Should you need to modify the reverb filter, right click on the plugin in the **Track** window and choose **Properties**. This will open the control panel for the effect, where you can change the attributes of the effect.

Automation in Qtractor

Nearly every aspect of any track can be automated in **Qtractor**, from the basics like volume and panning, to the very minute like the LFO frequency of a soft synth, or the levels of an effect.

To work on the automation of your tracks:

1. Click the **automation** button in the track control of your track.

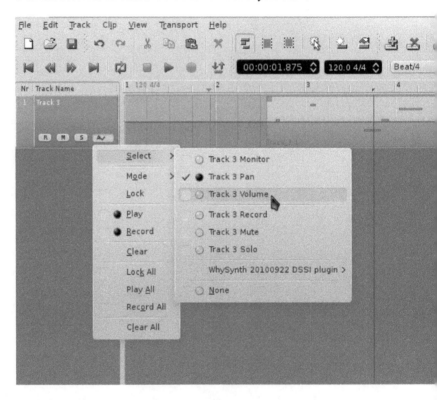

2. Choose from the popup menu the attribute you wish to automate.

3. Notice that an overlay appears over your track, representing the normal level of that attribute. To enter automation mode, click the **Edit** menu > Select Mode > Automation. In this mode, click the automation overlay to adjust levels.

4. To differentiate different attributes that you're automating, it can be helpful to modify the colour of the automation overlay. To do this, click the **automation** button in the track list and choose **Mode > Colour** and pick a new shade for that automation overlay.

To add automation for another attribute, click the **automation** button again, and navigate to **Select** to choose the next attribute. The new automation overlay appears in the default colour, and you can now modify its levels.

5. Leave automation mode by toggling off **Edit** menu > **Select Mode** > **Automation**

Bouncing the Project

Once you've finished your song, you obviously want to export the piece so that people can listen to it without having to have your **Qtractor** source files. This process is sometimes called "bouncing" a track, or exporting a "mixdown" or simply "exporting" the song.

Since it's possible to have multiple sources contributing to your final product (external hardware synths feeding sound into Qtrator while soft synths play over pre-recorded audio files to the beat of a Hydrogen drum machine on another virtual desktop, for example) it would make no since to treat the exporting process in the same way as a wave form editor (such as **Audacity**) would. **Qtractor**'s bounce process is literally to play all the sound sources in sync whilst recording what is playing back into **Qtractor** itself.

Note

Different people deal with bouncing and exporting in different ways, depending on their preference, their creative needs, and the capabilities of their computers. For instance, you could bounce each MIDI track individually to an audio track and then export all audio tracks into one self-contained track. Or you can simply set **Qtractor** to record and then play everything back into one audio track, which you then export.

There is no right or wrong way to do it. Either do it all in one go at the end or do it step by step. Usually the raw power of your computer will be the deciding factor.

To perform the final export of your completed work:

1. Create a new Audio track: **Track > Add Track**

2. Label the track, ie, "Bounce"

3. Open the **Connections** window: **View > Windows > Connections**

4. In the **Connections** window, connect the Master/Out of **Qtractor** to the Master/In of **Qtractor**, such that the output of all sound managed by **Qtractor** is being directed to the input of **Qtractor** for recording.

Warning

Be sure to disable any capture device such as microphones or unused line-ins. You'll be recording all the live sound going into **Qtractor**, so you don't want accidental line noise, hums, or room tone.

5. Set the in and out points for your recording by clicking once on the top timeline at the point you want the recording to stop; a blue transport line will be anchored where you click. Scroll back to the beginning of your project and click again in the top timeline to mark the in point with an opening blue transport bar.

Click the **Punch In/Out** button in the top menu bar to limit playback between your markers.

Note

If you do not set in and out points, you will need to stop the recording manually.

6. Arm your *Bounce* track for recording. Click the **Record** button in the top menu bar.

7. Make sure that your transport (playhead) is at the beginning of your track! When ready, press the **Play** button in the top menu bar.

Warning

Bouncing a track is a realtime process. Do not use your computer while you're bouncing a track!

When you've bounced your song to its own track, save the project! Solo the bounce track and listen to the recording for quality assurance, and then you are ready to export that track as a self-contained, distributable file.

To export a single track to disk:

1. Select the track or tracks you wish to export. If you bounced everything into one track, then it will just be that track, which you can solo using the **Solo** button on the track controls. If you are exporting a project consisting of only in-project audio, then leave them all activated and continue.

2. Choose **Track > Export Tracks > Audio**

3. In the **Export Audio** dialogue, choose a location and filename for your file. Choose the range of what will be exported; you can export the entire session, or manually set a Punch In/Out range, or specify the range in timecode, frames, or bars/beats/ticks.

    If you have multiple output sources, choose the appropriate source (probably your Master Output).

4. Click the **OK** button to begin the export.

Part 2. Advanced Qtractor

How to navigate and use the many features of Qtractor for audio production.

The Qtractor Interface

Qtractor's interface will be familiar to anyone familiar with Digital Audio Workstation software.

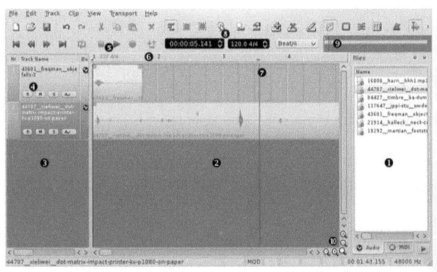

1. Files - a list of audio and midi files you've imported into your **Qtractor** project

2. Workspace - a view of the audio or MIDI data contained in each track in your project

3. Tracks - a list of tracks and some track-specific controls and information

4. Track controls - titles, bus information, recording and playback toggles, and automation controls for each track in the workspace

5. Transport controls - rewind, forward, play, pause, record

6. Timeline - your music workspace's timeline in bars, measures, and timecode

7. Transport - the playhead

8. Timecode and BPM - counter for SMPTE timecode, and the tempo or beats-per-minute setting

9. Overview - the entire project in one thumbnail view

10. Zoom - zoom in and zoom out (horizontally and vertically) buttons

Starting a new session

The first step in so many pro applications is one that is most overlooked by new users: create and save a new session. Saving a session before actually doing any work in it seems counter-intuitive, but it's important to save first so that any and all files created or required for your work can be contained in a pre-determined location.

To create a new session in **Qtractor**:

1. Launch **Qtractor** for a fresh new session, otherwise go to the **File** menu and select **New** or use **Ctrl+N** to start a fresh session.

2. Go to the **File** menu again and select **Save As** (or **Save** if you've already been working in the opened session), or just hit **Ctrl+S**

3. In the **Session** dialogue box, name the session and provide a description as needed. Click the **directory** button on the right to enter a file chooser dialogue.

4. In the **Session Directory** dialogue, create a new folder in the directory of your choice; for example, you might make a **myGreatSong** folder for your session in your ~/ music directory.

5. Click the **OK** button once you've created a directory for your session files.

6. Click the **OK** button in the **Session** dialogue box to proceed

7. A **Save Session** window will appear, which is a prompt for you to save the session file itself into the destination you've just created for it. Navigate to your new folder (in this example, **myGreatSong** in the ~/music directory)

8. Name your session file; by default it will already be named the same as the name of your session itself, but if you are versioning the file or have different notation you'd like to use, you can give it a customized name as well. The extension for **Qtractor** session files is **.qtr**

9. Click the **Save** button, and now your **Qtractor** session is saved in a self-contained, dedicated folder. This helps your project maintain its integrity and increases its portability

Managing Audio Tracks

There are four typical scenarios for dealing with sound in **Qtractor** and, indeed, for most digital audio workstations:

- Import existing audio files from your harddrive, a recording device, or a loop collection

- Record audio into **Qtractor** via your computer's built-in microphone or an external microphone

- Import MIDI data

- Create MIDI data

All three of these methods of acquiring sound for your work can be, and very often are, combined to produce a richer audio production.

1. Importing Audio Files

The easiest way to get sound into **Qtractor** is to import an audio file from your harddrive. Whether you are using sampled loops to construct a new musical piece, or importing a performance transferred from a recording device, importing audio in this way does not involve recording sound directly into **Qtractor**.

To bring audio into your project file, right-click in the **Files** pane and select **Add Files** or use **Ctrl+F**. Choose what file or files you wish to import from the file chooser window that appears.

To place an audio file in a track, drag and drop it from the **Files** panel into the **workspace**. You can add it to an existing track, or drop it directly into empty workspace and a new track will be created automatically.

2. Recording Audio

Recording audio into **Qtractor** requires a microphone and at least one audio input channel. Many laptops and webcams have built-in microphones, so in theory you could use this as an input source, but for best quality, purchase an external microphone and use it as your audio capture device.

Note

For simultaneous multitrack recording, rarely will the soundcard that was bundled with your computer be sufficient. Almost all soundcards embedded on motherboards are set to mixdown the input signals to a stereo mix. If you wish to record three separate musicians at the same time, each to a separate track in **Qtractor**, you will require a soundcard with separate dedicated inputs.

The way that Linux displays available sound inputs and outputs can be dauting at first, until you understand the logic behind it. A Linux system displays sounds devices the same way it displays hard drives and available network interfaces: the first device (regardless of actual inputs or outputs available via that device) is labeled hw0, the next hw1, the next hw2, and so on.

It is safe to assume that hw0 would be the built-in sound card on the system; being embedded in the motherboard would certainly qualify it as the first available sound device. So, hw0 represents, in almost every case, your built-in sound card. Hw1 might represent, for instance, a webcam that you keep plugged into your desktop, and Hw2 could represent, perhaps, a USB microphone or a USB interface that you've plugged in. You can usually determine which device is which by looking at the vendor name associated with the Hw labels; if I have two devices plugged into my system and one is labeled **Blue** and the other **H4**, then I would know from these terms that one is my Blue USB microphone and the other my Zoom Studio H4n.

With regards to outputs, these can sometimes be confusing due to the many possible ways you may wish to output your sound. Typically the stereo mix of you system sound is available as the first two output devices. If you have more than just two speakers and you wish to split your sound to each, then utilize the outputs labeled appropriately (Front, Center, and so on).

If the sound input and output labels confuse you, take a few minutes to learn them by playing sound on your computer and plugging speakers into each output on your computer. For the inputs, plug a microphone into your different inputs and see where they are received and how they are labeled. It won't take long before you understand the logic behind the labels, and you'll be able to use **Qtractor** all the more fluidly.

2.1. Analogue vs USB Inputs

There are many kinds of microphones, each intended for certain kinds of sounds and situations, but on a purely technical level, without the question of aesthetics and microphone design, there are only about three scenarios you will encounter:

- Microphones with an 8th- inch (also called a mini) jack

- Microphones with a quarter-inch or XLR jack

- Microphones with USB connectors.

The recording process is different, depending on your input type.

2.2. Recording from Line-In

If your microphone has an 8th-inch jack, then you can plug it directly into the line-in of your computer. No external sound interface is required. Your built-in sound card is JACK's default input, so no changes are necessary.

If your microphone can easily and cleanly adapted to the standard 8th-inch input with a cable or a simple plug adapter, then you can use this method of recording, as well.

To record from the line-in of your computer into **Qtractor**:

1. Go to the **View** menu and select **Windows > Connections** to verify that the **Capture** devices on your **System** are routed to the **Master/In** of **Qtractor**, and the **Master/Out** channels are routed to the **Playback** channels of your System.

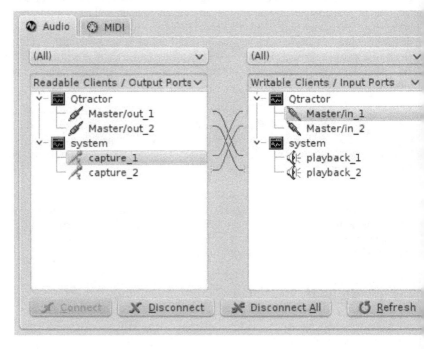

2. Go to the **Track** menu and choose **Add Track** or use **Ctrl+Shift+N**. In the **Track** dialogue box, give the track a name, set the **Type** to Audio, and set the **Input/Output** to Master. Click the **OK** button to proceed.

3. Arm the new track for recording by clicking the **R** button in the track listing on the left of the **Qtractor** window. This sets the destination for the recorded sound.

4. Click the **Record** button in the top toolbar

5. Click the **Play** button in the top toolbar

2.3. Recording from USB Audio

If your microphone has a quarter-inch or XLR jack and you choose not to use a plug adapter, then you will need an external sound interface. External interfaces are available from M-Audio, Fostex, Zoom Studio, and others; they serve as an intermediate converter from your input device and the USB port of your computer.

Similarly, a USB microphone plugs directly into the USB port of your computer.

If you input sound through USB, then (obviously) you are utilizing a different interface than your computer's built-in sound card. This must be set via **QJackCtl** for appropriate sound routing to occur:

1. In **QJackCtl**, stop the sound server by clicking the **Stop** button

2. If you have not already plugged in your USB audio interface or USB microphone, then do so. Make sure it's on.

3. Click the **Setup** button. In the **Settings** tab, locate the **Input Device** setting and click the **>** button to see your choices.

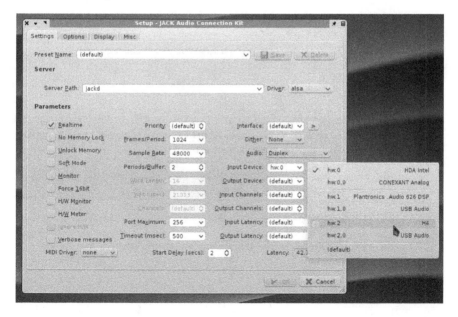

4. Click the **Start** button to activate.

Now your USB interface, whether it is a single USB microphone or a 4-channel Audio-to-USB conversion box, is managing your input sources. Plug your XLR microphone into your USB interface, set the interface's input source as your XLR jack, and then create a new track in **Qtractor** and begin the recording:

1. Go to the **View** menu and select **Windows > Connections** to verify that the **Capture** devices on your **System** are routed to the **Master/In** of **Qtractor**, and the **Master/Out** channels are routed to the **Playback** channels of your System.

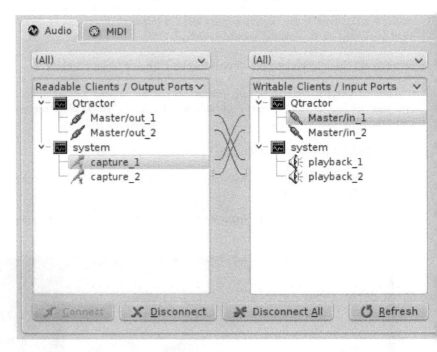

2. Go to the **Track** menu and choose **Add Track** or use **Ctrl+Shift+N**. In the **Track** dialogue box, give the track a name, set the **Type** to Audio, and set the **Input/Output** to Master. Click the **OK** button to proceed.

3. Arm the new track for recording by clicking the **R** button in the track listing on the left of the **Qtractor** window. This sets the destination for the recorded sound.

4. Click the **Record** button in the top toolbar

5. Click the **Play** button in the top toolbar

Managing MIDI Tracks

MIDI is a versatile format for triggering sounds; it can be used to trigger hardware synths external of your computer, software synths that are applications on your computer, samples, loops, automation functions, and more. There are basically three ways to get MIDI data into your **Qtractor** session:

- Import MIDI data from an existing file

- Enter MIDI data into a matrix editor (sometimes called a "piano roll" or "grid view")

- Play in MIDI data via a USB MIDI keyboard controller

Before beginning with MIDI, you should make sure that you have some software synthesizers installed on your system. A popular format for soft synths on Linux is **DSSI**, which is akin to **VST** or **AU** on other platforms. **LV2** is also quite popular, although in practice the bulk of LV2 plugins you'll find are audio effects units (reverbs, tape delays, EQ, and so on).

One of the easiest soft synths is **WhySynth**; it features enough presets to provide instant gratification, and enough control over the raw sound to become a permanent fixture in your studio. You can install **WhySynth** from your distribution's repository or directly from *smbolton.com/whysynth.html*[1]

If you've just installed soft synths now, then you should relaunch **Qtractor** so that it will detect the newly available plugins.

1. Importing MIDI Data

Since MIDI data consists of nothing more than digital signals to activate and deactivate sounds at certain times, MIDI files are small and easily distributed online. A simple internet search for MIDI files will result in thousands of MIDI files for nearly any song you can name. Taken alone, the MIDI file is useless. Imported into **Qtractor** and assigned instruments, the files come to life like a player piano.

The MIDI file you import into **Qtractor** could be from the internet, or it could be a MIDI files you yourself created on any given MIDI input application, or even from data dump from a MIDI-capable hardware synth. In this example, we will use one from the internet:

1. Download a MIDI file, such as *kunstderfuge.com/-/midi.asp?file=bach/sankey/ prelude_and_fugue_bwv-894_(c)sankey.mid*[2] and save it to your hard drive. Preferably, in your **Qtractor**'s session directory, to keep your project self-contained.

2. In **Qtractor**, go to the **Track** menu and select **Import Tracks > MIDI**.

---

[1] http://www.smbolton.com/whysynth.html
[2] http://kunstderfuge.com/-/midi.asp?file=bach/sankey/prelude_and_fugue_bwv-894_(c)sankey.mid

---

Alternately, you may click on the **MIDI** tab of the **Files** panel on the right of the **Qtractor** window and right-click or use **Ctrl+F** to import the MIDI file to your files panel and not automatically add its tracks to your session. If you do this, then you'll need to manually drag the MIDI file into the workspace in order for the data to appear as tracks.

3.   The MIDI tracks will appear in your **Qtractor** session, in this example's case it is even pre-programmed for General MIDI instrumentation.

Imported tracks will often have embedded General MIDI instrument assignments. General MIDI was an effort to standardize a set of 128 instruments to provide similar results in playback across all systems.

If you have a soft synth bank compliant with General MIDI, then you can press the **Play** button in the top toolbar of Qtractor and you will get a good approximation of how the original author of the file wanted the tracks heard.

You can also use the list of Generic MIDI instruments found in the appendices of this book to guide you in the instrumentation of an imported file, making the sound of the tracks truly your own.

1.   To assign instruments to a track, right-click on the track title and select **Track Properties** from the contextual menu.

2.   In the **Track** dialogue box, click on the **Plugins** tab.

3.   In the **Plugins** tab, click the **Add** button on the right to see a list of available sotware plugins.

4.   In the **Plugins** dialogue, select the type of plugin you wish to use with the top right button. Software synths on Linux are usually of the DSSI variety; from the list of DSSI synths, select the one you want to play and click the **Activate** checkbox in the lower left corner.

5.   Click the **OK** button in the bottom right corner of the window to proceed.

6.   Back in the **Track** dialogue, select the **Track** tab again. In the MIDI/Instrument panel, choose an instrument from the top dropdown menu; using **WhySynth** as an example, you would select **WhySynth_20100922 DSSI plugin**.

7.   Choose a **Bank** and **Program**. If you're not familiar with **WhySynth**, you can select any of its three Banks and any of the Programs contained in them. You should be able to instantly audition the sounds on a USB controller.

8.   When you've selected the sound you'd like to use, click the **OK** button.

Repeat these steps for each track to wish you want to assign an instrument, incrementing the MIDI channel you use for each new instrument you assign. Press the play button in the top menu bar to hear the MIDI file play.

Note

Note that you must increment the MIDI channel used, or keypresses on your MIDI controller will be using the same MIDI channel to trigger different sounds. In otherwords, if Track 1 and Track 2 are both using MIDI Channel 1, then a note played on Track 2 will also trigger the instrument assigned to Track 1.

2. Creating MIDI data with a MIDI controller

A MIDI controller is a piece of hardware to help you play the software-based synthesizers in your computer. Typically, a MIDI controller is a piano keyboard with a few octaves and no built-in sounds of its own. It usually plugs into the USB port of your computer and, once configured, will pass on any key press to Qtractor, allowing you to play a software synth in realtime as well as record the keypresses themselves.

MIDI and USB are two technologies that, fortunately, have been kept universal enough that you almost don't need to question whether any given USB MIDI controller will work with your system. There are perfectly capable USB MIDI controllers being offered from vendors like Akai, Roland/Edirol, Digidesign/M-Audio, and many others. If you require realistic, weighted keys with high resolution touch-sensitivity then look at the upper price-range of controllers and go to a music store to audition them. If all your require are a few octaves of piano keys so that you can get a tune into the computer quickly and easily, then the basic controllers will be enough.

To use your USB controller to input MIDI data:

1. Plug in the USB MIDI controller to your computer

2. Launch **QJackCtl** and start it

3. Launch **Qtractor** and click on the **View** menu, and select **Connections** from the **Windows** category

4. In the **Connections** window, click on the **MIDI** tab. Listed on the **ReadableClients/ Output Ports** column, find your USB controller device. Open its category to see the available outputs.

Note

If you do not see your USB controller listed in the left column, check to ensure that your controller is powered on (some require external power, others are powered by the USB port), and check the cable connection. If you still cannot see the device in the left column, make sure your computer sees the controller by checking `dmesg | tail`.

If your computer registers the device but you are not seeing it in **Connections**, try restarting both **QJackCtl** and **Qtractor**.

5. Connect the output of your MIDI device to **Qtractor** in the **Writable Clients/Input Ports** column

    Qtractor is now configured to receive MIDI events from your USB controller.

To play your composition (or parts of your composition) into **Qtractor**. you will need an empty track. To begin with, create an empty track by selecting **Add Track** from the **Track** menu, or by clicking the **New Track** button in the top toolbar.

1. To assign instruments to a track, right-click on the track title and select **Track Properties** from the contextual menu.

2. In the **Track** dialogue box, click on the **Plugins** tab.

3. In the **Plugins** tab, click the **Add** button on the right to see a list of available sotware plugins.

4. In the **Plugins** dialogue, select the type of plugin you wish to use with the top right button. Software synths on Linux are usually of the DSSI variety; from the list of DSSI synths, select the one you want to play and click the **Activate** checkbox in the lower left corner.

5. Click the **OK** button in the bottom right corner of the window to proceed.

6. Back in the **Track** dialogue, select the **Track** tab again. In the MIDI/Instrument panel, choose an instrument from the top dropdown menu; using **WhySynth** as an example, you would select **WhySynth_20100922 DSSI plugin**.

7. Choose a **Bank** and **Program**. If you're not familiar with **WhySynth**, you can select any of its three Banks and any of the Programs contained in them. You should be able to instantly audition the sounds on a USB controller.

8. When you've selected the sound you'd like to use, click the **OK** button.

Now that you've create an empty track and assigned it a soft synth, you can record MIDI data:

1. Create an empty clip in your destination track by choosing **New** from the **Clip** menu, or by clicking the **New Clip** button in the top toolbar

2. In the **Session** window, type in a name for your MIDI clip, choose the Directory into which you want to save the clip, and provide a description for yourself as needed. Click the **OK** button when finished

Note

Unlike pre-recorded loops or sounds, which already exist on your harddrive, a new MIDI clip doesn't yet have a home. Some music programs bundle your MIDI data into your project file, which can make it difficult to share one MIDI loop between projects. But **Qtractor** saves all MIDI tracks as independent files, meaning you can easily re-use them

3. Arm your track for recording by clicking the **R** button in the track control

4. Click the **Record** button in the top menu bar to prepare the track for recording. Click the **Play** button to start the transport recording

5. Every key press you make on your USB controller will be recorded in realtime. Depending on the feature set of your controller, velocity, pitch, and other data may also be recorded

3. Creating MIDI data with the matrix editor

If you have no USB MIDI controller, you can still create MIDI data using **Qtractor**'s MIDI Editor (sometimes called a "matrix editor" or "piano roll" in other music programs). This enables you to mark on a grid when a note should be triggered, how long it should be sustained, and at what velocity it should be played.

Broadly speaking, the steps are:

1. Create a destination track

2. Create a MIDI clip

3. Enter the data in the MIDI editor

To create a new track select **Add Track** from the **Track** menu, or click the **New Track** button in the top toolbar.

1. To assign instruments to a track, right-click on the track title and select **Track Properties** from the contextual menu.

2. In the **Track** dialogue box, click on the **Plugins** tab.

3. In the **Plugins** tab, click the **Add** button on the right to see a list of available sotware plugins.

4. In the **Plugins** dialogue, select the type of plugin you wish to use with the top right button. Software synths on Linux are usually of the DSSI variety; from the list of DSSI synths, select the one you want to play and click the **Activate** checkbox in the lower left corner.

5. Click the **OK** button in the bottom right corner of the window to proceed.

6. Back in the **Track** dialogue, select the **Track** tab again. In the MIDI/Instrument panel, choose an instrument from the top dropdown menu; using **WhySynth** as an example, you would select **WhySynth_20100922 DSSI plugin**.

7. Choose a **Bank** and **Program**. If you're not familiar with **WhySynth**, you can select any of its three Banks and any of the Programs contained in them. You should be able to instantly audition the sounds on a USB controller.

8. When you've selected the sound you'd like to use, click the **OK** button.

Now that you've create an empty track and assigned it a soft synth, you can input MIDI data:

1. Create an empty clip in your destination track by choosing **New** from the **Clip** menu, or by clicking the **New Clip** button in the top toolbar

2. In the **Session** window, type in a name for your MIDI clip, choose the Directory into which you want to save the clip, and provide a description for yourself as needed. Click the **OK** button when finished

 Note

Unlike pre-recorded loops or sounds, which already exist on your harddrive, a new MIDI clip doesn't yet have a home. Some music programs bundle your MIDI data into your project file, which can make it difficult to share one MIDI loop between projects. But **Qtractor** saves all MIDI tracks as independent files, meaning you can easily re-use them

3. Click on the clip to select it, and choose **Edit** from the **Clip** menu to open the clip in the MIDI editor.

The MIDI Editor is very intuitive, with simple but effective tools in the toolbar, such as an arrow to select and move notes, a pen tool to draw note into the grid, and a disk icon to save your work.

Vertically, the grid corresponds with notes on the chromatic keyboard. Horizontally, the grid corresponds with beats per measure.

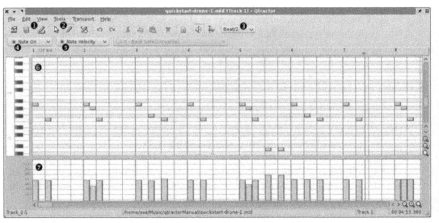

1. Properties of the MIDI Editor workspace, Save, and Track Properties

2. Arrow - to move notes, increase and decrease note length, and selecting

    Pen (Edit On) - to draw note into the grid

    Edit Draw - dynamically draw multiple notes with a click-and-drag of the mouse

3. **Snap/Beat** menu - determines the resolution of drawing and editing notes. In a 4/4 project, for instance, a setting of **Beat/2** would cause a pen tool click to produce an eighth note, while **Beat** would produce a quarter note, and so on.

    Regardless of the default note length, a note block can be extended by clicking and dragging the border of the note to increase (or decrease) its length. The resolution of changes to the length of a note is also determined by the **Snap/Beat** menu.

4. **Notes Type** setting indicates that the notes you draw in the grid represent the length of the note. The **Key Press** setting indicates that the notes you draw in the grid represents a MIDI event without a defined duration, such as triggering an external MIDI sequence to begin playing.

5. The **Value** menu lets you control note velocity, program changes, pitch bending, and other extra MIDI data.

6.   The main editor grid represents the notes being played. Use the pen tool to draw notes into the grid according to the keyboard on the left of the window.

Whether you are drawing in notes or only key presses can be controlled by the **Notes Type** menu.

7.   The value grid controls extra MIDI data, such as velocity, program changes, pitch bends, and so on. The data represented here will change according to the **Value** menu setting.

The MIDI Editor can be invoked either for raw entry or to modify existing MIDI data that you've either imported or played into **Qtractor**.

3.1. Additional MIDI Editor Features

In addition to input and editing tools, the MIDI Editor features functions to make it easy to modify your composition, such as Quantization, Transposition, Timeshifting, and more.

To access these features, use the **Tools** menu in the MIDI Editor window. If no notes are selected, then the **Tools** will be unavailable; select a note or block of notes with the arrow tool to make them available.

•   Quantize - allows you to automatically structure notes in stricter uniformity with your time signature. This is especially helpful if you've played the notes in and were not perfectly on the beat.

You can quantize notes such that the notes occur on the beat (or one 16ths of the beat, or 8ths, or so on), such that the duration of notes are extended to be on the beat (or divisions thereof), such that notes play with some degree of "swing", and even such that the notes played match a specific scale from Minor to Major to the extremely obscure.

•   Transpose - moves the block of selected notes up or down some number of steps.

•   Normalize - adjusts note velocity by either a percentage or an absolute value. A percentage value will adjust the velocity of the notes equally by the percent given in relation to the original velocity, while an absolute value adjusts velociy of each note to that value regardless of original velocity.

•   Randomize - provides random changes to the Note, Time, Duration, or velocity (Value). Adjust how extreme the changes will be with percent values.

•   Resize - allows you to control the duration of notes to any number of beats (or divisions thereof), or the Velocity to any value.

•   Rescale - changes the selected notes by some percentage; you may alter the time that the notes are triggered, the duration for which they sound, and the velocity at which they are played.

•   Timeshift - alters the timing of the selected notes on a curve, such that the acceleration from the beginning note to the ending note is either increased or decreased.

In order for Qtractor to know how to accelerate the timing of the notes, you must define a range of time for the acceleration to occur. Do this with the **head** and **tail** markers (the blue markers in the timeline above the MIDI Editor gride). Mark the out point (tail) of your range by clicking on the timeline, and then set the in point (head) of the time range by clicking somewhere to the left of the original marker.

Once the range is defined, select the notes you wish to timeshift with the arrow tool. Open the **Tools** menu and select **Timeshift**.

Use the slider to either cause an acceleration in your selected notes over the course of the defined time range, or a deceleration, and then click **OK** to commit the change.

3.2. Customizing the MIDI Editor View

The **View** menu provides cutomization for how the MIDI Editor is laid and how the notes are presented to you. The default layout is clean and pleasingly minimalist, but take a look at some of the other options to see what works best for you:

- Menubar - turns off the top menu bar; use **Control+m** to toggle it on or off.

- Statusbar - turns off the status bar at the bottom of the window.

- Toolbars - defines what icon toolbar is visible at the top of the window; choose from File (file opening and saving icons), Edit (cut, paste, undo), View (preview modes, snapping quantization), Transport (fast forward, rewind), and Scale (key signature and scale information).

- Windows - toggles on or off event information, a panel which will provide detailed information on each MIDI event in the MIDI Editor grid

- Tool Tips - toggles whether tool tips are visible

- Note Duration - defines whether the note's duration is reflected in the length of the velocity bars at the bottom of the grid

- Note Color - assigns differing colours to each note; if this is not active, all notes appear as one colour.

- Value Color - assigns the colours of the corresponding notes to the velocity bars; helpful when you have many overlapping notes but want to adjust their velocities.

- Zoom - zoom in or out on the grid.

- Snap - define what division of the beat your notes snap to, or turn snapping off entirely.

- Scale - change the key signature or type of scale being used.

- Refresh - for the MIDI Editor to redraw in the event of latent images.

- Preview Notes - turn on or off whether you hear the notes of the scale as you input or move notes along the grid.

- Follow Playhead - define whether the MIDI Editor grid scrolls with the playhead when you are playing the track.

Qtractor Options and Preferences

Qtractor's preferences can be accessed via the **View** menu, via the **Options** selection. The options are divided into tabs:

- General - contains options for overall preferences, such as file formats of project files, behaviour of windows and confirmation requests, and the transport

- Audio - determines how **Qtractor** stores newly recorded audio (ie, microphone or line inputs, as well as re-routed sound within its own mixer), and whether an audible metronome is used

- MIDI - controls how MIDI data is stored, captured, and what defaults it uses for quantization, playback, and metronome

- Display - controls whether your timeline uses timecode, frames, or beats, some default colours and fonts, and where log files are stored

- Plugins - the paths to folders containing your plugins. An empty list is OK, since **Qtractor** defaults to the typical locations such as /usr/lib/ and so on, but if you have customized your system heavily then you may need to specify the locations of your synths, effects, and plugins here

Soft Synths

Strictly speaking, soft synths are not a part of **Qtractor**. However, it is common to use soft synths within **Qtractor**. Acquiring free software synthesizers online is a simple matter of locating them online at *sourceforge.net*[1], *ccrma.stanford.edu*[2], your distribution's repository, or the project's homepages directly.

Software synths for GNU Linux come in a few varieties:

- Independent synth applications that launch separately from **Qtractor** but that plug into JACK so that the synths can be used as sound sources within **Qtractor**. One such example is **Qsynth,** written by the same programmer as **QJackCtl** and **Qtractor**.

- DSSI Plugins which are launched and controlled entirely from within **Qtractor**.

- LV2 Plugins which are launched and controlled entirely from within **Qtractor**.

- VST Plugins; the format from Steinberg does in fact support Linux technically but the number of Linux-native VST synths are few.

1. Installing Soft Synths

Installing any soft synth, whether it is a plugin or stand-alone application, is done through your distribution's package manager (yum, apt, slackbuilds, pacman, emerge, ports, and so on) or from the installers on the project's website.

Once the synth is installed, you may launch it and try it out; if it's a stand-alone application, then it can be launched like any other application on your system. If it's a plugin for Qtractor, then launch Qtractor and create a new MIDI track, choosing your new soft synth as the MIDI Instrument as described in *Managing MIDI Tracks*

To verify that **Qtractor** knows where all of your soft synth plugins are located, open the **View** menu and select **Options** and choose the **Plugins** tab in the **Options** window.

---

[1] http://sourceforge.net
[2] http://ccrma.stanford.edu/planetccrma/software/

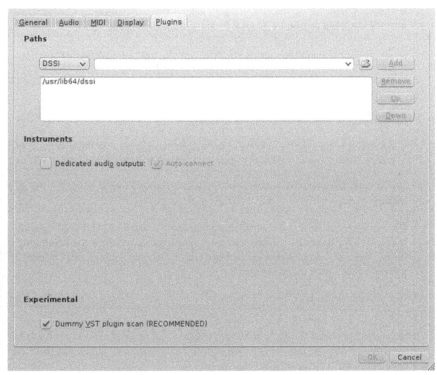

In the **Plugins** tab, define any non-standard paths to DSSI, LADSPA, LV2, or VST plugins on your system by selecting the type of plugin from the dropdown menu on the left and then adding the path with the **Add** button on the right. When finished, click the **OK** button to save your change.

2. Using Soft Synths as Plugins

Using soft synths as DSSI or LV2 plugins is probably the easiest model, as it does not require any additional routing of sounds through JACK. The synth is integrated into Qtractor's interface, the sound is directed to the appropriate track, and the fact that you are using a separate application is almost entirely abstracted away from you.

From *Managing MIDI Tracks* , you already know how to create a MIDI track and assign a synthesizer plugin to that track. Most soft synths, however, have some level of control over the sounds they produce, which you can access by editing the properties of the synthesizer:

1. Open the **View** menu > **Windows** and select **Mixer**.

2. The **Mixer** window shows all available tracks; on the far left are the Master Inputs and on the far right are the Master Outputs; in the middle are the tracks in your project's workspace.

In the top plugin list of your track, right click on the soft synth currently associated with the track and choose **Properties** from the contextual menu.

3.   In the window that appears, notice the three buttons in the top right corner:

-   **Params** toggles the view of available attributes you can modify (such as oscillators, resonance, envelopes, and so on)

-   **Edit** toggles whether the plugin is editable

-   An **active** plugin is "on" and will play sounds when receiving MIDI signals. If a plugin is not active, it will not produce (or affect, if it's an effect unit plugin) sound

If you do not see editable parameters in the synthesizer window, click the **Params** button.

4.   Change the parameters you wish to change using the controls the soft synth provides. If you create a patch that you want to save, type a name into the **Preset Name** field in the upper left corner and click the **Save** button and your settings will be added as a Preset in the Preset dropdown menu.

Whether you use DSSI, LV2, or VST plugins, the process for using a soft synth or effect is the same.

All parameters provided by the soft synth's interface can also be automated such that attributes like LFO or resonance can be programmed to change over time during playback. For more information on automation, see *Automation*

3. Using Stand-Alone Synths

The other kind of software synth you might use in your **Qtractor** workflow are stand-alone synthesizers such as **Qsynth** and **amSynth**.

Installing these stand-alone synths from your distribution's repository or from the projects' websites. Launch **QJackCtl** first, and then launch the software synths the same as you would any other application on your system.

 Note

Keep in mind that if your distribution requires you to set your own realtime permissions, you will want to add the stand-alone software synths to your RT list.

Once you've launched your software synth, it will become a source for sound and a destination for MIDI signals in the **Qtractor**. Verify that your settings are correct:

1. Select the **View** menu in **Qtractor > Windows > Connections**

2. In the **Audio** tab appear all possible sources of sound. If you have launched **QSynth** or **amSynth**, for example, they would be listed in the left column. Also listed will be **Qtractor** itself, since it also produces sound, and your computer's sound input (labeled as **System > capture**)

   In the right column are the sound destinations available. At the very least, you should see **Qtractor's Master In** and your computer speakers (labeled as **System > playback**)

   By default, the sound from **Qtractor Master Out** is patched to **System playback** so that you can hear, from your speakers, everything that **Qtractor's** mixer manages.

3. This is where the logic of audio engineering as well as the workings of your own studio setup should be considered. The sound produced from your stand-alone synth can logically be patched into either:

   • **Qtractor Master In** so that the sound produced by the synthesizer can be recorded back into an empty audio track in **Qtractor**

   If you're not sure what kind of setup you have, then choose this method.

   • **System playback** if you have an external mixer or recording device that will be recording the audio being produced by the MIDI-driven synths.

4. To patch the sound from the synth to its destination, click the left channel of the synth output, and then the left destination channel, and click the **Connect** button. Repeat this for the right channel if stereo is required.

This takes care of routing the sound; now you must route the MIDI signals controlling the synthesizer. As with the routing of sound, there is no "right" way to route the MIDI signal; you must be somewhat familiar with the equipment and workflow you are implementing and decide for yourself how you want it to all work together.

1. In the **MIDI** tab appear all possible sources of MIDI signals. At the very least, your stand-alone soft synth will be listed in the left column. If you have a USB MIDI controller, it will also be listed. **Qtractor** itself and a MIDI Through channel are also listed.

   In the right column are the sound destinations available. At the very least, you should see **Qtractor's Master** and the **MIDI Through** channels, and the soft synth you are running.

2. As with audio routing, there are many ways to design your production process:

   • The MIDI signal from **Qtractor** should be patched into the soft synth(s) that you are running so that the data in your MIDI tracks will trigger the sounds of those synths.

   If you are using an external USB MIDI controller, you might want to route the signals generated from it into the **Qtractor** destination so that you can play MIDI into **Qtractor** MIDI tracks (which in turn gets passed onto the soft synth, which plays sound back into **Qtractor** and/or into your computer speakers).

   If you are not sure about what you want, this is probably the method to use.

   • Alternately, you could route the MIDI signals from your controller straight into the soft synth. This would trigger the synth directly, playing sounds which could be routed into **Qtractor** for live recording.

   This method does not record any MIDI data.

3. To patch the MIDI signal from the source to its destination, click the MIDI source in the left column, and then the destination in the right column, and click the **Connect** button. Repeat this for all MIDI signals that need routing.

   If you're not sure what signals need routing, then you probably need to route **Qtractor** to your synth. If you are using a USB MIDI controller then you also need to route your controller to **Qtractor**.

All signals have been patched now, so playing MIDI into **Qtractor** should cause your external synthesizer to sound.

4. A Bit about MIDI

If you have had limited experience with MIDI, it's important to have a basic understanding of how MIDI talks to the devices it controls.

MIDI was originally developed for hardware, with the only software involved being MIDI sequencers, which were as frequently embedded systems as they were traditional software applications like the modern DAW's we are used to today.

MIDI signals are divided into channels; each channel is a discreet signal that can be directed to a specific device or a number of devices. If you generate a MIDI signal on MIDI Channel 1 and send that signal to a group of synthesizers, then any synthesizer programmed to play a note on either MIDI Channel 1 or MIDI Channel Omni will play. Any synthesizer programmed to respond to MIDI Channel 2 through 128 will not play.

Most musicians had more than one synthesizer, so the problem became how to get MIDI data from one controlling device (the sequencer; either a dedicated piece of hardware or a software running on a Personal Computer) to more than one synth. The answer was to daisy chain the synthesizers together, so that each synth could receive MIDI data pertinent to it as well as MIDI data for the next synthesizer in the chain.

Therefore, any MIDI-capable synth could have:

• MIDI IN used to receive playable MIDI data

• MIDI THRU to receive MIDI data to pass along to the next synth in line

• MIDI OUT to send MIDI signals from MIDI THRU (or its own internal sequencer) to other devices

Modern digital audio workstations don't necessarily have this problem, since many musicians are making music with no hardware synthesizer whatever. MIDI is generated by the sequencer (**Qtractor** in this case) and is passed to each software synthesizer over virtual MIDI ports.

A virtual MIDI THRU port is nevertheless available, so in the event that you do require MIDI data in a passthrough configuration, you can use the MIDI THRU port in **QJackCtl**, via the **Connections** window in **Qtractor**

The concept of MIDI channels are also equally relevant even without hardware. If you set up **QSynth** to generate a bassline for your piece on MIDI channel 1, and **WhySynth** to play the melody, then you must not set **WhySynth** to use Channel 1, or else all notes being triggered on **QSynth** will also be triggered on **WhySynth** because they are being triggered by the same MIDI Channel. With 128 channels to use, you are free to use 128 soft synths, but unless you are seeking unison, each should have a distinct MIDI Channel.

Note

You can set the MIDI Channel in the Track Properties of each of your **Qtractor** tracks.

4.1. Using Multiple Sequencers

If a synthesizer has a built-in sequencer, then the only MIDI signals that need to be sent to that device are START and STOP. This is common in external drum machines, which inherently manage their own sequencing so that you can create drumbeats and loops on them using a fairly familiar interface (familiar as long as you've used drum machines, anyway).

On the software side, **Hydrogen** is a good example. **Hydrogen** is a self-contained drum machine for Linux which allows the user to create custom patch sets and which does all of its own sequencing. Therefore, if you were to use **Hydrogen** as a stand-alone drum machine, you wouldn't sequence your drum tracks in **Qtractor**'s MIDI editor, but in **Hydrogen**'s sequencer. Since **Hydrogen** is **JACK**-aware, sending a START signal to Hydrogen to start the sequence playing and a STOP signal when the song is finished, is all that Qtractor will do; the clock and syncronization of the drum beats with the rest of the sequence is handled by **JACK** just as it would have been on hardware synthesizers via a MIDI clock.

Working in Qtractor

Editing audio in **Qtractor** is done directly in the workspace, with a small set of powerful tools. There are three types of audio within the **Qtractor** workspace:

- Audio files - the representation of the actual audio file on your harddrive, which is being referenced by **Qtractor** because you imported it into your project. It may or may not be actually used in the project yet, but it you have linked to it and so it will appear in the **Files** panel.

- Track - the representation of a mixable channel in **Qtractor**'s workspace. It may or may not have audio in it, but it is a bus which can hold audio, effects (or, technically, MIDI data, but that hardly applies in a chapter on audio editing).

- Clip - a piece or the whole of an audio file, as it appears in your **Qtractor** project. Audio clips are always contained in an audio track.

You can edit and effect the latter two; the first (the audio file itself) is merely referenced in **Qtractor** and cannot be directly manipulated by any of **Qtractor**'s tools. In fact, it should be noted that **Qtractor**, like most other digital audio workstations, is not a waveform editor; for cosmetic corrections such as removing pops or blown-out plosives, or removing lip smacks or dampening roomtone, you should use a waveform editor such as **Audacity**.

1. (Not) Editing Waveforms

Cleaning your source sound is frequently one of the first tasks you'll do, so ideally your sound will be sanitized before ever reaching **Qtractor**. However, in the event that you have imported audio and started working and then you decide that something needs some detail work, you can export just the clip that requires cleaning from **Qtractor**, clean it, and then re-import it.

To export a clip of a sound file for cleaning outside of **Qtractor**:

1. Right-click on the clip in its track and select **Clip > Export** from the contextual menu.

2. Edit the exported clip in a waveform editor such as **Audacity** and save export your changes.

3. Import the modified clip back into **Qtractor** and move it into place over the previous clip.

2. Audio Clip Tools

Outside of cleaning the sound of an audio clip, there are plenty of modifications you can do to the audio clips you record or import into **Qtractor**, such as splitting, punching-in, looping, and more.

2.1. Moving Clips and Controlling Snapping

You mouse cursor has four selection modes. Its default mode is **Clip** select, which allows you to click and drag clips within and between tracks. The precision with which you can move clips back and forward in time is determined by snapping. To deactivate or change snapping, click the **View** menu and select **Snapping** to choose the resolution you want to use when moving clips; you can move clips by beats, quarter notes, sixteenth notes, and so on, or none to deactivate snapping.

2.2. Truncating (Splitting) and Extending Clips

Also in clip mode, you can split audio clips nondestructively. To split a clip:

1. Position the playhead in the timecode bar at the top of the **Qtractor** workspace to the position at which you'd like to split your audio clip.

2. Click the clip you want to split so that it is selected.

3. Click the **Clip** menu and choose **Split**. The clip has now been split at the position of the playhead.

Since **Qtractor** never affects the original audio file it is referencing, any split you make to an audio clip is reversible. The easiest way to undo a clip (aside from using **Edit > Undo**) is to extend the clip. To extend a clip, click on the edge of the clip with your selection arrow and click and pull the edge to reveal more of the audio file within the track.

Note

Extending or truncating clips by dragging the clip's edge is also affected by the **Snap** setting, so if you are having difficulty modifying the end or beginning of a clip, check to make snapping is deactivated.

A second way to split clips is to use the Range or Rectangle selection tools.

2.3. Range and Rectangle Selection

The default selection tool is the **Clip** selection, which allows you to click on clips and select them as a whole so that you can move them within the workspace. The other two modes are **Range** and **Rectangle**.

The **Range** selection tool spans all tracks in your workspace and allows you to arbitrarily select any portion of clips regardless of where the clips begin or end. In otherwords, you can select a range in the very middle of a clip, and all other clips above and below it because you are selecting a block of time, rather than basing your selection on the nature of the clips in your workspace.

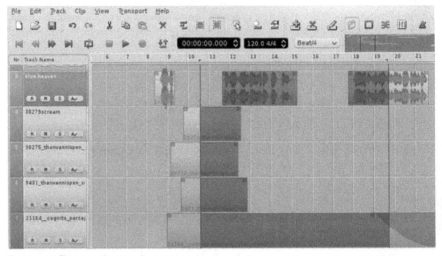

To use the **Range** select mode:

1. Click the **Edit** menu > **Select Mode** > Range

2. Click within an audio clip and drag your selection.

The **Rectangle** selection mode is similar to **Range** but is track-specific. Using the **Rectangle** selection tool permits you to draw the range of selection over one or more tracks, and a selection will be made wherever a clip is present.

To use the **Rectangle** select mode:

1. Click the **Edit** menu > **Select Mode** > Rectangle

2. Click within an audio clip and drag your selection. You may select portions, or the whole, of clips on as many tracks as you wish. Or you may confine your selection to one.

With both tools, your selected areas can be cut, copied, pasted, deleted, or even lifted out from their clips and moved elsewhere (the splits will be made automatically for you).

To lift a selection from a clip or a set of clips, click and drag the selection.

To copy and paste, click on the **Edit** menu and select **Copy** or **Cut** or the usual keyboard shortcuts of **Ctrl+C** or **Ctrl+X**. When you are ready to paste, click the **Edit** menu again and select **Paste** (or use **Ctrl+V**) and click in the time line where you want to paste the clips.

Note

If you have multiple clips copied, then they will be pasted relative to how they were copied (so if you paste a clip originally from tracks 1 and 2 into track 3, then the pasted clips will fall into tracks 3 and 4).

2.4. Using Range Markers

An alternate way to select a range in your workspace is with the marker transports, which appear in the timeline above the workspace alongside the play transport.

1. To bring the markers to your cursor, click in the timeline above the **Qtractor** workspace. Both the In- and Out- markers will appear at your cursor's position.

2. The position of the markers is the out-point for what will become your selection. Move your cursor left and click again to set the in-point.

3. The space between the two blue markers is now the active range. Click the **Edit** menu and use the options in the **Select** submenu to select areas based on the currently active track, the range spanning all tracks, and so on. You can also use this range to define a loopable area, or to delete or copy and paste its contents.

2.5. Paste Repeat, or "Looping"

In electronic music especially, there's a common need to record one or two measures and then loop those measures to create standardized basslines or drumbeats.

The "right" way to achieve that would be to use a drum machine or a sequencer, which would literally play the same data (either pure MIDI data or audio samples) for as many measures as the composer programs. However, the effect can be emulated in **Qtractor** with a **Paste Repeat**, which allows you to copy an audio or MIDI clip and then paste it back-to-back for as many repetitions as you want.

To perform a **Paste Repeat**:

1. Check your snapping settings in the **View** menu (usually when looping clips, the user wants precision snapping to the first clip's edge).

2. Click to select the clip you want to copy (or use a range selection to extract a portion of the clip) and use **Edit >** to **Copy** the clip.

3. Click **Edit** and choose **Paste Repeat**.

4. In the **Paste Repeat** window, enter the number of iterations you want to paste, or the duration (in timecode, frames, or beats) you need to fill with repetitions. Click the **OK** button to confirm.

5. Click in the timeline to complete the paste and anchor the newly pasted clips in their track.

2.6. Punch In/Out

If one or two measures of a track doesn't quite measure up to your standards, you might want to re-record just those measures without having to record the entire track over. This process is called "punching in".

1. To perform a punch-in (and punch-out), use the **Range** select tool or the range markers to define a region of your timeline as the active area as described in *Section 2.3, " Range and Rectangle Selection "* and *Section 2.4, " Using Range Markers "*

2. Once your range is set, click the **Punch In/Out** button in the main toolbar, or use the **Transport** menu and select **Punch Set**.

3. Arm the recording destination track by clicking the **R** button in the track list.

4. Click the **Record** button in the main toolbar, and then the **Play** button. Qtractor will play back your piece, and you can play along but nothing you play will actually be recorded except within the punch range. Recording will automatically stop once the transport leaves the punch range.

5. To stop playback, click the **Stop** button in the main toolbar, or use the **Spacebar**.

Punching in and out is a common task used in both MIDI and Audio recording.

2.7. Looping Playback

To play a section of your composition in a loop (often done so the musician can practise for a punch-in or improvise), select a range as in *Section 2.3, " Range and Rectangle Selection "* and *Section 2.4, " Using Range Markers "*

Once your desired loop range is selected:

1. Click on the **Transport** menu and select **Set Loop**.

2. Move the transport into the loop range, or start playing immediately; when the transport reaches the end of the loop range, it will return to the in-point of the loop and seamlessly continue playing until stopped.

2.8. Simple Fades

Fading in or out of an audio clip is common enough that there is a quick shortcut to achieve the effect on any clip. Notice in the top corner of any clip in the workspace there is a semitransparent square node. Clicking and dragging this node further into the clip will create a fade in (if done at the beginning of a clip) or a fade out (if done at the end of a clip). The fade is given a slight curve to give it a more natural feel.

Most of the time, these simple fades achieve the effect you need but should you desire finer control over your fades, see *Automation* .

2.9. Merging Clips

After a long day of editing, your workspace might start to look fragmented, with pieces of audio clips appearing in their tracks with long stretches of empty space. This is not necessarily a bad thing, but it does sometimes allow for accidental moves of precisely timed sound cues and it also may reflect a number of disparate files on your harddrive even though you consider the track one instance of music.

By merging clips, you can change a number of clips into one consolidated file on your harddrive:

1.   Select the clips within a track that you want to merge into one.

2.   Click the **Clip** menu and select **Merge**.

3.   In the **Merge/Export** window, enter a new name for the merged file and save it to a logical location on your harddrive.

4.   The merged audio clip immediately replaces the old files in your project.

3. Track Edits

As audio clips contain the sound (and MIDI) files you are using in your **Qtractor** project, so do Tracks contain the clips themselves. Tracks allow you to mix the audio clips in relation to one another, apply effects to whole groups of clips without ever affecting the waveform files themselves (ie, non-destructively), and even automate everything from volume to panning to the functions of effect units and synths.

A special window is dedicated to managing tracks: the **Mixer** window; set up like a traditional mixing desk with a user-friendly interface to allow for Aux Sends, Returns, Sub-mixing, and more. You can also manage many aspects of your tracks through the track list on the left of the **Qtractor** interface, but since the Mixing desk interface is so ubiquitous and useful, it's common to have it open on a separate monitor or virtual desktop for quick reference.

To open the **Mixer** window, click on the **View** menu, select **Windows**, and choose **Mixer**.

Note

Most track functions can be done through both the main **Qtractor** interface as well as through the **Mixer** window.

3.1. Track Order, Height, and Properties

It's a good idea to keep related musical parts grouped together. If your drums appear on track 1 and your bass on track 14, it's difficult to edit the two tracks in unison as one might reasonably attempt to do. To keep a logical order to your track listing, you can rearrange where each track appears in the **Qtractor** workspace.

To move a track up or down the track list, either click and drag the number on the far left of the track label, or use the **Track** menu and select **Move** to move the currently highlighted track either up, down, or straight to the top or bottom of the list.

In addition to changing track order, you can change the height of tracks with the **Height** selection in the **Track** menu.

Other track properties, such as track name, the color of the clips, the type (audio or midi) of track data, and more, can be modified through the **Track** menu, especially the **Track Properties** selection.

Mixing

Mixing in **Qtractor**, like most digital audio workstation software, is modeled after mixing on real-world equipment. With **Qtractor**, as with hardware mixing equipment, you are able to define inputs, outputs, auxiliary sends and returns, effects, and automation.

Generally, mixing in **Qtractor** utilizes three different toolsets:

- Mixer - used to control the stereo separation and levels of the track, route sound, and configure effects and other outboard "gear"

- Effect Units and Filters - plugins used to sweeten, degrade, fix, or control sound

- Automation - makes **Qtractor** your live mixer so that levels, effects, and pans are adjusted during playback

Just as with a hardware-based studio, you'll use a combination of techniques to achieve the mood, sound, and quality you want. The central hub, however, is the **Mixer** window.

1. Mixer

The **Mixer** window can be accessed by click the **View** menu and selecting **Mixer** from the **Windows** category. The **Mixer** opens in its own window, making it a prime candidate for occupying a second screen if you have a multiple-head setup.

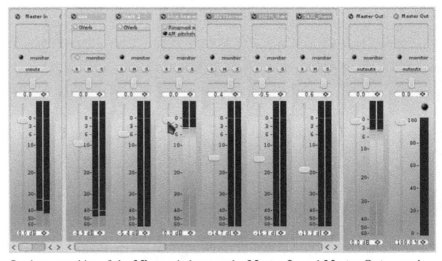

On the extremities of the **Mixer** window are the **Master In** and **Master Out** controls. These are independent of any one track and control everything coming into or going out of the mixing board. You can adjust the master levels of the input and output, and place any effect processors you want to apply globally (such as a compressor to control peaks on an outboard microphone, or to prevent peaks on outgoing audio).

The middle portion of the **Mixer** window represents the tracks in your project, both audio and MIDI (distinguished by the Audio or Midi icon next to the name of the track).

These control the individual track, allowing you to set the level of the track with the volume slider and gain control, the stereo position with the pan/pot control, and mute, solo, or arm for the track for recording.

1.1. Setting Levels

When monitoring the levels of your tracks, make sure that your sound does not enter the red zone on the volumeter. In audio production, any sound that goes above 0 dB hits its peak and will cause distortion. It's not uncommon to flirt with 0 dB to truly maxmize the impact of important sounds, but leaving sounds above 0dB in your final mix is a surefire way to ruin your project.

Using the volume level slider, adjust your track volumes into safe settings while listening to your project. Then listen to your project again to refine the levels in relation to one another.

If the sound source is too low (or too loud), you can add (or subtract) gain at the input point with the **Gain** adjustment at the very bottom of the mixer window.

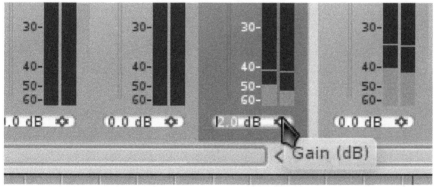

This adds or subtracts gain level at the point of the sound's entry, meaning that you are changing the amount of sound reaching any effects processors. Generally, gain adjustment is avoided and other tools, like a Compressor or Equalizer, are favoured.

Note

Tracks levels don't exist in a vacuum; the levels are cumulative, so if you have two tracks with near-maximum levels that produce very loud sounds at the same time, the Master Out level will peak even if each track was "safe" independently.

There is no authoratative way of achieving a balanced mix; some professional sound mixers prefer an additive mix, in which they start all levels at a reasonable and safe level and then accentuate important parts by adding volume to tracks. Others prefer a subtractive method by starting everything at the highest safe (or unsafe) level and then bringing volumes down so that everything falls into place. Predictably, still others prefer a combination of these methods.

1.2. Stereo Separation

By default, tracks are set to play sounds from the center point of the stereo space, meaning that to the listener the sound will feel as if it's situated directly in front of them, or evenly between their left and right ear.

To diversify the sound, sometimes in order to emulate a live setup or to suggest that a sound is just next to the listener, or to broaden the scope and impact of the piece, you can pan sound between the left and right speakers.

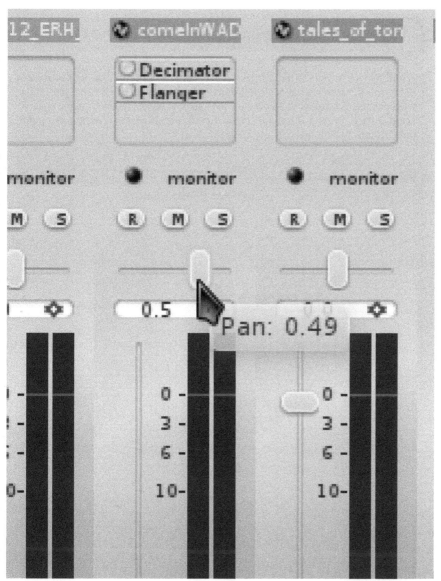

When panning a track, "less" is often "more" and an even spread is usually best. In other words, do not arbitrarily assign tracks in stereo space just to give a spread to your sound; consider where the sound would realistically come from if the listener were watching a live performance.

Note

Avoid moving sounds to the extreme stereo positions, since in real life sounds are rarely only heard in one ear and not the other (the sound of extreme stereo separation was common in early stereo mixes from the 1960s, in which the drums might only be heard in the right ear and a guitar only in the left; the effect was revolutionary at the time but largely considered utterly unnatural now).

A gentle spread of sound is most natural, with sounds at the extreme edges of the stereo space being used for atmosphere, emphasis, or effect.

Plugins

In the **Mixer** window, effects processor can be added to any track (the Master In, Out, or individual tracks in the project):

1. Right-click the plugin window in the track into which you wish to add the effect or synth.

2. Select **Add Plugin** from the contextual menu.

3. From the **Plugins** window, choose the LADSPA, LV2, DSSI, or VST plugin you want to plug into the track. Click **OK** to continue.

A plugin may also be a MIDI soft synth that you wish to associate with a track of MIDI data.

The order of processors is important; applying a reverb effect first and then a distortion filter will render a track with distorted reverb. Applying the distortion filter first and then the reverb will render a track with reverberating distortion.

To move an effect up or down the order of processing (ie, to place a reverb effect before a distortion filter), right-click the effect you want to move and select **Move Up** or **Move Down** from the contextual menu.

Once a plugin has been inserted into a track, control its settings in the pop up window that appears for the plugin. After your initial adjustments are made, you can access a plugin's controls at any time by right-clicking on the name of the effect unit in the track and selecting **Properties** from the contextual menu.

A green light to the left of the plugin name indicates that the plugin is active. You can temporarily deactivate (by-pass) the effect by right-clicking the effect in the track and toggling off the **Activate** menu item. If you wish to by-pass all effect units in a track, choose **Deactivate All**

If you want to remove an effect or plugin from a track entirely, right-click on the effect in the track and choose **Remove** or **Remove All** to remove all plugins from that track.

1. Send and Returns

What we call a "plug-in" in a DAW would be most akin, in a hardware-based studio, to a built-in reverb effect or gain adjustment on some of the more general-purpose mixing desks on the market. Mostly, however, there are no "plug-ins" in a traditional studio setup; everything is outboard and the mixer plugs into the effect unit, the effect unit processes the sound, and then the affected sound is send back into the board to be integrated into the mix.

This model is still useful in the software world, since not all sound applications are available as plugins, or you prefer to run them as separate applications.

To be able to utilize Sends and Returns, you should have some external, JACK-aware, sound application installed. In other words, the application should run outside of **Qtractor** but be programmed to utilize **JACK** when available.

A few examples of such applications would be

- **Jamin** - a sound mastering application

- **CALF** - an audio plugin set that is available as a stand-alone application as well as a plugin

- **amSynth** - a soft synth

- **QSynth** - a fluidsynth frontend

- **Schismtracker** - a MIDI tracker

- **Hydrogen** - a stand-alone drum machine

For this example, launch the **CALF JACK Host** plugin client. Click the **Add plugin** and select **Reverb** and turn the **Wet Amount** nearly all the way up so that it will be easy to hear that the sound is being effected in this test.

Bring in or generate sound into a track in **Qtractor**. To create a Send and Return on that track:

1. Locate the track you wish to affect in the **Mixer** window in **Qtractor**.

2. Right-click the plugin inset and choose **Inserts**.

3. In the **Insert** window, click the **Sends** button in the lower left corner.

4. In the **Connections** window that appears, choose the **Insert Out** connection in the left column and then then **reverb in** of **calf** in the right column. Click the **Connect** button to route the sound. Repeat this for both left and right channels.

5. At this point, you are successfully sending the sound from your track to the **CALF** effect processor, but if you were to play the track in **Qtractor** you wouldn't hear anything.

   Of course, the reason is because there is no Return yet. Back in the **Insert** window, click the **Returns** button.

6. In the **Connections** window, choose the **reverb out** connection in the left column and then then **insert in** of **Qtractor** in the right column. Click the **Connect** button to route the sound. Repeat this for both left and right channels.

7. Now your track is routed out to the **CALF** effect unit, processed, and sent back into **Qtractor**. Click the **Play** button in Qtractor to hear the results.

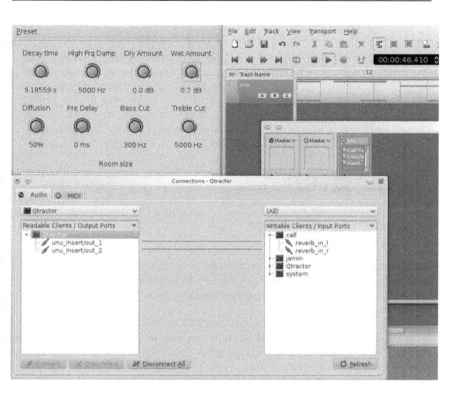

Effect Processors and Filters

There are many theories, personal styles, and preferences when it comes to mixing a project. One producer might opt for no effects at all while another might use compressors, limiters, levellers, EQ, and more, and those same producers will abandon their style depending on what band they are dealing with.

The best way to know what effects to use is to experiment; discover what different filters do, find out which ones you like or dislike, and do whatever your ear tells you to do.

There are some staples in any audio engineer's toolkit, and between the **Steve Harris LADSPA collection**, **CALF**, and **Jamin**, you'll find everything you need to achieve the sound you want:

1. Compressors

As a sys admin has **ssh** and **emacs**, an audio producer has Dynamic Range Compressors. A compressor's job is to reduce loud sounds or to increase quiet sounds by reducing (or "compressing") the signal's overall dynamic range. It has a number of uses in music production.

A compressor on a track that is inconsistent in dynamics will produce a more consistent track that might be easier to mix into the rest of the piece, and also provide a better listening experience for the audience; it's difficult to follow the lyrics of a song, for example, when the voice track continually drops behind the other instruments.

Compressors are very common on drums, as well, since when drums are mixed the loudest hits and crashes tend to rise to the surface while all the subtleties, like little touches of ornamentation and the decays of drum and cymbal hits, are lost. A compressor will even out the range between those softer sounds and the harder sounds, so you still get the hard-hitting beats but get to keep the personality.

There are at least three good compressors for GNU Linux:

1.1. CALF

The **Calf** plugin suite contains a compressor which you can use either as a plugin from within **Qtractor** or as a stand-alone app as an Aux Send/Return. Its features are typical of an all-purpose, general-use compressor, and running its full GUI with **calfjackhost** might help you understand the theory behind compression if you are new to it.

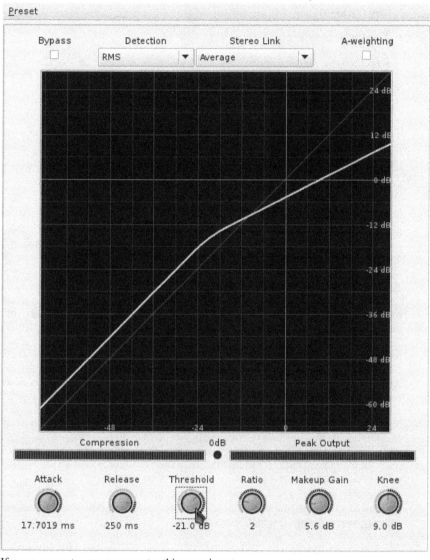

If you are new to compressors, try this experiment:

1. Open the CALF compressor by launching **calfjackhost**. Click on the **Add plugin** menu and choose **Compressor**.

2. To launch the user interface, click the **Compressor** button in the lower left. Change the settings to:

   • **Ratio** to 1

- **Makeup gain** to 0dB

- **Threshold** to -43.2

- **Knee** to 0dB

Notice that this causes the green line to align perfectly with the gray line that runs diagonally through the compressor screen.

This achieves, essentially, a pass-through effect. You have set a limit for every possible level of sound equal to itself, and since no possible level of sound will ever be greater than itself, nothing will be constrained.

3. Now change the ratio to approximately 2 (a 2:1 ratio).

   Notice the green line now deviates from the gray normal line; you may think of the green line as a sort of ceiling. Measuring soundwaves by the numbers along the X-axis, you can see that 24dB in the input (ie, the gray line), it will be constrained down to 0dB (along the green line).

   Accordingly, a soundwave that reaches -12dB will be constrained to -24db.

4. For one last demonstration, turn the **Ratio** knob all the way to right so it reads **+inf** and the **Threshold** knob all the way to the right so it reads 0dB.

   This places a hard ceiling at the current threshold setting. This means that any sound louder than the threshold will be constrained to that level, no matter what. Set too severely this can cause a clipped sound, but the concept of leveling is ubiquitous in production, as a safeguard to ensure that the levels do not go over 0dB.

5. When exactly compression kicks in is controlled by the **Threshold** value. Try adjusting the threshold knob and notice that the bend (or "knee") in the green line changes.

   Turn the **Ratio** knob back to 2 and set the **Threshold** to -12dB.

   Setting the threshold to -12dB means that everything below -12dB will remain unchanged, while anything above -12dB will be constrained to some degree (depending on the ratio setting, of course).

6. Make the **Knee** more gradual and natural by adjusting the knee to 18dB; this gives a softer curve to the compression. Sometimes this is intentionally not increased, and a sharper knee is desired (it's a trick sometimes used in compressing drums, to create hits that "pop").

7. The **Makeup Gain** knob, currently set to 0, allows you to boost the output sound to account for the inherent loss in volume when using a compressor that constrains levels.

8. The **Attack** and **Release** knobs control how quickly the compression effect takes to take full effect, and how quickly the effect is released.

In otherwords, at a 0ms attack, a soundwave will be constrained the very moment it pushes toward the threshold setting. The result of this is often a very harsh and noticeable effect, usually undesirable (except, again, for some stylistic choice sometimes made on drum kits or special effects).

Setting the attack to 500ms (.5 second), for instance, renders a softer, more gradual effect that better allows a soundwave to retain its natural shape and curve but still suppressing it under the threshold's level.

Once you've designed good compression settings, save it as a preset by clicking on the **Preset** menu and choosing **Store preset** selection. You will need the preset saved (perhaps in your **Qtractor** project folder for better organization) since **Qtractor** obviously will not save or preserve your settings.

The **Calf** compressor is a capable and user-friendly compressor unit, available either as a stand-alone unit or a plugin from within **Qtractor**, so use it often!

1.2. Steve Harris LADSPA Dyson Compressor

The **Dyson Compressor** is included in the **Steve Harris** set of LADSPA plugins. It is very basic, with few adjustable settings, but if quick and basic compression is all you need then it may just be what you need.

Use the Dyson compressor as you would any other LADSPA plugin in **Qtractor**. Its interface offers four sliders for customization: the peak limit (ie, threshold), release time (in seconds), the fast compression ratio, and the compression ratio (both ratios are counted from 0 to 1, so some math is required, with 1:1 ratio being equal to 0).

1.3. Jamin

The **Jamin** mastering application contains one of the most powerful compressors available. Whereas the **Calf** compressor excels in its simplicity, **Jamin** provides three separate compressors, essentially, for the Low, Mid, and Hi frequencies of your input.

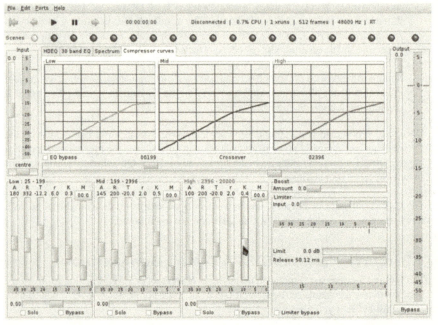

This obviously allows for a far greater degree of fine-tuning. As for what **Jamin** defines as a low, mid, or hi frequency: even these are adjustable with the middle horizontal **Crossover** sliders.

Your familiar Attack, Release, Threshold, Ratio, Knee, and Makeup Gain controls are found at the bottom of the window in the form of vertical sliders.

As with the stand-alone version of **Calf**, **Jamin** is used as an Aux Send/Return; unlike **Calf**, it has no plugin option.

Because **Jamin** also features a full-featured 30-band EQ, it might be best treated as the compressor/EQ filter for the **Qtractor**'s Master Out; something that **Jamin** obviously intends since it is advertised as a mastering application.

As with the stand-alone version of **Calf** compressor, you can and should save your presets in **Jamin** by clicking on the **File** menu and selecting **Save As**

2. Limiters

Directly related to dynamic compressors are limiters, which are basically compressors set to an infinite compression ratio. There are limiters available in the **Steve Harris LADSPA** set.

The **Hard Limiter**, for example, enforces the threshold by literally clipping off the offending portion of the sound wave. Its upper **dB limit** is 0dB and the harshness of the clipping can be set with the **Wet Level** (the more wet, the more clipping) and **Residue level**, which essentially control the attack and release times of the effect.

Limiters, compared to compressors, are by nature fairly harsh. However, slightly clipping the upper tips of offending soundwaves can create the illusion of loudness without actually crossing over into true distortion levels. It may also be used as a protective filter on the Master Out, just to ensure that levels absolutely do not rise above 0dB.

3. Normalization

The idea of normalization basically refers to dynamic range compression, since its job is to take irregular sound and make it more "normal". However, the term is imprecise and so it can mean many things.

In **Qtractor,** tracks that are too soft can have gain applied; manually applying gain can be dangerous, since you do not know how much gain you can safely apply without sending peaks over the 0dB mark. To have **Qtractor** calculate a safe clip-wide gain level:

1. Select the clip that is too soft.

2. Click the **Clip** menu and select **Normalize**

The clip has a safe gain level nondestructively applied.

What this does not do is compress the dynamic range of that clip. If you want to normalize a clip with dynamic range compression, then use either a compressor such as **Calf** or **Dyson**, or process the clip externally of **Qtractor**.

A good external normalization application is **normalize** (named **normalize-audio** in Debian), a command line application for GNU Linux that is available in most repositories and pre-installed on Slackware. The syntax is simple:

```
normalize -a -6db -l -3db nameOfFile.wav
```

In the above command, **-a** is amplitude and **-l** is limiter; so the command sets the average amplitude of the sound clip to -6dB and ensures that peaks do not exceed -3dB. Obviously these settings would need adjusting depending on what the sound file contained, but it's a marvelously efficient command for quick normalization.

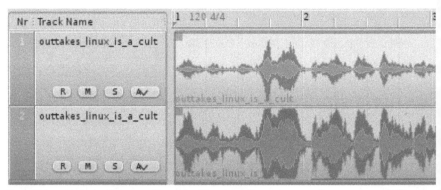

In addition to normalizing a clip to itself, **normalize** can normalize a group of files in relation to one another, set thresholds, and much more.

4. EQ

Sound waves, being oscillations of pressure, are measured by the cyclic standard of hertz. The human ear generally can hear from 20Hz to 16,000Hz (or 16kHz), with the human voice usually appearing around the 100Hz to 400Hz range.

A good equalizer can increase or decrease the energy of these frequency bands; this is used by audio engineers to boost bass, or possibly cut bass when it is overpowering, or boost the midtones where the human voice dwells, and so on.

There are a few good equalizers that can be used with **Qtractor**:

4.1. Jamin

The **Jamin** mastering application, which you can use as an Aux Send/Return, has two views of EQ: the graphical curve-based **HDEQ**, and a slider-based **30 band EQ**. They are literally two different views of the same thing, so it's typical to use both views depending on what kind of adjustment you need to make and which one makes that adjustment easiest.

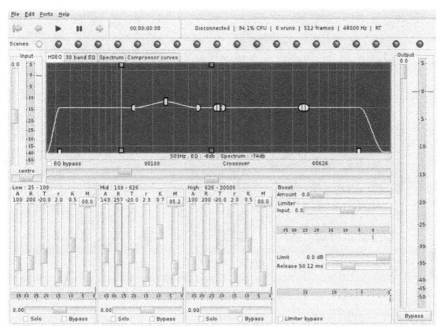

The practical theory behind EQ is simple enough; identify the frequency you wish to emphasize or supress, and then raise or lower its intensity in the equalizer. If you are unfamiliar with equalizers, you may have a difficult time at first being able to identify where in the spectrum of frequencies the sound lies. Put simply, the lower (bass) bands are on the left and the higher (treble) are on the right, with the mids (human voice and similarly pitched instruments) are in the middle.

For more precision, there is an old engineering trick that you can use in **Jamin** to identify where something you are hearing actually appears in the spectrum:

1. Send a track to **Jamin** as an Aux Send/Return

2. Open the **HDEQ** view of **Jamin** and use the yellow curve nodes to create the sharpest curve possible at its maximum value

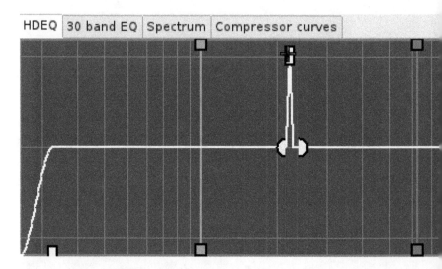

3. Using the middle node, drag the peak across the spectrum, listening to the sounds it emphasizes. Because of the drastic curve, the change will be obvious.

4. Once you find the sound you are searching for, lessen the volume of the curve and make it more gradual.

Less is more in EQ; rarely is there a time when huge increases or decreases of the existing frequencies are required. If you find yourself wanting to maximize the intensity of a frequency band then quite possibly you need to re-record to achieve the actual sound you were intending to capture.

The other view of the EQ in **Jamin** is the **30 band EQ** tab, which displays the same information as the **HDEQ** interface, but uses sliders instead of graphical curves and nodes.

The same principles apply; the sliders provide a quicker way to boost or cut frequencies when you know exactly what needs to be done and don't want to have to draw curves and move nodes around to achieve it.

4.2. Calf

The **Calf** plugin set provides a set of filters, which perform EQ through customizable presets. It is less precise than a 30 band equalizer but realistically is often all you'll need.

Calf offers four types of presets:

- Lowpass - low pass filters allow low frequencies to pass and cuts off high frequencies

- Highpass - high pass filters allow high frequencies to pass and cuts off low frequencies

- Band Pass - band pass combines low pass and high pass filters configured such that a targeted frequency range is allowed to pass while frequencies above or below that range are rejected

- Band Reject - band reject combines low pass and high pass filters with their intersection being a range of frequencies that will be rejected

You have control over the characteristics of these presets via the **Frequency**, **Resonance**, and **Inertia** knobs.

1. Open the CALF filter plugin by launching **calfjackhost**. Click on the **Add plugin** menu and choose **Filter**.

2. To launch the interface, click the **Filter** button in the lower left corner. When the interface for filters launches, it may only display a list of the presets, so be sure to expand the window until you can see the knobs and filter graph.

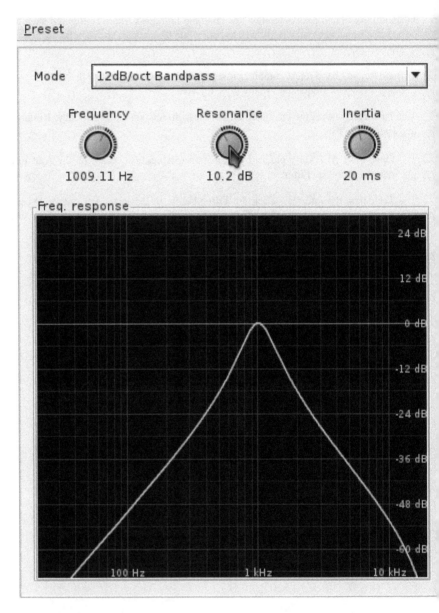

3. For the clearest example of how the **Calf** filters work, select the **18dB Bandpass**

   Set the **Frequency** knob to approximately 300 Hz. Notice how the filter shape moves horizontally along the graph as you adjust the filter. The green line indicates that sounds at 300 Hz will passthrough the filter, while the frequencies lower and higher than 300 Hz will be filtered down gradually until they are excluded entirely.

4. To control what frequencies are attenuated by the filter, use the **Resonance** knob. Setting it to 30dB, for instance, makes for a narrow filter, while setting it to 0dB makes it fairly broad.

5. Try a lowpass filter on bass parts, and a highpass on other instruments, and make adjustments by ear.

Note

Once you've designed good EQ settings for your track, save it as a preset by clicking on the **Preset** menu and choosing **Store preset** selection. You will need the preset saved (perhaps in your **Qtractor** project folder for better organization) since **Qtractor** obviously will not save or preserve your settings.

The **Calf** filters are more specialized than the **Jamin** EQ but just as effective in what it does. Since **Calf** can be used as either a stand-alone application or as **Qtractor** plug-ins, they are flexible in how you choose to implement them.

4.3. Steve Harris LADSPA Multiband EQ

Simpler than **Jamin** or **Calf** is the Steve Harris LADSPA plugin **Multiband EQ**. It features 15 sliders for broad rangers of frequencies.

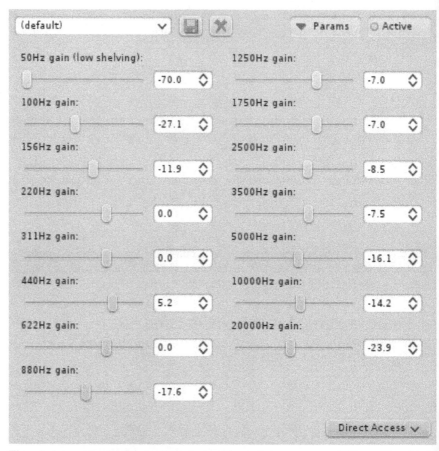

There is less customization available but well-rounded curves can still be achieved by staggering the sliders, a common practise on hardware equalizers.

4.4. Steve Harris LADSPA DJ EQ

A basic 3-band equalizer, the Steve Harris **JD EQ** LADSPA plugin allows you to easily control the three general areas of sound frequency: bass, mids, and treble.

5. Noise Removal

Noise removal is something of a myth borne of automatic filters bundled with recording applications. It is not possible, in spite of what the advertisements say, to isolate noise on a track and eliminate it without also removing that same frequency from what you deem to be signal.

The manual elimination of noise is easiest with **Jamin** HDEQ; first scan your sound for the frequency containing most of the noise as described in *Section 4.1, " Jamin "*, and then invert the resonance curve to eliminate the noise you've found.

Automated noise removal filters do the same process; analyze a sample of user-defined "noise" and then EQ the offending frequencies out.

6. Reverb

Reverb is an old ever-popular recording effect that simulates the phenomenon of a sound wave bouncing off of surfaces, causing the soundwave to bounce back in a new direction; our ears hear the original sound wave as the source and the reverberated sound wave as an echo.

Note

Common examples are large cathedrals, famous for very saturated and immediate echoes, and canyons, with the stereotypical distant and delayed echo ("Hello....hello........hello..."). You might also notice less drastic examples in, for instance, small empty closets, or you might try speaking into a coffee tin; the reverberation is immediate and subtle, but it's still clear that there are soundwaves bouncing back at you.

Reverb effect units simulate this phenomenon and allow the uesr to control different aspects of how the reverberation is generated.

6.1. Calf

As with the other **Calf** plugins, the **Calf** reverb can be used as a stand-alone application via **calfjackhost** or as a plugin from within **Qtractor**. It features a good number of the most important reverb controls:

• Decay Time - controls the length that the echo (tail) is heard before

• High Freq Damp - the tail of the reverb is dampened to simulate that sound loses energy and fades out over time and distance. The High Frequency Dampening knob determines the frequency at which the dampening begins

• Dry Amount - determines how much of the original sound is heard along with the reverb

• Wet Amount - determines how much of the reverb is heard

- Diffusion - structures the "spread" of the reverb; a highly diffused reverb effect spreads reverb widely across the stereo space, where as a less diffuse reverb effect is more centrally located

- Pre Delay - determines the distance between the source signal and the start of the reverb

- Bass Cut - determines the frquency at which bass frequencies are truncated

- Treble Cut - determines the frequency at which bass frequencies are truncated

- Room Size - sets the emulated space, determining the shape and character of the reverberated sound

Note

If you are using **Calf** as a stand-alone effect unit, remember that once you've designed good reverb settings for your track, you must save it as a preset. You can save presets by clicking on the **Preset** menu and choosing **Store preset** selection. You will need the preset saved (perhaps in your **Qtractor** project folder for better organization) since **Qtractor** obviously will not save or preserve your settings.

6.2. Steve Harris LADSPA GVerb

There are reverb units available in the **Steve Harris LADSPA** set. The **GVerb** plugin is particularly powerful.

- Roomsize - controls the size of the space being used to simulate reverb

- Reverb time - controls decay of the reverb; the longer the reverb time, the longer the "echo" is heard

- Damping - the greater the damping, the shorter and weaker the reverb effect will be

- Input bandwidth - the strength of the signal that reaches the reverb effect unit for processing

- Dry signal level - the volume of the unprocessed source sound

- Early reflection level - strength of the initial reverberated wave; a weaker early reflection level has the effect of hearing just the tail of a reverb, while a greater level brings more immediate sound

- Tail level - the level of the reverberated sound; increasing this will great a stronger signal, which will therefore continue even past the **Reverb time** setting, which can then also be controlled by the **Damping** setting

7. Echos, Delays, Distortion, and More

The range of effect units available for processing sound is nearly endless. With echos, tape delays, distortion filters, amps, decimators, chorus effects, ring modulators, and much more, Linux has no shortage of special effects. Explore **Calf** and **Steve Harris LADSPA** plugins to discover a wide variety of new possible sounds.

Automation

If you had to mix all of the tracks in a project, at the same time, in realtime, you'd not only need a lot of practice but probably two more arms and another mouse or two.

Qtractor features automation of nearly any aspect of any plugin, as well as basic track functions like volume and panning.

1. In the track you wish to automate, click the **Automation** button in the track list. From the pop-up menu, select the attribute of that track that you wish to automate first.

2. From the pop-up menu, select the attribute of that track that you wish to automate first. An overlay is placed on the track.

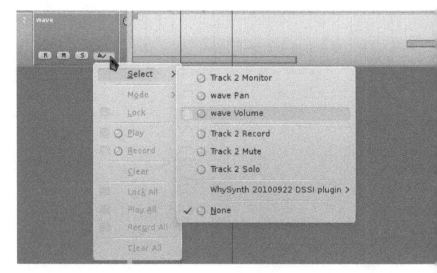

3. Click the **Edit** menu to go into the **Select Mode** category, and choose **Automation** selection tool.

    Alternately, click the **Automation Selection Tool** icon from the top menu bar.

4. Armed with your automation selection tool, click on the automation overlay on your track to create a node. Adjust the volume of this node to be the initial volume of your track.

5. Click again on the automation overlay to create a second node, and move it to another volume level. For the space between the two nodes, the volume will climb from the starting node level to the ending node level.

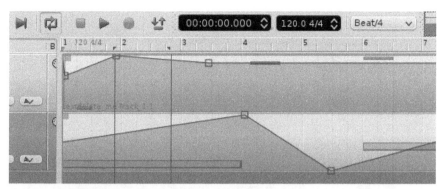

If you need a less gradual change, move the nodes closer together, or use more nodes to shape different movements for the mixer.

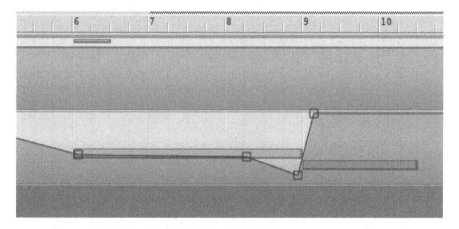

The automation is customizable via the **Automation** button in the track list, in the **Mode** category:

• Hold - places the automation nodes into absolute values until otherwise changed

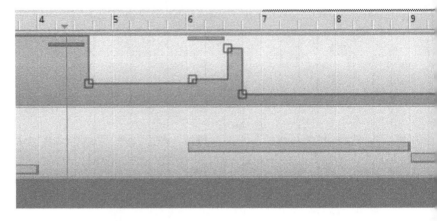

- Linear - represents the automation as even linear progression from one node to the next. This is the default automation mode.

- Spline - same as linear, except with b-splines instead of completely linear progress between nodes

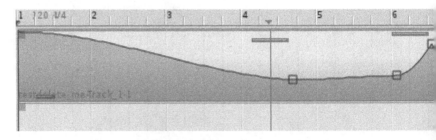

- Logarithmic - same as spline except that the degree of the bezier curves change proportionately to the difference between nodes

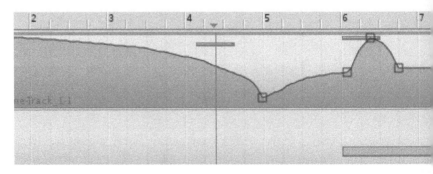

- Color - when you automate volume, panning, and an effect all on one track, it can get confusing. Use color to change the shade of the automation overlay so that you can distinguish one set of controls from another

- Lock - prevents accidental changes to automation, especially useful when working on a different automation function on the same track

1. Recording Automation

If you are a skilled live mixer and want to record your performance in realtime, you can override existing automation decisions, or record new ones, in two different styles, each available in the **Automation** menu:

- Play - with this enabled, you may make realtime changes to existing automation, and upon release of the slider or knob that you are automating, the value returns to the pre-existing value. This *may be* combined with the **Record** option.

- Record - with this enabled, you may make realtime decisions for automation and every move will be recorded, in realtime, as a node in your track. They can be manually changed later, if needed.

Note

if you have the **Play** option enabled, when you release the slider or knob that you are automating, the values will return to their existing level.

Without **Play** enabled, any change you make will persist until you change it again.

Delivery

At the end of the song-writing process, there is the final export. This of course combines all of the sounds being generated from all of the different sources you may be using, filtered through all of the effects and processors you have in place, and places them all into a self-contained file that your audience can play in their media player of choice.

Since everything in **Qtractor** is routed through its mixer, to combine the sounds into one audio file is as simple as creating a new track and using it to record the **Master Out**:

1. Go to the **View** menu and select **Options** to open **Qtractor**'s preferences.

2. In the **Options** window, click on the **Audio** tab. Select the kind of audio you'd like to use for your recording. It is generally prefered to export to a lossless format and use that file as the "gold master" from which compressed (ogg vorbis, mp4, mp3, and so on) versions can be produced. A high quality, lossless, free codec is **FLAC**.

3. Click the **OK** button to accept your changes.

4. Create a new track in your **Qtractor** project by clicking the **Track** menu and selecting **Add Track**.

5. In the **Mixer** window, right click the plugin window and click the **Inserts** category, choosing **Add Insert**.

    In the **Insert** window, click the **Return** button. This opens a **Connections** window.

6. Click the first (left) **Master In** jack in the left column to the first insert of your new track in the right column, and click the **Connect** button. Repeat this for the second (right) jacks. Close the window when finished.

7. You have now routed all of your mixer's outbound sound to the input of your new track. Arm your new track for recording by clicking the **R** button either in the track list or the mixer window.

8. Position the transport (playhead) at the beginning of the project (or the beginning of the portion of your song you intend to export).

 Note

You may wish to set an in and out point so that the recording stops automatically, or you may prefer to stop the recording manually.

9. Press the **Record** button in the top menu bar.

Warning

Before recording, double check your connections! If you have left a microphone plugged in and actively sending input to your **Master in**, for example, you might find later that you've recorded a layer of room tone behind all of your tracks!

10. Press the **Play** button to begin playback and recording.

11. When recording is finished, select the track by clicking on the new audio clip in the **Qtractor** project. Click the **Clip** menu and select **Export** to send the clip out as an independent file.

Your project is now complete. Create a new project file, and start over with your next song, and enjoy your time with **Qtractor**.

Appendix A. GNU Free Documentation License

Version 1.3, 3 November 2008

Copyright © 2000, 2001, 2002, 2007, 2008 *Free Software Foundation, Inc.*[1]

0. PREAMBLE

The purpose of this License is to make a manual, textbook, or other functional and useful document "free" in the sense of freedom: to assure everyone the effective freedom to copy and redistribute it, with or without modifying it, either commercially or noncommercially. Secondarily, this License preserves for the author and publisher a way to get credit for their work, while not being considered responsible for modifications made by others.

This License is a kind of "copyleft", which means that derivative works of the document must themselves be free in the same sense. It complements the GNU General Public License, which is a copyleft license designed for free software.

We have designed this License in order to use it for manuals for free software, because free software needs free documentation: a free program should come with manuals providing the same freedoms that the software does. But this License is not limited to software manuals; it can be used for any textual work, regardless of subject matter or whether it is published as a printed book. We recommend this License principally for works whose purpose is instruction or reference.

1. APPLICABILITY AND DEFINITIONS

This License applies to any manual or other work, in any medium, that contains a notice placed by the copyright holder saying it can be distributed under the terms of this License. Such a notice grants a world-wide, royalty-free license, unlimited in duration, to use that work under the conditions stated herein. The "Document", below, refers to any such manual or work. Any member of the public is a licensee, and is addressed as "you". You accept the license if you copy, modify or distribute the work in a way requiring permission under copyright law.

A "Modified Version" of the Document means any work containing the Document or a portion of it, either copied verbatim, or with modifications and/or translated into another language.

---

[1] http://www.fsf.org/

A "Secondary Section" is a named appendix or a front-matter section of the Document that deals exclusively with the relationship of the publishers or authors of the Document to the Document's overall subject (or to related matters) and contains nothing that could fall directly within that overall subject. (Thus, if the Document is in part a textbook of mathematics, a Secondary Section may not explain any mathematics.) The relationship could be a matter of historical connection with the subject or with related matters, or of legal, commercial, philosophical, ethical or political position regarding them.

The "Invariant Sections" are certain Secondary Sections whose titles are designated, as being those of Invariant Sections, in the notice that says that the Document is released under this License. If a section does not fit the above definition of Secondary then it is not allowed to be designated as Invariant. The Document may contain zero Invariant Sections. If the Document does not identify any Invariant Sections then there are none.

The "Cover Texts" are certain short passages of text that are listed, as Front-Cover Texts or Back-Cover Texts, in the notice that says that the Document is released under this License. A Front-Cover Text may be at most 5 words, and a Back-Cover Text may be at most 25 words.

A "Transparent" copy of the Document means a machine-readable copy, represented in a format whose specification is available to the general public, that is suitable for revising the document straightforwardly with generic text editors or (for images composed of pixels) generic paint programs or (for drawings) some widely available drawing editor, and that is suitable for input to text formatters or for automatic translation to a variety of formats suitable for input to text formatters. A copy made in an otherwise Transparent file format whose markup, or absence of markup, has been arranged to thwart or discourage subsequent modification by readers is not Transparent. An image format is not Transparent if used for any substantial amount of text. A copy that is not "Transparent" is called "Opaque".

Examples of suitable formats for Transparent copies include plain ASCII without markup, Texinfo input format, LaTeX input format, SGML or XML using a publicly available DTD, and standard-conforming simple HTML, PostScript or PDF designed for human modification. Examples of transparent image formats include PNG, XCF and JPG. Opaque formats include proprietary formats that can be read and edited only by proprietary word processors, SGML or XML for which the DTD and/or processing tools are not generally available, and the machine-generated HTML, PostScript or PDF produced by some word processors for output purposes only.

The "Title Page" means, for a printed book, the title page itself, plus such following pages as are needed to hold, legibly, the material this License requires to appear in the title page. For works in formats which do not have any title page as such, "Title Page" means the text near the most prominent appearance of the work's title, preceding the beginning of the body of the text.

The "publisher" means any person or entity that distributes copies of the Document to the public.

A section "Entitled XYZ" means a named subunit of the Document whose title either is precisely XYZ or contains XYZ in parentheses following text that translates XYZ in another language. (Here XYZ stands for a specific section name mentioned below, such as "Acknowledgements", "Dedications", "Endorsements", or "History".) To "Preserve the Title" of such a section when you modify the Document means that it remains a section "Entitled XYZ" according to this definition.

The Document may include Warranty Disclaimers next to the notice which states that this License applies to the Document. These Warranty Disclaimers are considered to be included by reference in this License, but only as regards disclaiming warranties: any other implication that these Warranty Disclaimers may have is void and has no effect on the meaning of this License.

2. VERBATIM COPYING

You may copy and distribute the Document in any medium, either commercially or noncommercially, provided that this License, the copyright notices, and the license notice saying this License applies to the Document are reproduced in all copies, and that you add no other conditions whatsoever to those of this License. You may not use technical measures to obstruct or control the reading or further copying of the copies you make or distribute. However, you may accept compensation in exchange for copies. If you distribute a large enough number of copies you must also follow the conditions in section 3.

You may also lend copies, under the same conditions stated above, and you may publicly display copies.

3. COPYING IN QUANTITY

If you publish printed copies (or copies in media that commonly have printed covers) of the Document, numbering more than 100, and the Document's license notice requires Cover Texts, you must enclose the copies in covers that carry, clearly and legibly, all these Cover Texts: Front-Cover Texts on the front cover, and Back-Cover Texts on the back cover. Both covers must also clearly and legibly identify you as the publisher of these copies. The front cover must present the full title with all words of the title equally prominent and visible. You may add other material on the covers in addition. Copying with changes limited to the covers, as long as they preserve the title of the Document and satisfy these conditions, can be treated as verbatim copying in other respects.

If the required texts for either cover are too voluminous to fit legibly, you should put the first ones listed (as many as fit reasonably) on the actual cover, and continue the rest onto adjacent pages.

If you publish or distribute Opaque copies of the Document numbering more than 100, you must either include a machine-readable Transparent copy along with each Opaque copy, or state in or with each Opaque copy a computer-network location from which the general network-using public has access to download using public-standard network protocols a complete Transparent copy of the Document, free of added material. If you use the latter option, you must take reasonably prudent steps, when you begin distribution of Opaque copies in quantity, to ensure that this Transparent copy will remain thus accessible at the stated location until at least one year after the last time you distribute an Opaque copy (directly or through your agents or retailers) of that edition to the public.

It is requested, but not required, that you contact the authors of the Document well before redistributing any large number of copies, to give them a chance to provide you with an updated version of the Document.

4. MODIFICATIONS

You may copy and distribute a Modified Version of the Document under the conditions of sections 2 and 3 above, provided that you release the Modified Version under precisely this License, with the Modified Version filling the role of the Document, thus licensing distribution and modification of the Modified Version to whoever possesses a copy of it. In addition, you must do these things in the Modified Version:

A. Use in the Title Page (and on the covers, if any) a title distinct from that of the Document, and from those of previous versions (which should, if there were any, be listed in the History section of the Document). You may use the same title as a previous version if the original publisher of that version gives permission.

B. List on the Title Page, as authors, one or more persons or entities responsible for authorship of the modifications in the Modified Version, together with at least five of the principal authors of the Document (all of its principal authors, if it has fewer than five), unless they release you from this requirement.

C. State on the Title page the name of the publisher of the Modified Version, as the publisher.

D. Preserve all the copyright notices of the Document.

E. Add an appropriate copyright notice for your modifications adjacent to the other copyright notices.

F. Include, immediately after the copyright notices, a license notice giving the public permission to use the Modified Version under the terms of this License, in the form shown in the Addendum below.

G. Preserve in that license notice the full lists of Invariant Sections and required Cover Texts given in the Document's license notice.

H. Include an unaltered copy of this License.

I. Preserve the section Entitled "History", Preserve its Title, and add to it an item stating at least the title, year, new authors, and publisher of the Modified Version as given on the Title Page. If there is no section Entitled "History" in the Document, create one stating the title, year, authors, and publisher of the Document as given on its Title Page, then add an item describing the Modified Version as stated in the previous sentence.

J. Preserve the network location, if any, given in the Document for public access to a Transparent copy of the Document, and likewise the network locations given in the Document for previous versions it was based on. These may be placed in the "History" section. You may omit a network location for a work that was published at least four years before the Document itself, or if the original publisher of the version it refers to gives permission.

K. For any section Entitled "Acknowledgements" or "Dedications", Preserve the Title of the section, and preserve in the section all the substance and tone of each of the contributor acknowledgements and/or dedications given therein.

L. Preserve all the Invariant Sections of the Document, unaltered in their text and in their titles. Section numbers or the equivalent are not considered part of the section titles.

M. Delete any section Entitled "Endorsements". Such a section may not be included in the Modified Version.

N. Do not retitle any existing section to be Entitled "Endorsements" or to conflict in title with any Invariant Section.

O. Preserve any Warranty Disclaimers.

If the Modified Version includes new front-matter sections or appendices that qualify as Secondary Sections and contain no material copied from the Document, you may at your option designate some or all of these sections as invariant. To do this, add their titles to the list of Invariant Sections in the Modified Version's license notice. These titles must be distinct from any other section titles.

You may add a section Entitled "Endorsements", provided it contains nothing but endorsements of your Modified Version by various parties — for example, statements of peer review or that the text has been approved by an organization as the authoritative definition of a standard.

You may add a passage of up to five words as a Front-Cover Text, and a passage of up to 25 words as a Back-Cover Text, to the end of the list of Cover Texts in the Modified Version. Only one passage of Front-Cover Text and one of Back-Cover Text may be added by (or through arrangements made by) any one entity. If the Document already includes a cover text for the same cover, previously added by you or by arrangement made by the same entity you are acting on behalf of, you may not add another; but you may replace the old one, on explicit permission from the previous publisher that added the old one.

The author(s) and publisher(s) of the Document do not by this License give permission to use their names for publicity for or to assert or imply endorsement of any Modified Version.

5. COMBINING DOCUMENTS

You may combine the Document with other documents released under this License, under the terms defined in section 4 above for modified versions, provided that you include in the combination all of the Invariant Sections of all of the original documents, unmodified, and list them all as Invariant Sections of your combined work in its license notice, and that you preserve all their Warranty Disclaimers.

The combined work need only contain one copy of this License, and multiple identical Invariant Sections may be replaced with a single copy. If there are multiple Invariant

Sections with the same name but different contents, make the title of each such section unique by adding at the end of it, in parentheses, the name of the original author or publisher of that section if known, or else a unique number. Make the same adjustment to the section titles in the list of Invariant Sections in the license notice of the combined work.

In the combination, you must combine any sections Entitled "History" in the various original documents, forming one section Entitled "History"; likewise combine any sections Entitled "Acknowledgements", and any sections Entitled "Dedications". You must delete all sections Entitled "Endorsements".

6. COLLECTIONS OF DOCUMENTS

You may make a collection consisting of the Document and other documents released under this License, and replace the individual copies of this License in the various documents with a single copy that is included in the collection, provided that you follow the rules of this License for verbatim copying of each of the documents in all other respects.

You may extract a single document from such a collection, and distribute it individually under this License, provided you insert a copy of this License into the extracted document, and follow this License in all other respects regarding verbatim copying of that document.

7. AGGREGATION WITH INDEPENDENT WORKS

A compilation of the Document or its derivatives with other separate and independent documents or works, in or on a volume of a storage or distribution medium, is called an "aggregate" if the copyright resulting from the compilation is not used to limit the legal rights of the compilation's users beyond what the individual works permit. When the Document is included in an aggregate, this License does not apply to the other works in the aggregate which are not themselves derivative works of the Document.

If the Cover Text requirement of section 3 is applicable to these copies of the Document, then if the Document is less than one half of the entire aggregate, the Document's Cover Texts may be placed on covers that bracket the Document within the aggregate, or the electronic equivalent of covers if the Document is in electronic form. Otherwise they must appear on printed covers that bracket the whole aggregate.

8. TRANSLATION

Translation is considered a kind of modification, so you may distribute translations of the Document under the terms of section 4. Replacing Invariant Sections with translations requires special permission from their copyright holders, but you may include translations of some or all Invariant Sections in addition to the original versions of these Invariant Sections. You may include a translation of this License, and all the license notices in the Document, and any Warranty Disclaimers, provided that you also include the original English version of this License and the original versions of those notices and disclaimers. In case of a disagreement between the translation and the original version of this License or a notice or disclaimer, the original version will prevail.

If a section in the Document is Entitled "Acknowledgements", "Dedications", or "History", the requirement (section 4) to Preserve its Title (section 1) will typically require changing the actual title.

9. TERMINATION

You may not copy, modify, sublicense, or distribute the Document except as expressly provided under this License. Any attempt otherwise to copy, modify, sublicense, or distribute it is void, and will automatically terminate your rights under this License.

However, if you cease all violation of this License, then your license from a particular copyright holder is reinstated (a) provisionally, unless and until the copyright holder explicitly and finally terminates your license, and (b) permanently, if the copyright holder fails to notify you of the violation by some reasonable means prior to 60 days after the cessation.

Moreover, your license from a particular copyright holder is reinstated permanently if the copyright holder notifies you of the violation by some reasonable means, this is the first time you have received notice of violation of this License (for any work) from that copyright holder, and you cure the violation prior to 30 days after your receipt of the notice.

Termination of your rights under this section does not terminate the licenses of parties who have received copies or rights from you under this License. If your rights have been terminated and not permanently reinstated, receipt of a copy of some or all of the same material does not give you any rights to use it.

10. FUTURE REVISIONS OF THIS LICENSE

The Free Software Foundation may publish new, revised versions of the GNU Free Documentation License from time to time. Such new versions will be similar in spirit to the present version, but may differ in detail to address new problems or concerns. See *Copyleft*[2].

Each version of the License is given a distinguishing version number. If the Document specifies that a particular numbered version of this License "or any later version" applies to it, you have the option of following the terms and conditions either of that specified version or of any later version that has been published (not as a draft) by the Free Software Foundation. If the Document does not specify a version number of this License, you may choose any version ever published (not as a draft) by the Free Software Foundation. If the Document specifies that a proxy can decide which future versions of this License can be used, that proxy's public statement of acceptance of a version permanently authorizes you to choose that version for the Document.

---

[2] http://www.gnu.org/copyleft/

11. RELICENSING

"Massive Multiauthor Collaboration Site" (or "MMC Site") means any World Wide Web server that publishes copyrightable works and also provides prominent facilities for anybody to edit those works. A public wiki that anybody can edit is an example of such a server. A "Massive Multiauthor Collaboration" (or "MMC") contained in the site means any set of copyrightable works thus published on the MMC site.

"CC-BY-SA" means the Creative Commons Attribution-Share Alike 3.0 license published by Creative Commons Corporation, a not-for-profit corporation with a principal place of business in San Francisco, California, as well as future copyleft versions of that license published by that same organization.

"Incorporate" means to publish or republish a Document, in whole or in part, as part of another Document.

An MMC is "eligible for relicensing" if it is licensed under this License, and if all works that were first published under this License somewhere other than this MMC, and subsequently incorporated in whole or in part into the MMC, (1) had no cover texts or invariant sections, and (2) were thus incorporated prior to November 1, 2008.

The operator of an MMC Site may republish an MMC contained in the site under CC-BY-SA on the same site at any time before August 1, 2009, provided the MMC is eligible for relicensing.

ADDENDUM: How to use this License for your documents

To use this License in a document you have written, include a copy of the License in the document and put the following copyright and license notices just after the title page:

```
Copyright © YEAR YOUR NAME

Permission is granted to copy, distribute and/or
 modify this document under the
terms of the GNU Free Documentation License, Version
 1.3 or any later version
published by the Free Software Foundation; with no
 Invariant Sections, no
Front-Cover Texts, and no Back-Cover Texts. A copy of
 the license is included in
the section entitled "GNU Free Documentation
 License".
```

If you have Invariant Sections, Front-Cover Texts and Back-Cover Texts, replace the "with... Texts." line with this:

```
with the Invariant Sections being LIST THEIR TITLES,
 with the Front-Cover Texts
being LIST, and with the Back-Cover Texts being LIST.
```

If you have Invariant Sections without Cover Texts, or some other combination of the three, merge those two alternatives to suit the situation.

If your document contains nontrivial examples of program code, we recommend releasing these examples in parallel under your choice of free software license, such as the GNU General Public License, to permit their use in free software.

Appendix B. Various and Sundry

Some software is not required for **Qtractor** to run, but are useful to have and can be run along with Qtractor. Optional installs include:

- *QJackCtl* [1] - a user-friendly control panel for **JACK**, which can help you fine tune latency settings, and wire your virtual instruments to your virtual mixer. The **JACK** subsystem will be installed automatically by your distribution; check to ensure that **QJackCtl** is installed.

  Being written by the same programmer, many control panels available in **QJackCtl** are also available from within **QJackCtl**, but unless you very familiar with **jackd**, you will probably find **JACK** easier to use with **QJackCtl**

- *Qsynth* [2] - a user-friendly controller for the **Fluidsynth** soft synth and a good example (for its familiarity) of how soft synths can be used external of the **Qtractor** interface and yet still send sound to **Qtractor**

- *Fluidsynth-DSSI* [3] - the **Fluidsynth** soft synth in plugin-form so that soundfonts can be used from within the **Qtractor** interface

- *WhySynth* [4] - a DSSI plugin that ships with a number of high-quality pre-sets, providing quick satisfaction as well as plenty of oscillators and dials to allow you to create your own patches

- *Steve Harris LADSPA Plugins* [5] - the famous must-have set of audio plugins. The LADSPA versions have been around for years, the *newer LV2 versions*[6] are also available and LV2 support is starting to become standard, so feel free to try the newer ones instead.

- *CALF*[7] audio plugin pack provides a compressor, chorus, reverb, flanger, delay, and lots more, as either DSSI, LADSPA, or LV2 plugins. They are easy to use and feature attractive interfaces.

---

[1] http://qjackctl.sourceforge.net
[2] http://qsynth.sourceforge.net
[3] http://dssi.sourceforge.net/download.html
[4] http://www.smbolton.com/whysynth.html
[5] http://plugin.org.uk/
[6] https://github.com/swh/lv2/
[7] http://calf.sourceforge.net/

Appendix C. General MIDI Instrumentation

This is the standardized list of General MIDI channels and the corresponding instrumentation. If you are composing using MIDI and want your piece to call a standard set of instruments so that it will sound the same across all systems, this is the list to use.

Distributing MIDI files of renditions of popular songs was fairly common in the early days of the Internet, when it was considered technologically advanced to have a MIDI song autoatically play in the background when someone visited one's homepage. With General MIDI, it could be ensured that the song sounded more or less the same no matter whose system it was.

Of course, this is rather rarely done now. It is far more common to use MIDI to trigger sounds and instruments in any format that works best for you, then to record the music and re-distribute the ogg or mp3 version.

Even so, this is a good reference list since General MIDI was widely used at one point.

1. Acoustic Grand Piano

2. Bright Acoustic Piano

3. Electric Grand Piano

4. Honky-tonk Piano

5. Electric Piano 1

6. Electric Piano 2

7. Harpsichord

8. Clavinet

9. Celesta

10. Glockenspiel

11. Music Box

12. Vibraphone

13. Marimba

14. Xylophone

15. Tubular Bells

16. Dulcimer

17. Drawbar Organ

18. Percussive Organ

19. Rock Organ

20. Church Organ

21. Reed Organ

22. Accordion

23. Harmonica

24. Tango Accordion

25. Acoustic Guitar (nylon)

26. Acoustic Guitar (steel)

27. Electric Guitar (jazz)

28. Electric Guitar (clean)

29. Electric Guitar (muted)

30. Overdriven Guitar

31. Distortion Guitar

32. Guitar harmonics

33. Acoustic Bass

34. Electric Bass (finger)

35. Electric Bass (pick)

36. Fretless Bass

37. Slap Bass 1

38. Slap Bass 2

39. Synth Bass 1

40. Synth Bass 2

41. Violin

42. Viola

43. Cello

44. Contrabass

45. Tremolo Strings

46. Pizzicato Strings

47. Orchestral Harp

48. Timpani

49. String Ensemble 1

50. String Ensemble 2

51. Synth Strings 1

52. Synth Strings 2

53. Choir Aahs

54. Voice Oohs

55. Synth Voice

56. Orchestra Hit

57. Trumpet

58. Trombone

59. Tuba

60. Muted Trumpet

61. French Horn

62. Brass Section

63. Synth Brass 1

64. Synth Brass 2

65. Soprano Sax

66. Alto Sax

67. Tenor Sax

68. Baritone Sax

69. Oboe

70. English Horn

71. Bassoon

72. Clarinet

73. Piccolo

74. Flute

75. Recorder

76. Pan Flute

77. Blown Bottle

78. Shakuhachi

79. Whistle

80. Ocarina

81. Lead 1 (square)

82. Lead 2 (sawtooth)

83. Lead 3 (calliope)

84. Lead 4 (chiff)

85. Lead 5 (charang)

86. Lead 6 (vox)

87. Lead 7 (fifths)

88. Lead 8 (lead bass)

89. Pad 1 (new age)

90. Pad 2 (warm)

91. Pad 3 (polysynth)

92. Pad 4 (choir)

93. Pad 5 (bowed)

94. Pad 6 (metal)

95. Pad 7 (halo)

96. Pad 8 (sweep)

97. FX 1 (rain)

98. FX 2 (soundtrack)

99. FX 3 (crystal)

100. FX 4 (atmosphere)

101. FX 5 (brightness)

102. FX 6 (goblins)

103. FX 7 (echoes)

104. FX 8 (sci fi)

105. Sitar

106. Banjo

107. Shamisen

108. Koto

109. Kalimba

110. Bag pipe

111. Fiddle

112. Shanai

113. Tinkle Bell

114. Agogo

115. Steel Drums

116. Woodblock

117. Taiko Drum

118. Melodic Tom

119. Synth Drum

120. Reverse Cymbal

121. Guitar Fret Noise

122. Breath Noise

123. Seashore

124. Bird Tweet

125. Telephone Ring

126. Helicopter

127. Applause

128. Gunshot

Index

Symbols

.el files
    installing , 83

A

adduser
    useradd , 18
amsynth , 43
animation , 65
applications , 41
audacity
    config file for , 55
audio
    conversion , 38
    export , 39
    grouping , 13
    importing , 41
    muting , 13
    tracks , 39
automation , 11, 83
    modes , 84
    recording a live mix , 86

B

blender
    compiling from source , 56
bouncing , 13, 87
brushes , 61

C

calf , 64
CCRMA , 72
changelog , 49
Chess Griffin , 23, 55
choma key , 23
chroma , 31
click track , 40
clips
    merging , 54
    moving , 50
    splitting , 50
codecs , 16
    forensics , 68
    installing , 35

transcoding , 17
color correction , 29
    3-point , 32
    stylistic , 35
compressors , 67
contrast , 30
converting , 16
creative commons, 11, 97
credits , 26, 48

D

DAW
    Digital Audio Workstation , 63
dependencies
    dependencies for Slackermedia , 33
desktop , 18
desktops
    alternative , 102
dissolve , 21
downloads, 11
    Slackermedia dependency queue files , 34
dssi , 71
dual booting, 17
DVD
    ripping , 62
DyneBolic, 1

E

editing , 49, 6, 11
    in the timeline , 11
    tools , 49, 8
effects , 9, 67
    compressor , 67
    equalizers , 73
    limiter , 71
    noise removal , 79
    normalizers , 72
    reverb , 80
effects processors , 75
elisp , 83
equalizers , 73
export , 87
exporting , 13, 43
ext4 , 51

F

fades , 53
fc-cache , 60
feedback
    contact information for this manual, x
file associations , 87
first launch , 1
fluidsynth , 73
fonts , 59
    installing manually , 60
    installing via KDE , 60

G

Gancarz, Mike, 3
gimp paint studio , 61
green screen , 23
GUI , 19
gverb , 81

H

hexter , 73

I

importing , 3
importing audio , 23
install
    installing slackware, 17
installation , 1
    soft synths , 41
iso
    how (not) to download Slackermedia, 1

J

jamin , 64

K

kernel
    compiling , 49
    panic , 51
    real time , 49
    realtime priority , 54
kernel panic , 53
keyboard shortcuts
    custom , 101
keyframing , 11

L

ladspa , 71
layout , 2
lilo , 52
limiter , 71
Linux From Scratch, 1
loops , 52
lpr
    printing with , 91
luma , 29
lv2 , 71

M

makepkg , 31
mastering , 75
menuconfig , 51
midi
    driver settings , 78
    editor , 33
    importing data , 6, 29
    overview , 46
    usb controller , 5, 31
mixdown , 13
mixer , 54, 57
modularity, 7

N

navigation , 15
nekobee , 73
noise removal , 79
normalization , 72

O

open with... , 87

P

package management
    installing applications on slackware , 19
packages
    slackware packages, 19
patchbay , 79
pdf
    from plain text , 91
playback
    looping , 53
plug-ins , 63

Kdenlive

A User's Guide

Seth Kenlon

Klaatu la Terible

Kdenlive
A User's Guide
Edition 0.8.x

| Author | Seth Kenlon | *seth@straightedgelinux.com* |
| Author | Klaatu la Terible | *klaatu@hackerpublicradio.org* |

A Guide for visual content creators both new and experienced.

Introduction to Kdenlive

GNU Linux has infamously been wanting for a good, solid professional-level free video editor for years. There have been glimpses of hope here and there, but mostly the editors that have the look and feel of a professional application are prone to blockbuster-worthy crashes, and those that have been stable have mostly been stable because they don't actually do anything beyond very basic editing. **Kdenlive** changes all of that.

In the production house where I work, **Kdenlive** is the Linux editor in production use, and matches (and sometimes out-performs) the proprietary boxen in cost, upkeep, flexibility, speed, and stability. The next few chapters will illuminate for professional editors how **Kdenlive** can replace proprietary tools with a fairly minimal learning curve.

A good video editor is one that is suitable for anyone wanting to edit video, with powerful features that enable the video professional to do any task required of the job, and yet with the simplicity that allows a hobbyist to quickly cut together footage off of their phone or point-and-click camera. **Kdenlive** can be both of those things, but regardless of the scope of your video project, there are right and wrong ways of doing things. Over the course of this book, we will review the practical usage and the common set of Best Practises that will ensure your projects are successful.

1. Installing

Kdenlive is a complex install, no question about it. It requires the **MLT** backend to deal with multimedia, and for maximum compatibility with all possible video codecs, it wants as many video decoding and encoding libraries that you can possibly throw at it.

The easiest fix, obviously, is to simply use the **Kdenlive** version provided by your repository. The watershed release for **Kdenlive**, in terms of stability and feature-completeness, was the 0.8 release; all major distributions currently provide 0.8 or above in their official repositories, their "official unofficial" add-on repos, or build services (like Slackbuilds, AUR, et cetera).

2. First Launch

During the first launch, **Kdenlive** will perform checks to discover what video codecs and sources it has available to it. You'll be given the chance to rectify anything you may have neglected to install.

The usual advice about troubleshooting applies; last month while setting up an editing workstation, there was an error with the **MLT-SDL** module, causing the new install of **Kdenlive** to not launch. A quick internet search for the issue provided the solution and we were up and running in no time.

You'll also be asked to create a default **Kdenlive** project folder. This isn't anything you'll be locked into later, and in fact it's often best to separate projects to distinct directories, but choosing a sane default ensures that you don't inadvertently dump important project files out into random folders without realizing it.

3. Your Workspace

Kdenlive uses **Qt4** for its interface, so customization is easy. It's pretty common for video editors to utilize a darkened theme to emphasize the video rather than distract the eye with a bright glowing interface (also, the dark theme helps during color correction). To change the theme of **Kdenlive**, use the **Settings Menu > Themes**. The available themes come from the available KDE4 themes, which you'll find in your **System Settings**.

Since I am often editing late into the night, I use the default theme during most of the edit (I find the light from the monitor precludes me from having to turn on a desk lamp and still prevents me from blindly knocking over my coffee) but during colour correction the bright theme is distracting. Good neutral themes for colour work are **Obsidian Coast** or **Wonton Soup**.

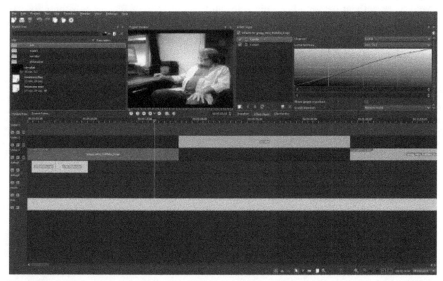

You'll probably want to use **Kdenlive** in full-screen mode (a near-kiosk mode is available by right-clicking on the window's title bar and selecting **Fullscreen**), but within its main window there are several different components. These sections can be popped out of the main window, tabbed, rearranged, and floated. All available components of **Kdenlive**'s visual workspace can be seen via its **View** menu.

The layout of **Kdenlive** is up to you and your own work style. You may choose to emulate the default layout of whatever video editor you might be used to, or you may find a layout that works best for you. Once you've created one that you like, you can save it via **View** menu > **Save Layout As**.

A typical layout will have at least these panels:

• **Project Tree**: otherwise known as a **bin** or **clip browser** in other video editors.

• **Clip Monitor**: a place to preview raw footage before commiting it to the final edit.

- **Project Monitor**: a place to watch your edited footage.

- **Timeline**: the destination for all selected clips you use in your project.

- We'll review what each of these panels is used for and how to use them, but first let's import some footage.

4. Importing Footage

Before importing footage, you should save your project. This may seem strange given that your project is currently empty, but giving your workspace a name and location on your harddrive will establish the default skeletal structure for all Kdenlive projects. **Kdenlive**, like most professional-grade editors, generates lots of cache files and meta data; starting your work without determining a place for all those temporary files to go simply means that you'll be dumping temp files into your default **kdenlive** directory and then abandoning them once you save.

Save your test project in its own subdirectory. I generally keep my **kdenlive** project directories in a **~/kdenlive** directory, with the default location being its own subdirectory called **~/kdenlive/default**. This tends to work well, and lends itself to being able to off-load old projects onto backup drives without worrying about whether or not that project is actually self-contained or whether I need to search through files to locate dependent media. Keeping the projects self-contained, even if it means replicating media, is quite liberating and should be used unless you are working in an infrastructure with stores of shared media that don't need to be saved along with your project data.

Creating a standard path for your projects is also helpful in the event that you need to migrate projects from one system to another. If the file paths are always ~/kdenlive/project-name then **Kdenlive** losing track of media files is less likely.

The path of your default **Kdenlive** project folder may always be chanced via **Project** menu > **Project Settings > Project folder**.

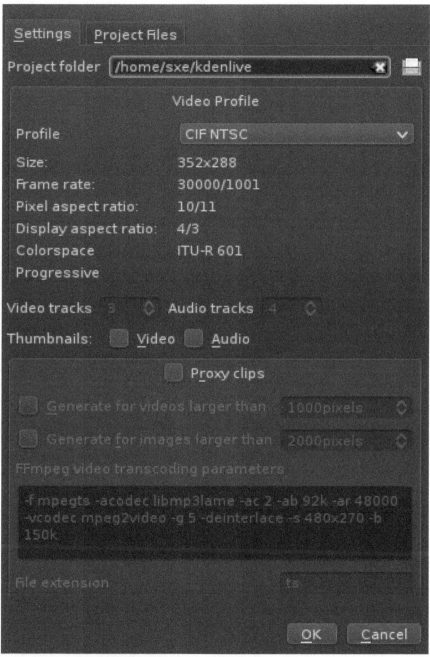

Now that you've saved your project, you can import footage. There are several ways to do this, and **Kdenlive** can handle them all. Since most cameras record to solid-state media now, "importing" footage often consists of little more than putting your camera into USB Storage mode, plugging it into your computer, and dragging and dropping the camera's directory tree to your **Kdenlive** project folder. Note that carrying over the entire directory tree is essential, since many cameras use complex muxed formats that require meta data about the clips in order to actually play the clips. Do NOT just drag over the "Streams" or "Clips" folder.

Once you've copied the footage to your harddrive, you can add those clips to your **Kdenlive** project via the **Project** menu > **Add Clip** (or by right-clicking in the **Project Tree** and selecting **Add Clip**). You may be notified by **Kdenlive** that the current project setting is not the same as the footage that you've just imported. This is telling you that your project setting has defaulted to, for instance, DV NTSC but that you've just imported CIF sized clips.

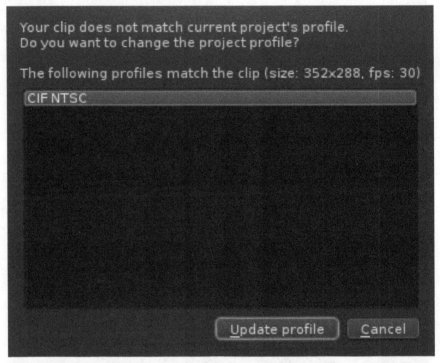

If this is the case, then you should accept **Kdenlive**'s offer to change the project profile to match your clips. It's best to edit in a native environment and perform any transcoding only when exporting, so regardless of what you actually intend to create, you should try to edit in the format that you shot, or else transcode up-front (a topic we'll cover in more detail in Article 5 of this series). Otherwise, you'll be capturing footage from some external source, like a tape-based camera, or even, in theory, a webcam. All of these options are accessible via the **View** menu > **Record Monitor**.

The **Record Monitor** is a robust video capture frontend; it currently defaults to Firewire, and will warn you if dvgrab is not installed on your system, but don't panic; you can change this. Click the wrench icon to configure what backend **Record Monitor** attempts to use.

The configuration menu for **Record Monitor** should give you a choice between Firewire (**dvgrab**), Video4Linux (USB and, accordingly, built-in webcams on laptops), Screen Grab (via **RecordMyDesktop**), and even third party capture cards. Choose the appropriate backend.

Once you've set the default capture device, return to the **Record Monitor** and select from the pop-up menu on the lower right and select the backend you'd like to use. You may need to click the **Connect** button on the left of **Record Monitor** in order to bring the capture device online. Finally, press the **Play** button to preview the external video, and **Record** to save it to your harddrive.

5. Three-Point Editing

The editing process was invented and refined over 100 years ago and is still just as applicable as ever. The first of these editing principles that we have inherited from men and women dealing with hundreds of feet of celluloid film is the three-point edit.

To perform a basic edit in your footage, click on a clip in your **Project Tree**; it appears in the **Clip Monitor** for you to preview. This is akin to a film editor taking a strip of film from the film bin and running it through a Moveola (a small, hand-cranked, personal film projector).

Once you've played the clip past the introductory footage (actors getting ready for their shot, the clapboard or slate, and so on), set an "In" point for that clip by hitting the **i** key on your keyboard. Allow the clip to continue playing until you find the end of the action you want to use in the clip. Mark "Out" with the **o** key on your keyboard. You've just set the first two points in your three-point edit.

The third point, then, is where in your timeline the clip should appear. If this is the first clip in your movie, then probably the logical place for it would be 00:00:00:00, ie, the very beginning of your timeline. To do this quickly, simply hit the **v** key on your keyboard, which will drop the video between the In and Out points of your clip into the selected Video track of your Timeline (by default, this will be Video Track 1, but you can select a different one by clicking the track label on the left of the Timeline). On some video editing applications, the video playhead in the Timeline determines where the clip is dropped; in **Kdenlive,** you get a dedicated target tool for this purpose, meaning that you needn't move your playhead from its parked position just to drop in a new clip. The target tool appears as a small white box in the top SMPTE ruler bar of the **Timeline**.

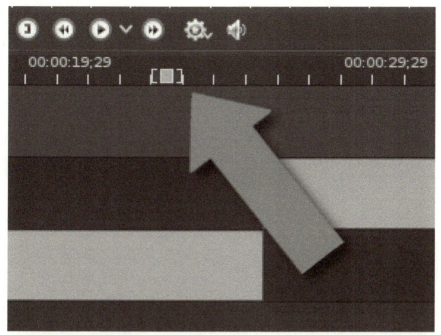

You can also do a drag-and-drop add by simply grabbing the video thumbnail from the **Clip Monitor** and dragging it down to the **Timeline**.

6. The Basic Tools

There are three basic tools in **Kdenlive**: the **Select Tool** (s), the **Razor Tool** (x), and the **Spacer Tool** (m). This is a fairly standard, albeit basic, toolset. There is no ripple edit tool, roll edit, or any of the power-user tools that some editors might have become accustomed to on other editing systems, but I've found that adapting to the simplified toolset is almost natural (and in fact many other video editing applications have been moving toward a simplified toolset). For the amount of use most of the specialized tools actually get, it's probably difficult to justify maintaining the associated code. In otherwords, I noticed the lack of some specialized edit tools when I first launched **Kdenlive**, but in practise haven't even noticed them missing.

- The **Select Tool** is exactly what you'd expect; click to select a clip, drag to move a clip. Use the **Select tool** for related tasks, as well, such as selecting the active track, creating Guides and Markers, extending or shortening video clips in the timeline, control-clicking to select multiple clips at once, and so on.

- The **Razor Tool** creates splices in a video region in the timeline. In theory this isn't really a necessary tool, since you could always just use the **Select Tool** to shorten a video clip manually, but in practice it's nice to be able to target a point at which you wish to cut out or in, make a splice, and then delete the excess footage.

- If you do shorten a clip with the **Razor Tool** and delete the excess footage that you've just sliced off, you will be left with a gap between your new out point and the beginning of the next clip in the timeline. To get rid of this empty space, you can right click on it and select **Remove Space**. Note that you need to **Remove Space** on both the **Video Track** and the **Audio Track** if you are using separate audio.

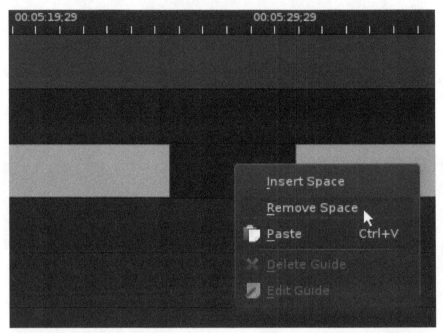

Rather than using the **Remove Space** function, you could manually move the video and audio regions over using the **Space Tool**. This tool simply selects everything to the right of where you click; ie, it selects all video and audio regions in the future and allows you to either move them to the left or right in your timeline. It's a common task, although unforunately the **Space Tool** is quite rigid in how it selects; it will select and move every media region on every track. Should you ever decide that you only want to select all regions on, for instance, track one, then you'll need to either lock all other tracks or you'll need to zoom out and just use your **Select Tool** to manually select the regions you want to grab.

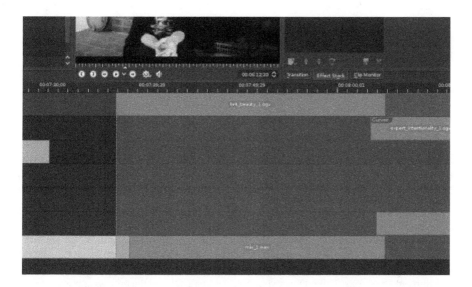

7. Conclusion

Kdenlive excels at a very difficult task: importing media from a myriad different sources, organizing them into projects, and allowing them to be manipulated in any variety of ways. It's user-friendly, powerful, simple and yet capable of so much. It is easily a drop-in replacement for industry standard video editors, as we shall continue to discover in the forthcoming chapters.

Advanced Editing with Kdenlive

In the previous chapters, we reviewed the different methods of importing footage into **Kdenlive**, best practises in organizing project files, and the layout and tools provided by **Kdenlive**. In this chapter, we will discuss advanced editing techniques and review most of the tools you'll be using on a day to day basis as a video editor.

1. A Brief History of the Editing Workflow

The initial edit of a movie is called a "Rough Assembly", and it literally consists of each take of each scene, from "Action!" to "Cut", lined up in a row on the timeline, in scripted order, one after another. The rough assembly might last for hours and is really just a good way to review all the footage available.

After this basic edit, a new cut is created, and it is called, simply, the "first cut". It's usually based around the master shot; a wide shot that encompasses all of the action of the scene as it appears in the screenplay. Close-ups, two-shots, and cut-aways are then added to a higher video track so that the end result is one continuous scene, with insert shots of more detailed actions and reactions. This edit is revised into a second cut, and the process continues from first cut to an editor's cut, a director's cut, and a producer's (or "final") cut.

This model might not be imposed on you, depending on your industry but its logic still applies and can help you organize the sometimes monumental task of making hours upon hours of footage into presentable content that people will appreciate sitting through.

The Rough Assembly is often done as described in the previous chapter; add a clip to the **Project Tree**, load the clip into the **Clip Monitor**, mark an In and Out point, and then add the clip to the timeline. Rinse and repeat.

This same technique may be used for the first cut, but after that many people find it impractical to work out of the clip monitor and choose instead to refine their edits in the timeline directly.

2. Editing in the Timeline

After your shots are all lined up in the timeline, you will find the need to adjust their in and out points. This can be done in three different ways:

The best way to refine an edit point of a clip in **Kdenlive** is to place your playhead on the frame you wish to cut in or out on. For instance, if a character is blinking in their close-up just as you cut away from them but the next shot has their eyes wide open, then you'll probably want to trim off a few frames before you cut. That is, you'll cut out earlier, such that their eyes are open before and after the cut. It's basic continuity.

Place your playhead on a frame where the characters eye's are open, and then make sure that **Snapping** is On (**Timeline** Menu > **Snapping**). Snapping, like in any graphic program, causes edges of objects to "magnetically" pull toward one another. Snapping is a feature that you'll find yourself turning on and off very frequently, so I generally assign it a handy keyboard shortcut. I use the completely arbitrary **control d**, simply because I find that my left hand is always on the keyboard as I edit with the mouse in my right hand. But you can choose anything (the **n** key seems a popular choice with graphic apps and other video editors, but that's never seemed convenient to me). Assign the shortcut by going to the **Setting** menu > **Configure Shortcuts**.

With the **Select Tool** (s) roll over the nearest edge of the video region. It should highlight itself with a flashing green arrow. Click and drag this video region to the left, and you've just adjusted the out point of your edit with frame-precision.

A more efficient variation on this is to place the playhead on a frame and then use `shift` `r` to place a splice in the region. Then select the excess footage and delete it as desired.

And one more step toward maximum efficiency is doing the same action with two clicks and one keypress only: position the playhead on a frame, select the clip, and hit the **1** key on your keyboard and the in point of that clip will be sent to the position of the playhead. Alternately, you can hit **2** for the out point to be repoisitioned at the playhead. It's a very convenient and fast way to adjust the ends of your clips and is one of my favourite features in **Kdenlive**.

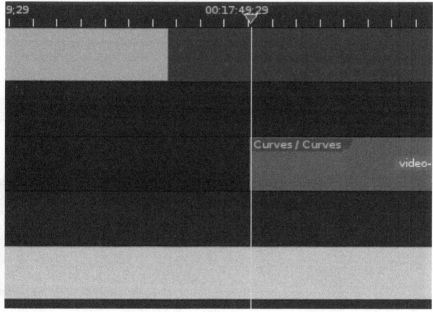

If it's not frame-precision that you need, you can opt to use the **Razor Tool**, which currently does not respect snapping. This makes the **Razor Tool** good for initial cutting, when you know that you like a shot but need it to be, more or less, half as long; grab the **Razor Tool** (x) and click on the video region at the point you wish to slice. A splice mark should appear and new thumbnails will be generated on the video region to demonstrate that it has been divided into two sections.

The final way of adjusting the length of a video region is precise but inelegant. If you double-click on a video region, you'll get a pop-up dialog box allowing you to modify the clip's position in the timeline, the clip's in and out points, and so on. Not only should you not require a dialog box for this action, there is also no way to quickly input the new values; you must select each portion of the SMPTE timecode, type in the new values, move to the next field, and so on. If you absolutely need to cut off, for instance, 6 frames from the beginning of a clip, then this might be a nice and exact way to do that, but aside from that it's impractical and clunky.

Keep in mind that the workspace resolution counts a lot when seeking frame precision. If you're zoomed out from your timeline so far that it is only able to account for every 10 frames or so, then any tool is going to snap to the nearest 10th frame. When you're so deep into your edit that every frame counts, zoom in on the region you're about to cut, and make sure you're cutting on the frames you think you're cutting on.

3. Audio Splits and Grouping Clips

Since most modern video devices also incidentally capture sound, most of the video clips you import into a project will have an audio stream in them. By default, **Kdenlive** displays this audio stream as a part of the video stream; you'll see a video region with its thumbnails overlaid with thumbnail representations of the audio stream's soundwaves.

If you've recorded to a separate audio device, you can keep the audio embedded in the video as reference sound, and you can turn it off by clicking the Mute Track button in the track label on the left.

If this is your primary audio track, on the other hand, you might want to separate it from the video region so that you can manipulate it separately. To do this, you can do one of two things:

1.   Right-click on the video region and select Split Audio.

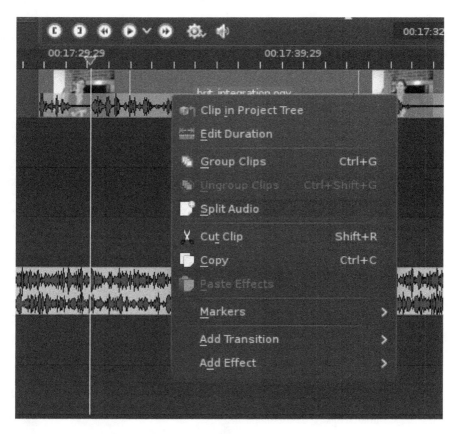

2. Set this as a default action by clicking the "Separate Audio and Video Automatically" button on the lower right of the bottom timeline control panel.

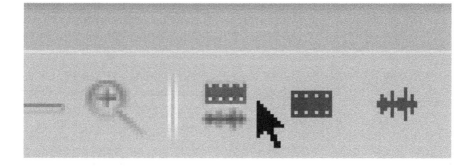

After you split the audio from the video region, you have regions on two tracks now: a Video Track and an Audio Track. The two regions are grouped together (indicated by yellow clip colour with blue space spanning any extra tracks between them). This means that if you shorten or lengthen one, then the other will also be shortened or lengthened. If you move one, the other moves, and so on.

Sometimes that's exactly what you want. Other times, you want to manipulate them separately; a classic example would be when doing the classic over-the-shoulder conversation scene; a close-up on one character intercut with the close-up coverage of the other. One each character's close-up, you want to use the audio associated with that clip, but if at one point you want to do an insert shot of a character's silent reaction, then you wouldn't want to cut their audio track, but allow the other character to continue talking offscreen even though the focus is on the silent character.

For this to work, you'll need to ungroup the clips. You can do this by right-clicking on the clip and selecting Ungroup, or using the keyboard shortcut (**Control Shift G**). This removes the invisible link between the audio and video, allowing you to, for example, cut and remove a piece of the video without affecting the audio.

You can always group clips together by selecting clips (use the Select Tool while holding down the Control key to add to your selection) and right-click on them or use **Control G** to choose **Group Clips**.

4. Basic Navigation in the Timeline

If you're spending your weeks in the timeline, you'll want to know a more efficient way of navigating it. There are all the usual video editing conventions in **Kdenlive**, albeit with some variation in keyboard assignments.

The now classic and ubiquitous **jkl** keyboard sequence is also present in Kdenlive. To play your timeline, you may press **l** once for standard speed, **ll** for double speed, **lll** for triple speed. **K** stops playback. Press **j** for reverse playback, **jj** for double speed reverse, and **jjj** for triple speed reverse.

You can also move by frame or by second. The left or right arrow will advance or rewind by one frame; **shift leftArrow** or **shift rightArrow** will move forward or back by one second.

To move your playhead to the beginning of a video region, use the **Home** key; for the end of the region, use **End**. To move along the timeline by splices, use **Alt leftArrow** or **Alt rightArrow**. And finally, you can jump to the beginning or end of the Timeline with **control Home** or **control End**.

By using these navigational tools, you'll find that for very long stretches of video editing, you won't need to bother with your mouse, which, as any Unix guru knows, is the real key to efficiency.

5. Notes on Video Formats

Video editing is a fairly intensive process, so for best results you will want to have a nice, powerful video editing computer with plenty of CPU cores, plenty of RAM, and a nice GPU with a robust and reliable video driver. That said, it is possible to edit on even a modest laptop, mostly depending on what kind of footage you're trying to edit.

Regardless of what you're editing, consider the format of the video you're using. If you've just imported a muxed video file then more than likely you'll want to transcode it for editing. My main workstation at the studio where I work can easily handle HD footage yet I continually run into stuttered playback when I import muxed footage. If i transcode it to a high-quality lossless matroska file or to something similar, I can edit it smoothly and quickly.

The opposite end of the spectrum sometimes has the same issues, in an odd way. Some phones and portable devices record video in such a highly compressed format that **Kdenlive** is forced to spends far too much energy decoding it to something that can be played back at a normal frame rate. I avoid this the same way; transcoding early in the project's life and leaving the compressed or muxed footage as backup source files.

To do this, go to the **File** menu and select **Transcode Clips**. Select the clip you want to transcode, choose what profile you wish to transcode into (Lossless Matroska is quite nice although depending on the source footage it may be overkill). Make sure the **Add to Project** box is checked, and then commence with transcoding. Note that for the transcoding process, an **ffmpeg** command is provided; if you have hours and hours of transcoding to do, feel free to steal the **ffmpeg** command and do the transcoding as a BASH script in a terminal.

For example, to transcode a folder of **.MTS** muxed video to something more easily managed by **Kdenlive**, open a terminal and navigate to the folder containing the source files. You may issue your command as:

```
$ for i in *.MTS; do $(ffmpeg paste-the-kdenlive-
command-here); done
```

This will cycle through each **MTS** file in the directory, run it through the **ffmpeg** command, and save it in the same directory without affecting the original file. To safeguard against even accidental file clobbering, you could establish a folder called "transcoded" and make sure that the final argument in the **Kdenlive ffmpeg** script is `./transcoded/%1.mov` rather than its default of just `%1.mov`

What codec you use when transcoding will depend on the project and its intended destination. If you require full quality for maximum output potential, then you should probably transcode to Lossless Matroska. If you feel confident that the video is destined for a limited distribution at a fixed maximum resolution, you might choose to transcode to DNxHD 720p or whatever resolution would be appropriate for the destination. Never transcode to something that will lose information before you edit; leave that for the final render and compression.

To further reduce strain on the computer system, Kdenlive has a built-in proxy (or "offline" in traditional editing terminology) system but I have found it unreliable so far. In theory, you should be able to establish proxy clips by enabling proxies in the **Project Settings**, and then by right-clicking on the clip in the **Project Tree** and setting it to generate and use a proxy. Unfortunately, the proxy generation has crashed every time I've tried it, so I've been unable to utilize this feature as yet.

Keep in mind that whatever footage you place in your timeline is occupying RAM. If you attempt to edit a one-track 30 minute project, then you'll find that your computer (provided it can handle the video format itself) will perform quite well. Start adding new tracks, compositing, two hours of footage in the timeline, and your computer will start to feel like it's working harder. Keep this in mind when constructing your projects. Don't hesitate to split a very complex project into separate **Kdenlive** project files, and edit on a scene by scene basis until you're ready to string your project together into a complete piece. This technique will be detailed in the final chapter of this series.

6. Conclusion

Kdenlive's editing tools provide functional and efficient editing options, as well as flexibility to suit your individual workstyle. Feel free to modify and customize your environment as much as you want, and try out the different tools to see what provides you with the most precise and satisfactory results.

Effects and Transitions in Kdenlive

It is expected that even a modest video editor will feature a set of basic video transitions. The challenge is to offer critical effects without becoming bloated and unfocused in scope. **Kdenlive** manages to offer the most commonly required effects with all the standard options without sacrificing stability or quality.

The famous first words of every screenplay are **FADE IN**, and in a way, that is the most commonly used effect of all. The classic fade would normally be considered a transition but in **Kdenlive** a "transition" is a visual effect that requires two video regions to function, while an "effect" works on a single region. This is an important distinction to bear in mind, since the terms are laden with preconceived interpretation.

1. Layout Mods

First, configure your layout (covered in the first chapter of this guide) to have the **Effect Stack** and **Transition** panel readily accessible. To do this, go to the View menu and select **Effect Stack** and then **Transition**.

This introduces two new panels into your **Kdenlive** interface. If your interface now looks crowded, you can use tabs. Since effects and transitions are applied to clips in the **Timeline**, you'll never use your **Clip Monitor** (which views clips in the **Project Tree**) and the **Effect Stack** or **Transition** panel (which operate on clips in the **Project Monitor / Timeline**) at the same time. You can make the Effect Stack and Transition panel a tab of the clip monitor panel by dragging the effect stack panel on to the clip monitor; it is now available in a tabbed view (located at the bottom of the panel). Do the same for the **Transition** panel.

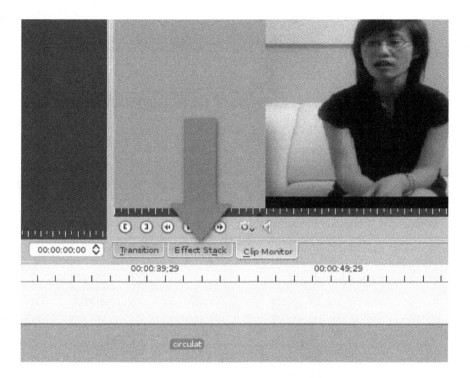

2. Fades

To apply a fade effect, right-click on the video region you wish to affect. Select Add Effect > Fade > Fade to Black, and the fade-to-black transition will be applied to the end of the clip. Scrub through the video (by clicking along the timelime's SMPTE ruler bar) or play (spacebar) to see the effect.

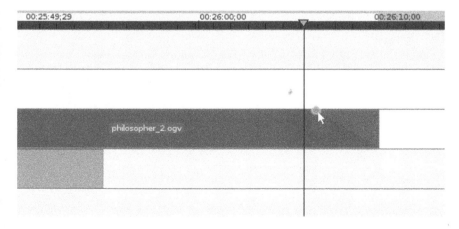

Once you've applied a fade, you can modify its duration by either using the Duration slider in the **Effect Stack,** or you can click and drag the corner of the red fade indicator that appears on the video region.

 Warning

> **Fade In** and **Fade Out** (not **to Black**) effects are Audio effects, not video effects. It's easy to get them mixed up, and you'll spend an hour wondering why your fades aren't working.

Armed with just these two simple effects, you most likely have all of the functionality expected from a typical video editing application. But for those peculiar clients and users who want more interesting visuals, **Kdenlive** features quite a bit more.

3. Dissolves

A dissolve is like a fade, except that they do not fade to black, but to another clip. This, then is a Transition and requires two clips in order to function.

To use it, place one clip on **Video Track 3** (the bottommost Video Track on the default **Kdenlive** setup) and another on **Video Track 2**. Overlap the end of Track 2 over the beginning of Track 3. The concept here, as with any transitional effect, is that in order to gradually move from 100% of one clip to 100% of another, there must be some material that overlaps so that the incremental transition can be built.

Once you've ensured the clips overlap for some duration, right-click on the region in Track 2 and select **Add Transition > Dissolve**.

You can adjust the duration of the dissolve by overlapping the video clips further, and stretching the yellow dissolve region to encompass more of the overlap.

4. Slides and Wipes

Another way of getting from clip A to clip B is the Slide transition. Being a transition, it also must be added to not just one clip, but to two clips that overlap.

Place one clip on Video Track 3 and another on Track 2. Make sure they overlap by at least one second. Right click on the top video clip and select Add Transition > Slide. Play the video to see the result; notice that one clips "slides" into frame over the other. If you've added the transition in a round-about way, you might find that the wrong clip is sliding in; if that happens during your experimentation, select the Slide transition region in the timeline and, click to activate the Transition Tab, and click the Invert checkbox in the Transition options.

Different wipe effects can be seen with the Wipe transition, easily accessible now that you have a transition region by clicking the drop-down menu in the **Transition** tab. Choose **Wipe** to change the transition, and notice the new options available. You can choose from multiple styles of wipes, and as with the slide you can invert them to control which clip supplants the other.

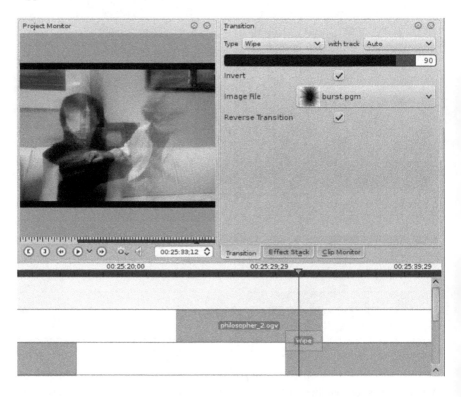

5. Chroma Key, aka Green Screen

With so many effects and even entire sets being generated digitally now, there's been a huge demand for the "blue screen" or "green screen" effect, which is technically known simply as a **Chroma Key**. It is called a Chroma Key because you are selecting (or keying) a specific chroma (colour) value, which you can then discard entirely or use as a matte, or any number of operations.

The Chroma Key in **Kdenlive** is a two-step process: first, you must select the colour you want to use as your key, and secondly you must composite the image.

The first step can be done, obviously, with the effect called **Blue Screen**, but it can also be done with the **Color Selection** effect, which turns out to have more options including choking and throttling the selection.

To set up the effect, place some footage on **Video Track 3**; it could be anything from a shot of a grassy field to a digital Tron universe that you want your character to be transported to. This is called a plate shot.

Above this, on Track 2, place the shot of your character in front of the green or blue screen. Right click on this region and select **Add Effect > Color Selection**.

In the **Effect Stack**, use the color selector to choose the chroma level you wish to key. Refine the selection with the **Hue** and **Chroma** sliders, the **Edge mode**, and other options.

The **Blue Screen** effect does exactly what's expected and replaces your selected chroma value with an alpha channel (in other words, it makes the selected colour become transparent). If you're using the **Color Selection** tool, it will do the reverse of tha; it retains the color selected rather than keys it out. However, there's a handy check box just under the colour picker for **Invert Selection** which loses the colour and retains everything else around it. Be sure to check this box if you're using **Color Selection**.

The less compressed the source video is, the higher the likelihood of getting a quick and easy chroma key, since you have more colour depth available for subtle keying. Should you need to apply multiple chroma keys or other effects, the **Effect Stack** is called a "stack" for that very reason; effects upon effects can be added to a single clip as required. If you had to, you wouldn't be the first composite artist to key one shade of blue or green only to add a second key for some other shade in that same spectrum, or to key out all blue in a scene and then add back in some element using a garbage matte.

Once you've successfully keyed out the color, you've essentially replaced that color with an alpha channel that is just waiting to become transparent. The second step, therefore, is to add a composite transition between the top and bottom video regions. Right click on the top region and select **Add Transition > Composite**.

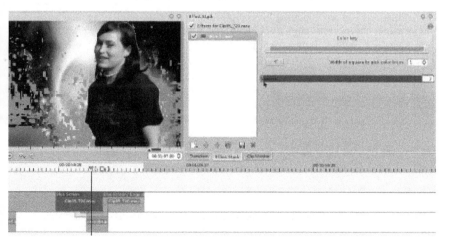

The composite transition is added to only the first second or so of the video region by default, so extend it with your select tool to the duration of the clip. You should see in your **Project Monitor** that the top video is visible except where there used to be blue or green (or whatever colour you keyed), through which the plate shot is visible.

Now, ideally, the subject in the first clip will match the plate's color temperature and will have nice smooth edges and look integrated into the shot. If that is not the case, you'll want to either add effects like a Blue Screen effect to key out the last vestigals of a colored edge, or do color correction to better match the shots. In the next chapter, color correction will be reviewed in detail.

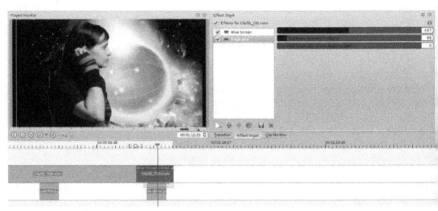

Overall, this is a powerful tool and provided me with surprisingly good results on even highly compressed video I'd shot with an Android phone. This is significant since other editing applications couldn't even ingest that footage, and even after trial-and-error transcoding to just get the footage into another editor, the chroma key was poor.

6. Composited Images and Titles

If the material you are importing for compositing is an image or an image sequence, such as an export of sequential png's from **Blender** or **Synfig Studio**, then they probably already have an alpha channel. In this case, all you need to do is use the **Add Clip** option to add the sequence to your **Project Tree**.

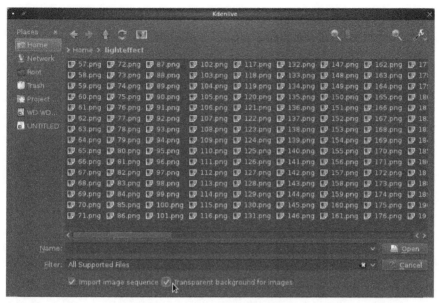

As long as you have checked the boxes at the bottom of the file chooser dialogue box (**Image Sequence** and **Transparent Background Images**) then the images will be imported as a single video clip with built-in alpha, meaning no color selection or chroma key is required. Simply place the image sequence over a video clip, add the Composite transition, and move on.

Titling in **Kdenlive** works much the same way as images or animations. You can generate titles from within **Kdenlive** by right-clicking in your **Project Tree** and choosing **Add Title Clip**. This will open a text creation interface, where you'll be able to choose fonts, styles, and even basic animations for the text. You can use the text in its default form (white text on a black background) or you can add a composite transition between the text and some video clip to have a text overlay.

I've never been a fan of doing anything but the most basic titling with the built-in text tools of a video editor. The editing apps I've used seem to agree with me, since all feature or are sure to integrate with external, dedicated titling programs. On free software, there is **Synfig Studio**, a traditional digital cel animation application, and **Blender**, the famous 3d modeling and animation application. There is a Youtube series dedicated to teaching video editors *Blender for Motion Graphic Artists*[1].

---

[1] http://youtu.be/7FBoegkgIho

7. Conclusion

Kdenlive features all the standard tools a "prosumer" would ever need for video production, plus quite a lot more. Its stability and feature set places it firmly in the professional market, and it integrates easily into the workflow of a busy post production schedule. With a little experimentation with the different effects, **Kdenlive** will prove itself as a versatile editing application with all the features demanding clients and producers expect.

Colour Correction with Kdenlive

Good photography doesn't just magically happen. Careful attention to lens settings, depth-of-field charts, and lighting will produce quality images but even these, since the days of the earliest photography, have been taken into the darkroom and adjusted.

Kdenlive's colour correction suite easily rivals any professional video editing application and in many ways surpasses the basic tools often found in the expensive industry application. Let's look at the typical workflow of colour correction, and then the tools.

1. Workflow

Colour correction comes into play fairly late in the post production process for two reasons. First, you don't want to spend hours colour correcting footage only to find that later in the edit, the scene is cut entirely from the movie. Second, adding color effects to all of your footage is burdensome on your computer and logistically difficult for you to keep track of during intensive editing.

So you'll wait until picture lock to start color correction; frequently it's done at roughly the same time as the sound mix is being done. The workflow of post production itself will be discussed in further detail in the final chapter of this series.

Without exception, colour correct your work scene by scene. Your eye treats colour very subjectively; a shade of blue that looks "too bright" one moment starts to fall into place after the eye has stared at it long enough, so you want to emmerse yourself in one scene, and adjust the colours only within that scene so that your eye accepts the colours and character of that scene as normal. When the camera cuts to a different scene, both you as the colourist and the audience understand that the colours should be different; we're in a different location now, so of course the colours of even our hero's skin tone can be drastically different.

2. The Human Element

The human eye naturally gravitates to other humans, and unless you're making a documentary about animals or plants, your audience mostly cares about the humans in your movie. Or at least, their eyes mostly cares about the humans. For that reason, a good colourist first targets the human in the shot. If you colour correct for the people in your frame, your audience will tell you that the colours in your film were brilliant (or, more likely, they won't notice the colour at all, but at least they won't walk out of the screening room talking about how bad the film looked; it's a thankless job).

3. Luma Values

Start with the Luma. "Luma" is a fancy term for the levels of your picture's brightness values; if you desaturated your picture so that it was black-and-white only, then you're looking, essentially, at the pure luma values of your image.

The reason this is significant is because celluloid has a wide tolerance for luma. Think of it as a resolution for the scale from darkest black to brightest white; first of all, celluloid can read darker shadows and brighter highlights, and second of all the gradiation between those two extremes is constant and even, so that even in the darkest shadows there is still great detail.

Film Response Sensitivity
Video Luma Potential

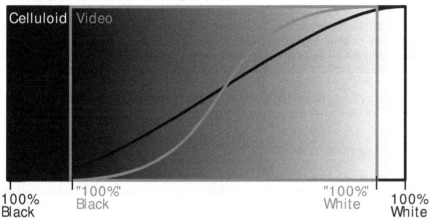

Video represents a relatively small inset within the celluloid luma spectrum, with its darkest value being early in the shadow levels of celluloid, and its potential white level being quite early in celluloid highlight. Anything below this dark level or above the light level bottoms out quickly and actually causes distortion (which is precisely why your video camera has a "zebra stripes" function on it). Furthermore, the progress from dark to bright is not constant and features less variation than celluiloid.

In other words, your audience is accustomed to seeing a medium with a colour range almost as rich as real life, and are instead being presented with a digital reproduction. Since most video is shot to capture reality (or suggest that it has captured some form of reality), and to the audience "reality" on film is The Look Of Celluloid" (yes, the film industry has trained audiences that film grain and perfect cinematography equals Reality) the colourist's goal is usually to fake a more filmic look and feel for their video.

The most effective way to fake celluloid-like luma in your video is to "crush" the darks and make the brights "pop"; in other words, increase the contrast. There are many ways to do this but my favourite is the **Curves** tool.

To add a curve to a clip, right-click the clip in the timeline and select **Add Effect > Colour Correction > Curves**. Activate the **Effects** Tab (see *Effects and Transitions in Kdenlive* on how to modify your layout and add tabs to your interface). The curve adjustment interface defaults to the Red/Cyan channel, so use the drop-down menu in the top right to select Luma instead.

Bring the bright level up by clicking the top part of the curve and nudging it to the left. Bring the dark level down by clicking the bottom end of the curve and nudging it to the right. This makes the gradiation between the two less constant, so the result is that the image now has more drastic dark levels and more drastic bright levels. Note that this is actually lessening your video's luma variance, in other words it's making it even less like celluloid by further restricting the luma potential. However, to the audience's eyes, it now looks more like celluloid because the dark areas of the image are richer and the bright areas appear brighter. Like on film.

Another Luma modification tool is the Levels effect, accessed by right-clicking the clip > **Add Effect > Colour Correction > Levels**. It's a less graphical interface so might be less user-friendly but it's a powerful way to control the input and output levels of each value. Its controls are available in the Effect Stack as long as the clip is highlighted.

As with the Curves, the default channel is Red, so if you want to target the Luma values first then use the drop-down menu in the top right of the Effect Stack to choose Luma.

4. Colours

Next, you can manipulate the chroma values of your image. This is done in the exact same way as you would adjust for celluloid: use your human subject as your guide. Human skin, regardless of tone, loves amber. Increasing the red and yellow values in a shot with human flesh in it makes the subject look warmer and more alive and vibrant.

You can use the same toolset as you did for Luma adjustment, but be sure to add a new effect for each channel you adjust. You cannot use the same effect for different channels; you will simply be overwriting the luma adjustment if you switch an existing curve over to the Red channel.

The order of the effects matter. It's a stack, so anything at the top of the stack is effecting all effects below it. This is why I start with the Luma values; I find that if I adjust colour first and then place a Luma curve on top of all these, I find that the colors are in danger of becoming posterized and need to be dialed down. So start with the Luma, and then move on to the colors.

If you're using curves for the colour adjustment, then knowledge of basic complementary colours will help. As I've stated in an chapter on a different video editing application (written back in the dark ages, before I'd switched to a free software solution), there's a simple mnemonic to remember the relation of colours in the digital world; it comes in the form of some stock trade advice: Buy General Motors and RC Cola.

Buy	General Motors	RC Cola
BY	GM	RC
(Blue and Yellow)	(Green and Magenta)	(Red and Cyan)

Ergo, if you add red to a shot you are necessarily reducing cyan. If you add green, then you reduce magenta, and so on. The Curves interface makes this abundantly clear, since one side of the curve will be, for instance, red, and the other cyan. You can target certain areas of the image according to which part of the curve you manipulate; you can add red primarily to the midtones (where human skin tone is) by moving the middle of the curve more into red. Constrain the darks and highlights to prevent their red levels from changing.

You can also use the Levels tool for color manipulation. Select the red channel to begin with, and adjust the different levels of red. I find this slightly less useful since it's not possible to target just the midtones, and yet sometimes it produces a rich result nevertheless, so try it out.

Yet another tool you can use for color adjustment is the RGB Adjustment effect. This is a straight-forward manipulation of the levels of the RGB values in the image. Again, there is no target just a specific range, ie, just the highlights or just the midtones so I tend to reserve it for overall adjustments. But combined with other filters, I've used it for primary skintone adjustment, depending largely on the lighting situation and colour depth of the video.

5. Things That Look Broken

The tool that most video editors and colourists will default to when looking for quick colour correction will be the **3 Point Balance** effect, because in some professional applications that's the name of the go-to tool for colour correction.

The **3 Point Balance** tool in **Kdenlive** is nothing more than a dumbed-down curve frontend. When it is first applied, the image inexplicably turns cyan, and the color-select droppers are completely literal, such that if you select some area of the image as your white point, it assigns cyan as your white point, turning your image into a bad parody of a cartoon effect.

The correct way to use this tool is not to use it; use the more powerful curves tool instead. But if you like this simplified interface, then manually select shades of gray using the colour picker (obtained by clicking on the color swatch by the Black Level, Gray Level, and White Level.

You'll also notice that there is not color wheel interface in **Kdenlive**. To any traditional colourist, this will probably be a deal-breaker. Luckily, I'm not a traditional colourist and neither should you be. The tools of the trade are changing and the colour correction tools in **Kdenlive** have proven themselves to be powerful, flexible, and effective. They have easily matched the colour tools in any other professional video editor used in the production facility I am a part of, and in many ways they are more efficient. The ability to manipulate colours on a curve, therefore having a built-in ability to immediately target the luma range that those colours are changing within, is an amazing time-saver.

6. Saturation

Finally, the saturation of the image can be adjusted; you can created a more vibrant look with very saturated colours, a dull and stark image with less saturated shades, or course go completely black and white with a saturation level of zero.

The tool for this is fairly staight-forward: **Add Effect > Colour Correction > SOP/ Saturation**. Add this to a clip and use the controls in the **Effect** Stack to modify the Slope/ Offset/Power of individual channels, or the levels of the overall saturation. A level of zero saturation will render a black and white image.

7. Copying Values Between Clips

Obviously if you had to re-apply and re-do the colour correction from one shot of your subject to the next, I wouldn't be recommending you do any colour correction in **Kdenlive**. But of course it's easy to copy colour settings between clips.

The first method is to right-click on the clip in the timeline containing the color effects. Move to the clip in need of the same (or similar, if you just want to start from approximately the same place) colour adjustments and right-click on it. Choose Paste Effects.

Now tweak the colour adjustments as needed.

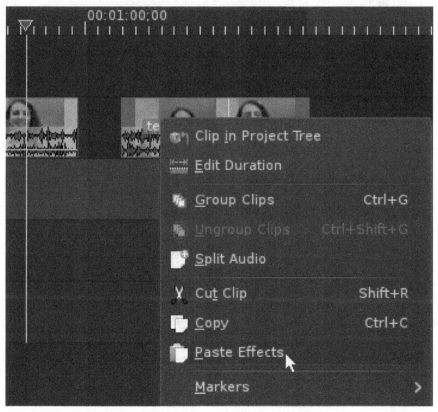

You can also save your own effect settings such that they will be available in your effect menu. In the Effect Stack, click the Save icon under the effect you wish to save. Enter a new name for the effect. From now on, you can apply that effect with those settings onto any clip by right clicking on the clip > **Add Effect** > **Custom**.

8. Colour Effects

As a final note on stylizing your image's look and feel, remember that you have different compositing options available via the right-click > **Add Transition** menu. By layering one clip on top of itself and adding a multiply transition between them, and then adjusting the saturation or color values of the bottom clip, you can create a new composited image with some very interesting effects, such as the classic "bleach bypass" look.

8.1. Selective Colour Correction and Rotoscoping

If your subject is not moving, or if they are moving and you have a lot of time on your hands, you can rotoscope the subject to isolate it from the rest of the image. You're then able to affect only what is visible within your selection.

Rotoscoping and masking is something of an art and is often considered a relative to animation, especially when your subject is moving around and you need to create a rotoscope that moves accordingly. But the basics are simple; add a rotoscope to your video clip, select the area you wish to keep, and composite.

To try this, place a video on Track 2, right click on it and select **Misc** > **Rotoscoping**. In the Effect Stack, set the Mode to **Alpha** so that anything not selected is converted to an alpha channel and ensure that the **Alpha Operation** is set to **Write on Clear**. In the **Project Monitor**, click around the object that you wish to effect on that layer.

After you close your selection, only that object will be visible in that video track. Now add another clip on Track 3, just under than clip and right click on the top track to add a composite transition (see *Effects and Transitions in Kdenlive* for more information). In the context of colour correction, I add the same clip under itself so that it appears that there has been no rotoscope at all. It looks like one complete image. But now add a new effect onto the top track, such as a curve, and adjust its color. You've successfully isolated adjustment on that object to only that object.

Obviously the use of rotoscoping goes far beyond colour correction, but since it's usually touted as a "killer feature" of dedicated color correction applications, it's worth mentioning here.

9. Conclusion

This chapter shows that Kdenlive is not just a capable video editor, but also a colour correction suite that matches some of the high end colour applications available. Not only is it flexible, but it's efficient. Don't let its lack of some traditional conventions fool you; powerful colour correction is easy with Kdenlive.

Audio

Traditionally, the film editing process was regimented and compartmentalized. The assistant editors helped organize footage, the editor cut the picture, a sound engineer mixed the sound tracks, and a music composer provided the score.

In today's quickly evolving landscape of film production, these roles are becoming less clearly defined and many of these tasks are falling upon the editor alone. And in the independent world it's been this way for a very long time. The results are that the video editor is responsible more and more for building the final film from its desparate pieces, and consolidating the tasks in this way tends to quicken the post-production process, and of course bring down costs.

Unfortunately, since video editors have mostly been trained on video editing applications, they tend to try to perform all of those different tasks (clip organization, dialogue editing, audio cleaning, and soundtrack mixing) in the one application that they are familiar with: their video editor.

On GNU Linux, we have the principle of modularity, and the well-known idea that a tool should "do one thing and do it well". **Kdenlive** hardly does one thing, but even if we broaden the idea of what "one thing" can mean, it would still be a difficult argument to make that you were ever meant to do anything but the most basic audio editing in a video editing application.

In this chapter, we'll discuss the different sources of audio, how to prepare it for editing, how to export it, optimize it, and finally re-import it.

1. Audio Recording and Synchronization

Most cameras that you'll use will have some ability to capture sound, but very rarely are the microphones embedded in the camera of very good quality or at a reasonable distance from the actors to capture good sound.

There are three scenarios that have become prominent in how to deal with this:

1. Ignore the onboard mic and set up an external recording system.

2. Ignore the onboard mic and use an external mic recording into the camera.

3. Use the onboard mic.

In the first case, you'll end up with separate audio files that you'll import from the external recording device, such as a Zoom H4, or similar.

In the second case, you'll end up with audio "embedded" into the video file that you import from the camera.

And in the third case, you'll have "embedded" sound in the video file, which you'll either have to use as your only sound or you can simply use as reference sound while you sync your external audio file to your video.

If you did record to an external device, then you'll need to synchronizing sound in your video editor. This is easier if you did get the reference sound via the onboard camera mic, and it is even easier if you actually bothered to slate each shot.

Slating is one of those often-overlooked parts of production that is probably the single most helpful thing you can do on set to aid in post production. A slate can be simple; I find that a legal notepad (like a tablet computer, but made of trees, believe it or not) and a Sharpie pen is perfect for the non-audible indication of what scene, shot, and take the clip is about to contain. To give something to sync sound to easily, make sure that both the camera and the sound recording are rolling, and then firmly clap your hands in clear view of the camera. This is a low-budget version of a clapboard and frankly it has the exact same results.

The only reason to not slate is because the shot is complex and there is literally no way to fit a slate in at the beginning of the shot. In this event, do a "tail slate", that is, the same thing only at the end of the shot. It's customary to hold the notepad (or clapboard, or whatever) upside down just as a visual cue for the assistant editor or editor that this slate isn't indicating that a shot is just beginning, but that it's just ending.

If you slate each shot, then synchronizing sound in your video editor is as simple as making sure that your audio files and video files have sane names (more on naming conventions in the final chapter of this series), dragging them both into the timeline, and lining up the loud sound of a clap in the audio track with the visual of that clap in the video track.

Once it's synchronized, group the video and audio tracks together by selecting them both with your **select tool** (s), right-clicking on one track, and choosing **Group Clips**.

If your sound is starting out synchronized but is then falling out of sync, then you should check your sample rates. **Kdenlive**'s project settings provides you with two options in terms of sound: 44.1khz and 48khz. If your sound files were recorded at 32 khz or 22050hz or worse, then you might find that the audio simply isn't playing at the correct speed. It will gradually fall out of sync, consistantly, regardless of how you move it or slice it.

To fix this, a simple sox command will suffice:

```
$ sox inputfile.wav -r 44100
outputfile_44100.wav
```

Of course you can do this to an entire folder of audio files with a simple **for** loop:

```
$ for i in *.wav; do sox $i -r 44100
$(basename $i .wav)_44100.wav; done
```

2. Best Practises for a Basic Mix

Even though you will be taking your audio out to an external application to for the final mix, the first draft of an audio mix happens within the video editor. The best way to make this happen is to stay organized with what tracks receive what kind of sound file.

You should plan on having at least two audio tracks for dialogue; the first will be your default landing track for audio, and the second you can use for overlapping dialogue, which sometimes happens in your typical over-the-shoulder (OTS) conversation scene.

In addition to these, you'll probably realistically want a track or two for sound effects. While I don't want to do much mixing in my video editor, I have to admit that sometimes when editing a cafe scene, it just helps to have a bed of cafe background noise to provide a little environment. *Freesound.org*[1] is an excellent resource for these kinds of effects, so I often download a few tracks and sound effects and drop them in on my effects and foley tracks. Even if I end up not using those particular sound effects, at least they serve as good refernce during the actual audio mix as to when the "real" versions of those effects should come in and when they should end; think of it as a Click Track 2.0.

And finally you might want to designate a track for music or musical elements. Again, strictly speaking this isn't something you should really be doing in the video editor but then again we're not editing for Cecil B DeMille, either. Modern editors frequently edit to music, and if nothing else, as with the effects, it will serve as a good indication of when the real music is supposed to come in and when it should swell and when it should be soft, and so on.

Be sure not to mix different types of sound into the same tracks; dialogue must stay in dialogue tracks, effects in effect tracks, and music in music tracks. If you need to add a track and designate it as a third or fourth dialogue track, then do so. They're free, I promise.

At some point during your edit, you should separate the audio from the video tracks if you are using any of the embedded sound streams that belong to a video track. By doing so, you ensure that all of your audio is consolidated into the correct tracks, and it enables you to safely and securely mute all sound off of the video tracks, which you'll want to do if you are ignoring most of the embedded audio streams.

3. Exporting

The audio tracks for your project will not be exported for the final audio mix until you have declared "picture lock", meaning that you've resolved that no changes to the sequence of images will be made, or that if they are made then those changes will in no way require shortening the audio tracks (ie, you are swapping out one establishing shot for another, for the same duration, and will not require any change to audio).

Once you are secure that your picture is locked, then you can do a simple export via the Render menu in Kdenlive. Access this via the big red button in the main toolbar, or via the **Project menu > Render**.

---

[1] http://www.freesound.org

For **Destination**, choose **Audio Only**. Select the format and sample rate you wish to export to; it's best to stay with your current sample rate. make sure your **Output File** is going to a logical directory and has a sensible name; I usually place my audio tracks into a directory call "mix".

You want to export each track as an individual file; so, in your timeline, mute all tracks but the first dialogue track. And then add it to the render queue by clicking the **Render To File** button on the lower left of the **Render** dialogue box. This starts processing in the background, so next you can mute the dialogue track and unmute your next track. Name the output file and add it to the render queue. Then mute that track and unmute the next one, and so on.

In the end you'll have 6 audio tracks (assuming two dialogues, two effects, and two music) that are each the full length of your project file. There will probably be a lot of dead space in each, since you may only have a sound effect every few minutes or so, or only one instance of music, and so on. The important thing is that each track is self-contained, independent of the others, and all of them are exactly the same length as one another and as the video project itself.

You, or your sound mixer, can then import the audio files into an audio mixing application; such as **Audacity**, **Qtractor**, or **Ardour**.

There's a little bit of an expectation now that an audio mixing application will have the ability to import a video track so that audio can be mixed exactly along with the video. This certainly does help with sound cues or subtle sonic touches like noticing a passing airplane outside a window and dropping in a faint airplane sound effect, and so on. The de facto audio mixers for Linux do not yet feature this ability out-of-the-box.

One solution is a click track. This is the time-honoured convention of having a spare audio track with either literal clicks or, in my personal version of the click track, temporary sound effects that indicate where an when some significant event is supposed to occur. This, combined with a lo-res temporary render of the movie that I can have open in Dragon or Mplayer, allows me to easily maneuver my audio mix and cross-reference the video as needed. So far I've not missed an audio cue yet, and I feel that the absence of a constant video track helps me immerse myself in the sound design.

The application *Xjadeo*[2] allows you to bind a video file to the **JACK** transport, which is sort of a meta playhead that synchronizes various sound sources on a system. **JACK** is usually used by musicians so that, for instance, the drum machine playing in **Hydrogen** will come in at the right moment in a sequence being designed in **Ardour** or **Qtractor**. **Xjadeo** uses **ffmpeg** to play back a video in time (and, accordingly, stop or scrub) with your audio in any **JACK**-aware audio mixer.

---

[2] http://xjadeo.sourceforge.net/ar01s03.html

4. Re-importing the Mix

Once your sound is mixed to your liking, you should export the sound as one complete mixdown. Obviously you will keep the audio project itself in the event that you need to re-mix or change the language or the dialogue (ie, for a dub track), but I see no reason to allow **Kdenlive** to do any of the mixing by keeping tracks separate.

Before importing the final mix into my project, I generally save a copy of the project as, for instance, **`project-name_mixed.kdenlive`** This, I open in **Kdenlive**, and eliminate the unneeded audio tracks, mostly just to avoid silly mistakes but sometimes also to save system resources.

Importing the final mix is as easy as adding a clip to the Project Tree, and then dragging the final mix to a new audio track in the timeline, starting at 00:00:00:00. You've now successfully made the round-trip with your audio mix.

Final Export and Notes on Workflow

Post-production is a long and involved process. As these chapters have demonstrated, **Kdenlive** is capable of handling every step with efficiency and flexibility. In this final chapter, we will discuss the final export of the full project from **Kdenlive**, as well as examine the over-all Free Software workflow of post-production.

At this point in the **Kdenlive** project, all editing has been completed, the picture lock has been declared, colour correction has finished, compositing has been perfected and titles inserted, and the audio mix has been finalized. The only step left is to export the movie from **Kdenlive** as a self-contained movie file.

The first export of your movie should be a full-quality, bit-for-bit copy of exactly what you see in **Kdenlive**. This serves a few different purposes:

1. Ensures that you have a full-quality backup "Gold Master" of your movie.

2. Ensures that everything you think you see in the small-ish windows and relatively chaotic interface of your video editor is actually true. Regardless of how good an editor you are, there is just something different about sitting back and watching a movie without the ability to stop it and make a quick adjustment or a quick edit. This isn't something you should reserve for the very end of your project, either; this is a step you'll want to do periodically throughout the edit. They're called "sanity" checks in the industry.

1. The Gold Master

To get a Gold Master from **Kdenlive**, click the **Render** button in the main toolbar, or access it via **Project** menu > **Render**.

As your **Destination**, choose **Lossless/HQ**. Name your output file as your gold master, or rc1 if it's merely a release candidate, or whatever notation you want to use.

Kdenlive, using **ffmpeg** as its render backend, offers **FFV1** and **HuffYUV** as its full quality master formats. Choose one of these (both are good; **HuffYUV** will have a larger file size as it uses **PCM** for audio while the **FFV1** preset uses **FLAC**), and click the **Render To File** button on the bottom left of the dialogue box.

Now that you have a full quality version of the movie, you can either use it as your transcoding source, if you wish to encode for distribution manually, or you can use **Kdenlive**'s interface. I use **ffmpeg** directly, mostly out of habit but the **Kdenlive** frontend is, to date, the most sensible **ffmpeg** frontend I've used.

2. Encoding

Encoding video for distribution is subject to artistic preference and per-project requirements. There is not a single "best way" to encode your project; you must consider your desired format, your intended delivery method, and so on.

Kdenlive takes into account most of the usual delivery methods, offering presets for DVDs, mobile devices, web sites like Youtube and Vimeo, and much more.

From the user perspective, video codecs are mostly all created equal (a gross over-simplification that should have **ffmpeg** and **Kdenlive** developers cringing). They take video and somehow compress it and ideally play it back on the desired device. So it's useless for a content creator to debate over which codec would be best for their film. Fact is, any codec will do. The deciding factor will be subtleties like bitrate, keyframing and GOP size, and frame size.

The bitrate of a video determines how much information each frame contains. This effects not just the visual quality of the video, but also the ability of the video to be streamed over a network or even a device (since the graphic chips of any device will have its limitation). A very high bitrate, like 35000 kbps (and higher, up to about 54000 kbps, or 54 Mbps) is common on a medium like Blu Ray. DVDs had a bitrate of about 8000kbps. Internet video, obviously, varies greatly, depending on just how much confidence the content provider has in the network connection of their audience.

Variable bitrates help lower the overall file size by throttling the bitrate during shots that don't actually require much information. A relatively still shot of a building, for example, is a lot less demanding on video playback than a high-speed car chase.

The best way to optimize this is to use the **2-pass** option. This takes twice as long to encode, but the results are invariably better in both quality and file size. During the first pass, **ffmpeg** reviews the footage and plans out the optimal method of encoding. On the second pass, ffmpeg does the actual encode.

If you're using the **Kdenlive Render** dialogue box, the bitrate and number of passes are really all you can control, aside from choosing your video format and frame size. The free video formats, **Xvid**, **MP4**, **Theora**, and **Webm** are all excellent codecs, most of which are gaining widespread adoption. I would argue that 9 times out of 10 these codecs alone are sufficient for most distribution channels. That said, there are those devices that require special options, and for this you simply have no choice but to encode into a format that you don't really own or control.

Frame size has a very direct result on file size, so if you're targeting a specific file size then the bitrate and frame size are the attributes you can target to help you achieve your goal. The lower the bitrate, the smaller your file will be, and if you reduce your frame size by 50% you'll often see nearly a 50% drop in file size. Of course, the trade-off in both cases is quality.

If you want to try some custom **ffmpeg** commands to run against your uncompressed Gold Master, then you can choose all the options you want and then, rather than clicking the Render to File button, click the Generate Script instead. This dumps the **ffmpeg** command that **Kdenlive** has generated to a file on your harddrive. You can customize this script using your favourite text editor and then run from the **Kdenlive Render** Dialogue box via the **Scripts** tab.

3. Workflow

The bigger picture of post-production warrants some consideration since **Kdenlive** is only one piece of the puzzle in a diverse industry that is filled with developing technologies. This guide has shown that **Kdenlive** is poised to easily be a drop-in solution for video editing, being able to ingest a variety of formats, combine all manner of visual effects, and be the final mix of all the different elements that go into a video production. The bigger question, then, is whether GNU Linux is ready to be a multimedia production solution.

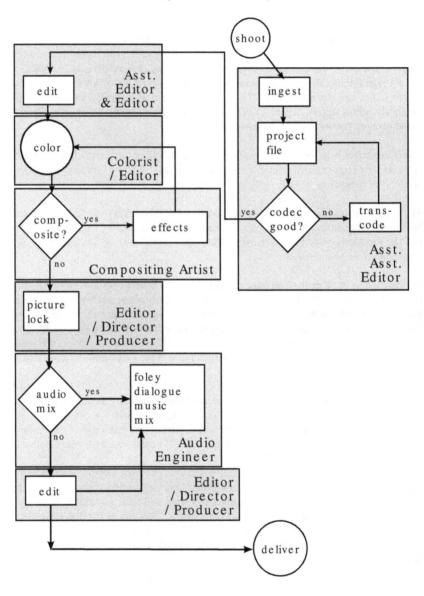

The general flow of post production revolves around the video editor, but requires a number of additional, specialized applications. Before the media even gets ingested by the video editing application, it must be organized and sorted in some useful way. Proprietary editing applications mostly encourage the editors to do this within their application. This often is very helpful as long as you're only accessing the media from within the application, which is rarely ever the case even when the proprietary application claims to be a turn-key solution.

Proper media management should be done in a file manager, such as **Dolphin** or **Nautilus** or the terminal of your choice. Here are some good principles that any good Assistant Assistant Editor knows:

1. Stay organized. Don't scatter your footage all over your computer and expect your project to retain its integrity for years to come. If your project is a quick one-off video that you're going to post to the internet or render out to a harddrive and then delete the source files from your computer, then you might not need to bother with proper organization. For a serious video project that is going to take more than an afternoon to edit, however, keep your files in one directory tree, keep them organized on your drive, and back them up.

2. Name your files so that they are useful. **MVI00087.AVI** and **DCS_000101.MOV** are not appropriate file names for video clips upon which your project relies. In a perfect world, we'd all be assigned an Assistant Assistant Editor to watch all of our footage and carefully summarize what's in the take, what take number it is, and then to name the clip accordingly. Until this happens, the responsibility falls upon you. So, watch your clips, give them logical names, such as **klaatuDrinksCoffee_21_MCU_2.mts**, where "klaatuDrinksCoffee" is the scripted action, 21 is the scene number, MCU is the type of shot (in this case, Medium Close-Up), and 2 is the take number. Stay with that convention and you'll never fail to know exactly what is in each shot and where in your project it should be used.

3. Don't edit off of a USB 2.0 drive. There are exceptions to this rule, but USB 2.0 really is too slow for serious high def editing and even, I find, for standard def editing once the project becomes very complex. Get an extra SATA controller if you have to, or a SATA external drive, or upgrade to USB 3.0, but try to avoid USB 2.0 for editing if possible.

Once the media has been properly organized, it's safe to import it into the video editing application. Kdenlive allows you to create folders within the project tree; use this to manage your scenes. Also remember to make copies of each major cut of your work. Versioning is important!

Note

At least two projects are geared toward media management on a larger scale. *dmedia*[1] aims for fully distributed workflows, and *mis*[2] from Nido Media provides editors with comprehensive details about shared media in a central media library.

Transcoding, if it needs to be done, is an area in which GNU Linux excels. Between **Ffmpeg** and **Mencoder**, you will usually have no trouble getting video into a format that is easily edited. In fact, at the production facility where I work, it's a Linux box, built at a fraction of the price of the computers around it and yet three times as powerful, that is the main conversion station when video comes in that nothing else will edit. (Some day, of course, it will be Linux that is used to edit everything in the first place!)

After the project has been created in your editing application and the media is ready to be cut, the next step is, obviously, editing the film. **Kdenlive**, as you've read, handles this with ease. A few things to keep in mind in any editing application, **Kdenlive** not excepted:

1. Whatever is in the timeline is in your RAM. In **Emacs** terms, the Timeline is your Buffer. If you are editing standard definition footage and have 4gb of RAM then you'll surely be able to edit about a half an hour of footage with numerous cuts and clips without noticing any burden on your system. High Def footage on 4gb RAM is quite another story. Keep this in mind. If you must, edit your project in two or three scene chunks, as convenient, and then marry it all together in the end.

2. I've edited on both my laptop and my main workstation. The laptop is, technically, able to edit, which is convenient when not in studio, but it's far more pleasant to edit on the workstation. Marketing ads showing professional editors cutting their film on a small laptop are doing just that: marketing. If you are about to embark on a serious video project, buy or build a computer appropriate to the job, with multiple CPU cores, plenty of RAM, and a healthy video card.

3. Unfortunately, my tests with the free video card drivers available for ATI and Nvidia have not yet proven to be capable of the same performance as the proprietary drivers. Intel cards are nice in this way, being both open source and, depending on the chip, capable, but if you are doing serious compositing you will most likely require Nvidia or ATI. Hopefully the free drivers will be able to develop quickly so that they can be used for heavy lifting, or Nvidia or ATI will come to their senses and open source their drivers.

---

[1] https://launchpad.net/dmedia
[2] https://github.com/nido

Once the picture is locked, or nearly locked, effects, composites, and titles can be worked on. While **Kdenlive** could do basic versions of all of these things, there are better tools in the GNU Linux world for the job. In fact, we have two excellent tools that, again, equal or rival the tools available in the proprietary world: **Blender** and **Synfig Studio**.

In the FX world, it is typical to work with image sequences rather than video. To export just a scene from your movie to deliver to the composite artist, you can utilize in and out points in the timeline just as you would in the clip monitor. It is common to deliver the scene to the FX artist with "handles", that is, a second or so of the shot leading into the FX shot and a few seconds of the shot following.

In the **Render** dialogue box, choose **Lossless/HQ** as your Destination, de-select the **Export Audio** option, and save the clip to some location. Then in a terminal convert that shot to a series of images with **ffmpeg**:

```
$ ffmpeg -i short_for_compositing.avi
./scene21_fx/sc21_%03d.tif
```

Important

The output target `%03d.tif` will provide three digit numeration for each image; ie, `sc21_000.tif`, `sc21_001.tif`, and so on. If you are for some reason exporting a shot longer than 40 seconds or so that requires compositing, then you'll want to make sure you have enough digits in your numbering scheme to preserve correct order of images.

Both **Synfig** and **Blender** will import such an image sequence, and export an image sequence that you can then re-import into **Kdenlive**.

Titling can be done a few different ways; for animated title sequences, **Blender** or **Synfig** will probably be the best choice. If you are simply going to use static title cards then you can also design your titles in **GIMP** and import a single PNG or TIF image to your project. You might have to adjust for pixel aspect ratio (ie, design your titles in **GIMP** at 720x534 or so, such that when they import into 720x480 projects they will appear properly proportioned) but aside from that, it's straight-forward.

While compositing is under way, it is common for audio work to begin, since both processes rely on a locked picture. In the previous chapter, preparing for the audio mix was discussed in detail. Free software offers a number of excellent options for achieving a professional sound mix, whether you know just enough to use **Audacity** or prefer a full-featured digital audio workstation like **Ardour** or **Qtractor**. With over 100 plugins available from the **LADSPA** and **Calf** projects and a few others, you'll have everything you need and quite possibly a lot more than you'd normally have if you'd had to pay for all of those features separately.

When the audio and composites are ready, they are re-imported into **Kdenlive** and integrated with the project. More than likely, a few last-minute revisions will be made by a picky director or the all-knowing producer (they are always all-knowing), but more or less the project is finished. Export it as a lossless Gold Master and compress for your targeted distribution.

4. Conclusion

GNU Linux has refined its multimedia capabilities to being both user-friendly, flexible, efficient, and stable. It is a realistic platform for post production and content delivery. It is also flexible enough to integrate into an existing non-Linux environment, with many tools such as **Blender** and **Audacity** and **ffmpeg** being completely cross-platform. Start converting your post production process today, and discover true independent filmmaking!

GODSTREAM.TAR

Listen to Godstream! A daring new experimental album inspired by the worlds of REVOLUTION RADIO and PRIVATE PROPERTY.

Download your free copy of this and more at http://aesdiopod.com/books or http://straightedgelinux.com/seth

As always, 100% Free Software
100% Creative Commons
100% Sci Fi

PRIVATE PROPERTY

Fear and Loathing in Post Apocalyptic Amerika

"I can't remember the last time a book made me feel so understood and so lonely at the same time." **JESS WEICHLER**
Filmmaker

"The idea that private property and *fun* have not changed in the aftermath of this future genetic change is interesting. The search for the meaning of life does not change either." **ARLENE RADASKY**
Author

"A bizarre, weird trip through dystopia that is feminist and humanist, anarchist, hopeful but morbid, and entirely unique. A novel few will understand, but those who do will know it." **SAMANTHA_CCOM**
Blogger

www.ingramcontent.com/pod-product-compliance
Lightning Source LLC
Chambersburg PA
CBHW051224050326
40689CB00007B/790